MUSKY SLAYER'S BIBLE

A GUIDE ON WHAT **NOT** TO DO

BY BRAD MATHEWSON

This book is based on
true fishing experiences.
Names of lodges and lodge
owners have been changed.

Musky Slayer's Bible:
A Guide On What Not To Do
Copyright © 2021 Brad Mathewson

All Rights Reserved. No portion of this book may
be reprinted or reproduced without permission,
except for journalistic or educational purposes.

Author and owner:
Brad Mathewson
bradmathewsonoutdoors@gmail.com
facebook.com/muskyslayersbiblebook

Let's go fishing!

Graphic design and illustration by:
Shawn Brook Williams
www.shawnbrookwilliams.com

1st Printing: January 2021
Printed by KDP

"An F for "failure" isn't always a bad thing, if it's what's needed to motivate one to succeed."
— *Ron Steinhorst, 1997 New London High School*

"When the eagles are fishing, so should you. If they just hang out in the trees, then you should be enjoying a cocktail instead of wasting time washing baits."
— *Brad Mathewson*

"The underling factor in becoming a successful musky hunter is time on the water."
— *Bill Gradner, Time On The Water, Copyright 1982*

"The muskellunge brain is the same size as the people who spend all their time and money chasing them."
— *Brad Mathewson*

"Conservation is a state of harmony between men and land."
— *Aldo Leopold*

CONTENTS

INTRODUCTIONS

Canada here we come! My greatest fishing times have been with Brad Mathewson in Canada. I've know Brad for almost 20 years, both professionally and personally. Brad has a way of making our fishing trips very memorable as we usually have a large group of 8 to 12 guys and rent half the resort in Lake of the Woods. The days are long as we begin musky fishing at sunrise and don't stop until 9:00 pm at night, followed by grilling out and telling the days fish stories over several drinks. We fish two to a boat and rotate every day so we can experience fishing with all the guys. Each day brings a story of the one that got away and by the end of the week that same fish story has grown by at least 10 inches in size!! One of my favorite memories of fishing musky with Brad was on a hot summer day - he took his shirt off and asked me to rub lotion on his back. I replied, "WRONG ANSWER - you're gonna burn!" Brad has many stories he can share of our fishing experiences and yes, I've caught more fish than Brad at times and I'm sure you'll enjoy reading this book!
— *Steve Hoelzel*

Brad is a good family friend who has fished with myself and five of my brothers through the years. One of our best trips to Canada was in Sabaskong Bay at Lake of The Woods. During this seven day musky trip we were challenged with unseasonably HOT weather for Canada. We were still able to land a few and had great fun trying. The missing of a "monster musky" was a bit of a let down, but Brad and I moved past it and continued to pound the water some more. Even if one misses a musky, it is still a great memory on the water! I have found Brad to be very passionate about fishing especially for Musky.

– James Hoelzel

Brad Mathewson is an interesting person with whom I have had the honor of going on fishing trips to Canada with several times. We have had some interesting trips. No mater what the trip, I have always enjoyed his many conversations whether it was politics, fishing, or another topic somewhere in between. We have had days where we saw three fish over fifty inches and even if we were lucky enough to land one, we are strictly catch-and-release, so they won't be hitting the grease, though we do have a few Northern pike fish fries. Brad has brought some interesting food on our fishing trips to eat, besides the fish we caught. One time he even brought Antelope loins which were absolutely delicious! I am positive the stories in his book will be very interesting.

— Stew Hoelzel

Brad is an industrious hard working young man. He is very diligent in what he does. He is not afraid to try something different in the sports world of fishing and hunting. He is a

former bass fisherman turned musky hunter still learning the ropes. Just because of his short stature it doesn't mean he needs to cast short, but he is very persistent. He is always looking for the right angle to get the job done. Behind every good sportsman there is a good wife that can put up with him. He will instill the love of the outdoors to his family. P.S. There is always a bigger fish lurking around the corner. Happy endless casting!
— *Jan Hoelzel*

I'm sitting here in my gun stand writing this documentary about Brad, we had a great time in Canada, caught lots of musky and Northern pike. Brad is an awesome guy to fish with, knowing where to cast for the best potential chance at active musky. He's more than welcome to fish with me again. God bless him and his family.
— *Tracy Schadrie*

Brad as a musky fisherman is a very good cabinet maker. I first met Brad at one of my jobs (I built homes, I was a general contractor). My brothers and I told him stories about musky hunting, and did he suck it up!! We had him hooked. His brother Eric and his dad were great to work with also. Brad wanted to learn how, so we took him up to Boulder Junction, WI and Canada and had a lot of fun and interesting incidents as he will tell you. We still Love YA Brad
— *Jerry Hoelzel*

To know Brad is to know his love of the Great Outdoors. One also knows that once you get this man talking about fishing or hunting, you better sit back and be prepared to listen because you are in it for the long haul... He's a bit of a talker. So it's only fitting that he had a dream of retelling his Lake of the Woods musky fishing adventures through a book. I once heard Brad say that he considers himself a "Teller of Stories". I'm so excited for readers to relive the many tales and laugh along as the adventures unravel through his stories.

Brad, this book has been a true labor of love for you. I admire your continued passion in writing and fulfilling your dream of publishing a book. I've watched you spend countless hours scribbling down all your memories and ideas in a notebook, then watching them transform on the pages as you typed. Despite life's distractions, limited quiet time alone, continuous knocks and wiggles on your locked office door by a toddler, and a few frustrated eye rolls from your wife, you persisted. We are beyond proud of you and admire what you've accomplished.

Hah! I guess this book is proof that at least something good came out of almost dying on my "dream" musky fishing honeymoon. Looking forward to all our upcoming adventures together that are hopefully more romantic than a desolate cabin with twin beds and endless hours of casting in the pouring rain. Love you! Congratulations on your book.

— *Laura Mathewson "Brad's Wife"*

PROLOGUE

Canada: Wild. Untamed. The beautiful gemstone of the great North. A lush, uninhabited vastness of pure God's country. A conifer and hardwood paradise. Where the horizon is shaped by ancient mountains that have been readily whittled away over millions of years by the gentle rolling of crisp, clean streams. All of which is pure, unfiltered, and unmolested by man's grubby mitts. Nature at its most powerful and free form.

Florida: Relentless. Oppressive. Sweltering. Fungus-inducing moist air. Overrated splashy ocean shores littered with polluted waters and decaying retirees. Where insects the size of grapefruit stalk your blood while you sleep. The land of hanging chads, overstuffed and overpriced amusement parks, and tourists. Oh, the tourists. Lots and lots of tourists. Swamps, sweat, man eating gators, and swimming pools. Where locals, even if it's sunny and seventy outside, go to tanning booths.

The choice was obvious. In fact, it was no choice at all. To spend one week in either of these two destinations wasn't rocket science. (Oh, yeah, include 'rocket scientists' to the list above for Florida). Only one problem existed. This was to be a democratic decision between myself, and the love of my life. Newly wedded, it was to be our first major collective decision as husband and wife. The challenge was on. In her eyes, Florida was more than just America's spring break frat party. Florida's marketing department is really good at conjuring images of sunsets on the beach, fantastic nightlife, and Margaritaville. Sure, those may actually exist. It's the other ninety-nine percent of Florida, to me, that was laden with medical waste and gated communities.

In any normal democratic decision (except the United States Presidential vote), majority rules. The problem lies that in all marriages, there are at least three votes: The Husband's, the Wife's, and the Wife's. (All married men know, the wife gets a minimum of two votes to every one vote of a husband. I don't make the rules. That's just how it works and as a man, you just have to deal with it.) So before any ballot was cast, I knew the odds were stacked against me. The early exit polls showed Florida with a healthy two-to-one advantage in the race for our Honeymoon destination. If Canada was gonna win this derby, I was gonna have to plea to the voter and get some high rollers to fund my marketing campaign, if not buy this election outright.

Don't get me wrong, Florida, I'm sure, is a great place to visit for a very short period of time. But Canada has been a dream of mine since I was a lad. To experience the great Canadian Shield and toss a cast out for the chase of a lifetime, the elusive and diabolical Canadian Musky, was more than just a vacation or even a honeymoon. It was a pilgrimage for my personal Holy Grail. Just the thought of pollution free water, some bodies of water without even as much as a name to them, bloated with so many fish that they ignore hooks and baits and launch themselves right into your boat (it's my dream, I'll believe what I want) was enough to go on the honeymoon solo if I had to.

To make this journey complete, though, I truly wanted the love of my life, my bride-to-be, to come along. Therefore, I needed to figure out a way to convince her that a trip to God's country was better than a trip to the Sunshine State. Chasing muskies was better than chasing the sun at the edge of the ocean. That drinking a Labatt Blue was better than Sex on the Beach. This was not gonna be easy.

CHAPTER I

HOLE IN THE WALL-ET

The All-Canada Show, one of Green Bay, Wisconsin's best annual exhibitions, was just a few short weeks after our nuptials. Coincidence... maybe, but not unforeseen. I circle this date on my calendar each and every year. Only this year, it was gonna have a whole new meaning. There was a sense of urgency like that of a late fourth quarter drive down by six points. This show was to be my one and best shot at convincing my wife that our kissing cousins to the great north had just as much, no, MORE to offer than the retirement home of America. I'd have to scout this show like a late summer jaunt into the woods to set up a new bow hunting stand. I needed to hit every nook and cranny, and find every ounce of sugar sweet ole' Canada had to offer. Since maple syrup is a key export of our neighbors, I figured this undertaking should not be mission impossible.

It was a bitter cold late Saturday afternoon when we took the half hour jaunt north to frigid Green Bay, Wisconsin. (I know, redundant. Bitter cold, frigid and Green Bay all kind of mean the same thing.) After plowing through the icy parking lot, we finally arrived inside the Expo Center for the All-Canada Show.

Once inside, we immediately stumbled on an enormous amount of large, burly men decked out in red and black flannel and blue jeans. The thought popped in my head "If it's true, it's not a stereotype." Each outdoors man was lobbying his own kiosk, adorn with trophy mounts of whitetail deer, bear, walleyes, pike, and yes, the majestic musky. Those monstrous mounts put a cast out for me, and I bit hard. Like a school boy unhooking his first bra, my heart pounded as I streamlined right to a number of great Canadian fishing kiosks.

I was immediately greeted heartily by a macho north woodsman. He reached out his gigantic paw to shake my hand. Once my hand entered that vice, I knew I was in for a world of pain. His bratwurst-sized fingers wrapped around my string beans and absolutely crushed them, but in the nicest way possible. This guy looked like Paul Bunyan, but his demeanor was so innocent and kind he made Mr. Rogers look like an ISIS terrorist on crack cocaine. Somehow, when he shook my newlywed's hand, he found a moment of finesse. This happened numerous times with the clad of Mounties.

Aside from the hand pancaking, the All-Canada Show was everything I could have hoped for. As I expected, aside for the glorious mounts, each kiosk was adorn with glorious photos of the deep green forests with crystal blue lake gems sprinkled between. Numerous times, I'd catch my newly minted wife gasp at their beauty. And every time, I'd point out how wonderful it would be to see that in person someday. Yeah, I was playing the subliminal message game. I grabbed brochures from dozens of lodges in hopes that on the way home, she'd fall in love with at least ten to twenty of them for me to plead my case to go to. As we head back through the arctic winter night to our vehicle, my heart sped knowing that this drive home was gonna be my now-or-never moment for a trip of a lifetime. Even in the subzero temperature, I was sweating. It closely resembled buck fever, of which I never, ever, ever, ever get. NEVER! (OK, just once)

I ground the starter on the truck until it finally fired up. After sucking in a deep breathe, I began to lawyer up my case for a honeymooning in God's Country. The entire drive home, I pointed out every single way I could think of, that Florida was a pile of steaming hot garbage compared to Canada. How everybody went to Florida for their honeymoon, but how we were different and more adventurous and that our first get-away as husband and wife should be no different. After a half hour straight of pleading my case, maybe a little whining, definitely some crying, but in the manliest way possible, of course, I finally convinced her to say those words I'd been dreaming about for years. Let's go to Canada!!!!

We pulled the truck into the garage to escape the brutal winter. She quickly dashed into the house, but I just sat there. My dream was coming true. I was going to chase muskies and drink maple syrup with our neighbors to the great north. Little did I know at that time, it was a decision that would haunt me for the rest of my life. Looking back on it, I should have realized I had just given my wife a lifetime pass to shove this back in my face any and every time I did something wrong. Oh well, live and learn. I'M GOING TO CANADA MUSKY FISHING!!!

Canada is a big country and the province of Ontario is crammed full of potential landing spots for dynamite musky fishing. The dilemma at this point was where the hell to go? Each possible destination had its merits, pros and cons. Some of the decision influence was gonna be just how much I was willing to lighten my wallet for this grand adventure. As much as I'd prefer that not be an influence, it did play a part, to a certain extent.

The next day had me yapping to a contractor, Jerry, that we do a ton of work for. I knew he was a died-in-the-slim musky hunter who had been on many fishing adventures to Canada. He suggested the majestic White Birch Lodge on the famous Lake of the Woods in Ontario. He thought it was a fantastic place, as it was close to many good fishing holes that held tons of quality fish. Secondly, you could drive right to the lodge. Many of the resorts on L.O.T.W. are out on islands which require you to either be picked up at a boat landing (ka-ching) or you drive your own boat to them. I definitely didn't feel comfortable or safe staying on an island if I didn't have to. Maybe I've seen to many horror movies, but that's between me and my psychiatrist.

After schmoozing with Jerry for a bit, he got the sense of my excitement about musky fishing. Out of the blue, he invites my wife and I to join him, his brother Steve and son Allen, along with his buddy Kenny to go to White Birch Lodge with them that coming summer. They had planned to camp out, but Jerry suggested the wife and I should ruff it in one of the luxurious log cabins, being that it would be our honeymoon. Out of gut reaction to his invitation, and before I talked to my wife about much of anything, I agreed with exuberance. Now, for you newlywed men out there, a word of sound advice: Don't agree to anything without consulting you wife first. Period. End of discussion. This will save you from many a cold night alone, because believe it or not, my wife was none too thrilled to spend 8 days in Canada with 5 crazy musky hunters on our honeymoon. Go figure.

I hopped online and dug up the phone number for the White Birch Lodge. This wasn't something that came to my mind, but was at the urging of Jerry to feel things out. Jerry and his wife have been married a long time, and even he didn't think it was such a great idea to say yes to his offer without checking what special offers they might have for newlyweds. As you can probably tell, my mind was a bit one-track at that point. Not that I wasn't thinking about my new wife, but at the time, my only concern was how can I keep my lovely wife entertained in the boat all day so I can achieve my goal of catching my first Canadian musky.

As the phone rang, my mind raced with all the nice ol' Canadians I had met at the All-Canada Show only days earlier.

BY **BRAD MATHEWSON**

When the line picked up on the other end, a crotchety, drowsy voice muttled, "Ya. What da ya vant?". My first thought was I had called some poor old bastard struggling to sleep off a night of Crown Royal. I apologized for dialing the wrong number and mentioned I meant to call the White Birch Lodge. To my shock, and mild dismay, he admitted, "Ya, dis is White Birch Lodge." It was the owner of the Lodge himself, Ben. After sputtering a few pleasantries as I regained my focus, I lobbed him a myriad of questions, ranging from the weather, fishing conditions, water levels, allege blooms and rates. Somewhere in there, I believe I asked about the accommodations, I think. Most of the questions were answered by Ben with either a "no", "ya" or "I dunno". Come to think of it, most were the latter. Not one subject was touched with any further depth. After two long, agonizing, and slightly embarrassing minutes of his time, his annoyed accent yelped, "You can get the rest of yer information from er website."

With that, the phone slammed down. One nice thing about modern technology is that the phones are much harder to slam down without needing replacements. In Canada, it's good old fashion corded phones, made solely for busting eardrums on the other end when you're riled up. It took me a few minutes to figure out what had just happened. From every personal meeting I'd ever had with a Canadian, I believed Canadians were a happy and carefree lot. This lodge owner, who you'd think would be performing his best to get my business and hard earned American cash, was just a denim dickhead.

The next day, Jerry quizzed me on how my discussion with Ben went. After a replay of the quaint conversation, or lack thereof, Jerry admitted that Ben is pretty much a jerk that only helped run the place. His mother actually owned White Birch Lodge. Jerry, well aware of my disgust, suggested I should maybe reconsider going. At minimum, at least call back that night and talk to Amy, the pants wearing head of the family. Not going was not a consideration. This was my dream we were talking about. I wasn't this close to just give up and say forget it.

Later that evening, I called up to White Birch Lodge again, but this time knew to ask for Amy. A woman answered the phone and informed me that Amy wintered in the United States. That being said, the woman stated she would be more than happy to answer any question I might have. The woman introduced herself as Ben's wife, Jenny. That made the skin perspire a bit. You had to wonder how this would turn out. I prayed opposites attracted, and Jenny had some resemblance of brain between her ears, unlike Ben. I eased into the conversation by notifying her that I was searching for a nice place for my new wife and I to spend a pleasant, romantic honeymoon, and maybe do some musky and walleye fishing. I also briefly mention my wife's concern that if the weather turned bad, we'd need to be sure we had other activities at the lodge or surrounding area. Jenny informed me of the plethora of things to do on rainy days. (We regrettably found out later, Jenny was really good at giving sales pitches.) Our conversation flowed nicely, and Jenny assured me that my wife and I would have a very memorable vacation. Before our chat ended, she promised, "Brad, I don't want you to worry one bit. I'm gonna setup something real special to make sure you and your wife have a fun, romantic honeymoon." At that moment, I thought, "How nice! This woman really wants to go the extra mile to make sure we have a good time." I should have gotten that last part in writing. I was so taken aback by her hospitality, I booked our trip immediately. I couldn't fetch my wallet fast enough. Jenny presumably opened her desk calendar, asked what time frame we were thinking about for our romantic getaway, and without ever asking my wife, I blurted out, "Whatever time frame my friend Jerry has." I hope you newly married guys take notes. At least, get a highlighter out and mark these mistakes as you read them. It will save you from many a cold night on the couch. Trust me.

Before I realized the mistake(s) I had made (or better yet, before they began taking their toll on me), I decided old Brad needed some new, high-grade equipment for his big musky trip, err, honeymoon. Off to the local musky shop for some much needed supplies! My first purchase was a fantastic, sturdy net. I had always borrowed my buddies whenever I wanted to go. I didn't ever recall using a net in my previous musky escapades, mainly because I was always catching hammer handle sized muskies. But hell, we were gonna do this honeymoon right. No expense was too large for our first big trip together!

I dug through my lure selection. It wasn't much better than a half dozen small bucktails, a few discount bin crank baits, a couple Bull Dogs, and two of my favorite Bucher Top Raiders. This certainly would not do for a honeymoon trip to the

America's top hat. It was time to pull out my Rollie & Hellen's catalog and jot down a wish list. I had done this in the past, only to watch it collect dust and end up in the recycling bin. This time, these wishes were gonna be granted. I hopped online. I clicked here. I clicked there. I stuffed that cart like shooting for a record high score on a video game. Only problem here was, this high score definitely wasn't a winner, at least for me. It turned out to be one of those bills that if you paid attention to the final score, and you thought about it for any length of time (a second or two), you'd pull the plug on the game system and force it to reset before it counted against you. Luckily (or unluckily) for me, I had the propensity to not think about things too much, and let that "Pay Now" button compress. It was one of those cases where it was, "Ask for forgiveness rather than permission"... from myself. Can you plead 'ignorance is bliss' when you do it to yourself?

After already lightening my billfold to an extreme level, I decided I needed a place to store my shiny new baits. Only one acceptable place for that: a new tackle box! This would replace a broken old foam cooler I had been using. Plus, all of my newly purchased double 10s wouldn't stand up in that little stink box. They always ended up all tangled on the bottom. I hopped on another site. Click, click, click, done. My high score would have challenged the Black Friday mobs. Sure, in a month I'd complain like there was no tomorrow, but at that moment, I think I peed a little from pure adrenaline.

Once the dust settled on my shopping spree (or more accurately, the dust took over my now empty wallet), I met up with

Jerry at the job site. To my surprise, he had something in hand for me. "Got ya a map for Sabaskong Bay. Study it. Memorize as many of the landmarks as you can. Know where the track lines are in relation to where you will be fishing."

Now for those of you that haven't been to Lake of The Woods and don't know what track lines are, they're lines drawn on a map that indicated safe travel routes by boat. You'll see red and green marker buoys. These keep you off reefs or other obstructions in the water. Once off those lines of travel, you are purely on your own. The map isn't a completely accurate guide, as there are many things that aren't found on any map, so slow, cautious travel is strongly recommended.

I opened this newly acquired map, and its dotted with so many Islands and reefs it may as well have been a map of our solar system. My eyes brighten as I see there's a second side to this map. And it's only then that I realized I'm not gonna be on one of my little five hundred-acre Wisconsin musky lakes. This realization made me pee myself for a different reason. Safety is always important, but doubly important when you're bringing along a new bride.

Jerry must have sensed my nervousness, or just saw the urine dribbling down my pants leg. He uttered, "Brad, it might be a wise decision to pick yourself up a GPS for your boat, along with a Lake of the Woods map chip." My butt-hole puckered. That meant much more money than I wanted to spend. And that's before I realized how much I had spent the days leading up to this. Jerry watched me wince. "How much money would it cost if you tore your lower unit off, not to mention hoping nobody gets injured in the process? This big water mistake could cost you your life or your loved one. My brothers' and I all have GPS units. And we've been coming up here for the last twenty years." No matter how good a point is, when it comes to dropping a ton of coin, it always stings a little. In this case, logic outweighed butt-hole tightness. Looked like another road trip to the local sporting goods mega store to break out the credit card. "By the way, what do you have for a boat?" At this point, I'm thinking the bastard is just piling on. "A16.5 foot Modified V- Smoker Craft, with sixty h.p. Yamaha," I squeak out. "That will work just fine," nods Jerry, to my elation. NOTICE: Get the highlighter out. This little under site would cost me dearly, and I'm not talking monetarily.

Thinking I'd avoided a massive bank account apocalypse, I scurried back to the big box sporting good mega superstore toting a new, extensive list from Jerry. Top of the list, begrudgingly, was that GPS unit. Now, I'm not the most tech savvy guy, so I'm prepped for a deep sales-crew bombardment of questions. After a good half hour of peppering some poor schmuck, I found out there were basically two major brands of quality GPS units to choose from: a Lowrance or a Hummingbird. You'd think this would be easy to figure out, but of course, it was pulling teeth. After another half hour, I finally settled on a mid-range Lowrance. Mind you, I'm not sure if it was the right decision being made, or just being sick of the big box store occupancy for that amount of time and anxious to get the hell out of there. Either way, it was done and I was moving on for the next mandated purchase: a lake chip for

Lake of the Woods, and a swivel mount for my boat. I waddled up to the register with the commission-only sales dork, and he chimed in the grand total of just a catfish whisker under the magical $1,000 mark. I think my balls dropped a few inches watching the digital screen ring up a number like that. "Now, that's money well spent. Quality products for a quality trip!" Shut up douche bag and take my card before I swipe it up your ass, I thought.

Before I could drag my depressed butt home, Jerry mentioned that when they head up to Canada, they usually don't buy expensive Canadian gasoline. They literally lug up tanks of fuel to fill up at the dock each morning before heading out for the day. It was cheaper, and time efficient. I'm sure you're probably reading this and thinking, 'what a cheapskate'. But at that time, gas was outrageously priced to begin with, and I knew it would be even worse out in the middle of Nowhere, Canada. I trusted Jerry, a guy that had been there, done that many times before, so I followed his instructions to the letter. He stated to bring a minimum of thirty gallons, so I purchased five six-gallon gas tanks and plop them in the back of the truck. That's it. List completed. Wallet sufficiently empty (and then some). I'm excited, but became very aware of what was in store in the near future: Overtime at work, and a ton of it, to pay for this crazy musky trip. Err, I mean honeymoon.

Once I get home from my wife-like shopping spree, I realized I gotta sneak all my new boy toys into the garage before the wife got home. I wasn't in the mood to explain this mauling of the bank account, so I stuffed bags into the back of the boat just as my wife pulled into the driveway. It took me a moment to realize I should have closed the garage door before climbing into the boat with bags of goodies. She emerged from her car with a quizzical glance, and it's on. Yeah, another highlighter moment.

Needless to say, the conversation was a bit one-sided. It reminded me of the old taunt 'there will be two hits: me getting hit, and me hitting the floor.' I stuck to my guns and waxed on a long discussion about safety and did everything I could to convince her that I did it because her life was worth the grand I had just spent on a GPS unit for my boat. To this day, I'm not sure if I convinced her or not, but I do know I convinced her this wasn't going to end any differently than attaching the GPS to the boat and using it, regardless of whatever she thought or said. I told you, I really wasn't in the mood to argue about it. High quality husbandry in full display.

Later that afternoon, after a very quiet lunch by myself, I yanked my boat apart struggling to install my new Lowrance. If you are anything like me, instructions don't work. Maybe it's because I don't read them. I don't know. Anyway, I called probably the only guy I knew who DOES read instructions, my buddy Mark. Mark used to run wire in airplanes, so he's very adamant about reading instructions. I, on the other hand, probably shouldn't be allowed within a hundred yards of any electrical unit. I learned that the hard way by miswiring some navigational lights on my first boat at the age of eighteen. It fried the entire system like a Kentucky chicken. Mark saved my ass in that mess, so I knew he was the guy for the job. After some scheming, the plan was to take my Hummingbird fish locator off the console and move it to the work station on the front of the boat. Then, place my new Lowrance on the console. I know you Lowrance and Hummingbird guys are reading this, thinking, "Why don't you have two of one brand and network the two together?" Frankly, the boat came with a Hummingbird, which was in good shape and filled my basic needs. But when I researched and decided to buy new, there was something about the Lowrance's features that tickled my ivories. I figured someday, once my wallet wasn't so dusty, I'd eventually replace the Hummingbird with a new Lowrance and have my matching set. For now, this had to do. I'd spent enough already, so I was told... numerous times... by my wife... every damn day.

When April finally arrived, and the ice had left the area lakes and rivers, it was time to work out my new Lowrance and ascertain all this high tech, high priced unit could do. In the past, I only had the most basic fish finders. The ones that could only show the depth and have those goofy preprogrammed fish symbols waddle past your screen every thirty seconds or so. After a few hours of dinking around with my new toy, I was able to plot way points and navigate my way around my hundred-acre lake. For a minute, I felt like the smartest man alive. I'm cocky. I got a newly found confidence and was convinced I could navigate the Atlantic. Shortly after my cock-sureness subsided, a moment of reality sets in. Would I be able to find my way if I couldn't see the boat landing? Hell if I knew. All I did know was, I got a great new toy and I'm anxious to whip it out and play with it! (That didn't come out right).

Two weeks before the big trip, my anticipation practically dripped off my bones. I couldn't wait to have a fifty-inch Canadian Shield musky throbbing on the end of my pole. I'm wet dreaming on the job site, attempting to not nail gun a spike into my palm. While I muddled around with a kitchen cabinet install, a familiar voice broke my wet dream. "Hey, Brad. You all set to catch your first Canadian musky?" asked Jerry. "Hell yeah! Just hope my wife can tie into a couple herself." After some quick pleasantries, Jerry got to the crux of the matter: Did I get everything for the trip? "Yeah, I bought every stink-in' thing. And it wasn't cheap, either. I probably dropped nearly sixteen hundred bucks!" Yeah, still a bit stung by that bill. "Been meaning to ask, what time are we gonna be leaving on Saturday?" Jerry raised a brow and gawked at me like I had mismatched lips.

"We ain't leaving on Saturday. We're hittin' the road on Friday morning." Son of a bitch. "Jerry, you told me months ago that we were leaving on Saturday! My wife and I both started our vacations from work on Saturday!" Jerry, either unamused or uncaring, sniped back, "We always leave on Friday. That way we get up there late afternoon so we can squeeze in some fishin' for a couple of hours before bed. Then we got a full day of fishing on Saturday." At this point, steam whistles blared to me more than his voice. "Well, Jerry. That's not what you told me when we set this up months ago."

Jerry turned to his brother next to him. "Steve, what day do we always leave for Canada?" "Friday. Come on, Brad. You know that." I'm beside myself. I'm too pissed to take the time to understand or care whom was at fault. All I knew was, it wasn't mine. "How the hell could I know that? I've never gone to Canada with you guys before? Now I have to call my wife at work and see if she can get off of work on Friday, too." Jerry contemplated for a moment. "If she can't get off on Friday, you guys could always meet us up there on Saturday." Remember, this is before GPS units came standard with vehicles. "I have no idea how to get up to White Birch Lodge! That's why we were going to follow you up!" Jerry scratched his brain in wonderment. "Oh, it's really easy," Jerry uttered. In my head, I screamed, "Of course it is! You've been up there over two dozen times you old coot!" Thankfully, I kept that one in my head.

After a minor debriefing on the directions to White Birch Lodge, I whipped out the cell to make a dreaded call to the wife. Having to tell her my friend has "planned" on leaving a day sooner than I thought contorted my guts. It took all of two seconds for even me to figure out that she was none too happy. After twenty agonizing minutes, Laura (my wife) called me. After a good, thorough guilt trip, with multiple references that she would have to burn her last day of vacation for the entire year, she revealed that she could get off on Friday so we could follow Jerry up. I praised and thanked Laura profusely and quickly got off the phone with her to track down Jerry. What felt like an eternity, I finally connected with him. After a brief download, we decided to meet at a local gas station. The one they always met at (how foolish of me not to have known!). "Time: 6:00 Am, just like always."

If you haven't figured it out, my friend Jerry and his brother, Steve, like to assume everything based upon their own personal knowledge, mingled with talks amongst themselves. They have this incredible ability to never tell another soul, and when asked about something, there response is "We always." It can be quite annoying, and embarrassing when done to you in public, but Jerry and Steve, along with their other brothers, are some of the absolute best musky fisherman in the state. Each would give you the shirt off of their own back if you asked. People like that are hard to find, and I am proud to call them friends. (Just don't tell them I said that.)

It was two days before my trip. I'm packed, err, we're packed, and all i's have been dotted and t's have been crossed multiple times. Everything was going exactly as planned, which always worried me. That worry was soon realized, because Murphy's law ALWAYS kicks you square in the nuts. Heaven forbid you manage to do something without cranking your head on the ceiling after hitting one of life's bumps in the road. I had my truck at the local mechanic a week earlier to scour for any glaring defects. It's an older truck and I may have been unnecessarily hard on it through its long life.

To ensure a safe trip, I dumped some more cash on it, installing a new set of tires, breaks, oil change, and wiper blades. Expensive to say the least, but I figured it was cheaper to do it now than miles down the road in a foreign country, where I think they still use horses and sled dogs as their main methods of transportation.

I was on my way home from work when I heard a loud Harley Davidson behind me.

This guy was compensating for something, because he was really cracking it loud. So I sped up to get away from him and save my aching ears, but this biker trash just kept getting closer and louder. I looked in the mirror to give him the old 'your number one' solute, but only then realized there was no biker there. That god awful, noisy jerk was me.

I pulled over to look under the hood. The oil dip stick and wiper fluid levels looked good. Nothing loose or on fire. At that point, I'd have preferred a raccoon jump out and claw my face. At least it would have justified this ill-timed pain in the ass. Anyway, I called up my mechanic and begged to get my truck into the shop. He informed me the books were solid for the week, and even then, I might not get my truck back until the following week. "Well shoot. I need it by Friday! We're headin' for Canada!"

Somewhere in my exuberant whine, my mechanic, a fellow fisherman and a veteran of many Canadian fishing trips himself, gained the proper understanding that my truck was obviously more important than anyone who just needed to get to and from work. "I'll see what I can do. But the next twenty-four hours will be touch and go." Fair enough, I thought. I dropped off the rust bucket at his shop and the next day, now Thursday, he gives me a call. "Brad, I hate to tell you this. Your head gasket and manifold are shot to shit on one side. That's why your truck sounds like a hog. Good news is, I think the parts will be in today and I'll try to get it done for you." I'm a mixed bag of emotions at this point. Yay that he was acquiring parts. Nay that there's a chance it ain't getting done.

Four in the afternoon had me receive another call from my mechanic. His tone was not overly optimistic. "I'm having a little trouble with a bolt." I'm a bit perplexed by this. What does that mean? What the hell was I gonna do about that? Wasn't he the mechanic?

"Well, a bolt broke off in your block and I'll have to grind it out and re-tap it. It's a long process since your block is made of aluminum" he stated. After an eternity of waiting for him to elaborate on the definition of 'long process', he muttered, "Can you take your old man's truck? Or maybe your brother's to Canada?" I shook my head, aiming to keep it from spontaneously combusting. There were a plethora of reasons this was a bad idea, but my main concern was with the new border laws. Mounties weren't keen on people driving vehicles into their country unless you owned them. Even then they'd look at you funny. "Isn't there a quick fix you can Band-Aid up the truck to get me through the trip? You can properly overhaul it when I get back." Clint mauled this over. "I might be able to put a vise grips on your new manifold and clamp it to your block until you get back. Can't guarantee it will hold, but it could work." I'm sold. Do it. "By the way, where is your spare tire? You're gonna need it for the trip". I paused, dumbfounded. "Uh, it's under the truck, right?" Clint hesitated in his response. "I'm sorry to tell you this Brad, but your spare tire is gone. Looks like someone has cut your support cable and made off with your tire." Typical bullshit at this point.

"The good news is, I think I have an old tire on a rim that's just one size larger than yours. I could sell it to you for eight bucks," offered Clint. That was about the only good news I'd heard at this point. I had to take what I can get. I know that if I didn't get it, I pretty much guaranteed what will happen on the way to or from Canada.

"Tack it on my bill," I pouted.

An hour later, I made it to his garage, ready to take my truck for an quick test drive to see if the clamp will hold. After a short drive around a country block, it seemed good as new. Would it hold for an eleven hour trip to Canada and back? Eh, details. I thanked good old Clint for his help. He wished me the best of luck, fishing and otherwise.

Now things began to truly settle in. I was going to get my first Canadian Shield musky. No matter how many thousands of dollars it took. What was the difference at this point whether I did or didn't have those thousands of dollars to spend. I would have the rest of my life to worry about bills. It was musky time! Oh, and my honeymoon, too.

CHAPTER II

THE ROAD LESS TRAVELED

The night before we leave had finally arrived. Our apartment was a shambled mess. Crap was cluttered across everything. Apparently, I didn't realize we were moving to Canada. My wife's pile alone resembled a Paris Hilton day trip. We spent hours packing and unpacking the boat and truck based upon what we really needed to bring, versus what we wanted to bring. Jerry had explained to us that Canada, in early July, could be up to ninety degrees, or down to forty degrees this time of year. Spring time tended to start later and end quicker, so I was told. Well, to a woman, that meant pack everything in the closet and both dressers 'just in case.' Our food for the trip was quite basic, but my wife is an incredible cook with whatever she has on hand. She even took the liberty of planning all our meals. I did try my best to convince her into letting me catch our supper every night instead of her pre-planned meals, but for some reason she wasn't so warm to the idea and even laughed at such a notion. I had a slight suspicion she didn't have the same confidence in my fishing ability as I did. I did bring along the cast iron skillet and peanut oil anyway, just in case.

We awoke to a beautiful July day and all I thought was T.G. I. F., and my musky itch was going to receive a good scratching. Jerry informed me the day prior that if we made good time, we could get a good three hours of musky fishing in later that day. After we bid our apartment a farewell, we were off to our rendezvous at the local convince store for some fuel and caffeine.

Once there, we meet up with Jerry and his fishing partner Kenny, and brother Steve, who brought his son, Allen. The game plan was simple: follow Jerry and Steve Hoelzel all the way to Canada, then fish. Since we had no idea how to get there, we were 'supposed' to stick together. But we were traveling with the Hoelzel brothers, who tended to make up the rules as they went. Once on the highway, it became an all-out NASCAR race. It felt like riding on 4 bald tires, low on fuel and a couple of laps down. No wonder they could leave Wisconsin and managed to cram in hours of fishing in Canada before nightfall! By the time we hit the interstate, horns were blowing, middle fingers were flying, and we passed anything that didn't have red and blue berries on their roof. It was like teenagers were given the keys to the family car for the first time, and then forced to drink 10 red bulls before driving. As the morning wore on and the miles slipped by, all that coffee got to work. The urge to take a whiz grew stronger by the minute. Damn thoughts of the Hoover Dam breaking and flooding my truck seemed like a real possibility. I placed a quick cell call to my drafting buddies, and pleaded for a quick, and much needed, bathroom break.

"That's fine, Brad. Do what you have to do, and you'll catch up with us later," Jerry said. I pulled the phone from my ear and gawked at it with a confused eye twitch. "Jerry. I have no idea where we are going! I thought we were going to stop together so no one got lost."

Jerry cleared his throat on the other end. "Oh, that's ok. I won't get lost. I've been to Canada over a dozen times," he replied. I couldn't help but laugh at that one, only because I thought he was joking. He wasn't. "I'm talking about me, Jerry!" I chuckled. "Well, if you can hold it for one more hour, it will be noon and we'll stop at the gas station we always stop at," Jerry explained. I glanced over at my wife. I was a newlywed, but even I could tell I'd better make a pit stop if I ever want to see the finish line again. "Where is this gas station?" I asked Jerry. "Well, You drive through Superior, and as you come into Duluth, Minnesota, you'll want to stay in the left lane. If you don't, you'll end up in the Twin Cities. You then drive five or six miles into Duluth, and you'll see a BP gas station with a Subway. We'll meet you there."

At this point, we understood that if a record pit stop wasn't accomplished, we might end up in the wrong Province. We tore into the first gas station that we find. I will tell you this, it was the most memorable pee I had ever had. There were flood gates that could rival the days of Noah's ark that were set loose, followed by a light-headed, almost orgasmic feeling that, to this day puzzles me.

On the road again. We worked to get our laps back because the pit stop didn't allow us to take in any liquids. It would be at least one hour to our next stop and we couldn't take any further chances. We had only lost eight minutes in our pit stop, but when you're driving in a twenty-four hour Le Mans endurance race, every second counted. I thought if I drove hard and fast enough, I could catch up. Dead wrong. One hour into our sprint, both Laura and I started getting nervous. We couldn't get a hold of Jerry or Steve, so we started looking for the specific BP gas station with the Subway. Trouble is, we couldn't find a BP and Subway combo just down the road from Duluth. We pulled into a regular Subway and waited. Thankfully, the phone rang shortly after we stopped. "Brad. Where are you guys? We're almost done eating and about to leave." My face burnt red. "Jerry, I have no idea where the hell I am! You told me to stop at a BP with a Subway just outside of town, and there is no such thing here!" Jerry mumbled to Steve on the other end of the phone. "Oh, sorry about that. You gotta drive two miles down the road yet to the next town and stop at the Mobile station with the Subway," Jerry explained. Sorry. That's on me. I should have searched for the opposite of what Jerry had told me. I was just shocked it was actually a Subway and not an Arby's. We high-tail it, and five minutes later we spot four stooges smiling and waiting next to their trucks. My wife was not amused. She silently marched by, with me in tow. "You guys better get a move on cause we are leaving soon. Muskies wait for no one," announced Steve.

Irritated, but unable to argue against Steve's simple brilliance, we ran up to the counter in a flash and requested two twelve-inch subs made by the finest young sandwich artist in this land of a ten thousand lakes. When she was through with her craft, she questioned if we wanted anything to drink. Laura and I, in unison, sing, "no thank you". Maybe it was a bit too forcefully, cause the artist offered us a strange look. I slide her a ten dollar bill and we're out the door. Just a little side note: those of you gonna Canada and have a ten plus hour drive, drink only as much liquid as it takes to keep you from dehydrating. When you arrive at your destination, go crazy with the liquids, preferably the alcoholic kind.

We screeched wheels down the road, us in my old Ford beater pickup truck, Jerry in his slightly used Chevy Silverado and Steve in his almost new diesel GMC 3500, with personal license plates reading "MR MUSKY". Note: it should read MR BS. Anyway, Laura and I struggled to keep up with the newer trucks. Each and every stinking hill we encountered ramped the RPMs on the old Ford up to five thousand. The gas gauge plunged at breakneck pace. Bottom line was my truck just couldn't keep up with their seventy mph speeds.

Within thirty minutes, Jerry and Steve were long gone, and once again, it's just Laura and me. I glanced over at my beautiful new wife and I could tell she was concerned we'd get lost. I decided to give Jerry a call to give her some peace of mind. Quite honestly, I really wanted to know if I was even going in the right direction.

"Hey Brad, what's up?" spouted Jerry on the cell. "Oh, not much. I see you guys have left me in your dust again." Jerry chuckled. "Well Brad, I told you to trade in that old Ford and buy yourself a real truck," says Jerry. Funny guy. Like I hadn't spent enough on every other thing, why NOT buy a new truck, too! "Where is Highway 53 going to be taking us?" I swear I could hear Jerry's gears grinding in his head through the cell phone. "Well Brad, you're gonna be on this road for approximately one hundred and fifty miles. You're headed for International Falls, so whatever you do, don't leave this highway. Seven miles before you get into International Falls, you're gonna take the short cut to Highway 11, and that will take you to Baudette." At least he let me know there was a short cut. Being that I've never been here before, I wouldn't know the difference between a short cut and a cross country marathon. "It's on a big bend in the road. You turn left about seven miles from International Falls, like I told you," says Jerry. "A road name would be really helpful to me." I literally have to spell out every single question to him. There was zero logic. There was no common sense. I assumed it was musky fever clouding his mind. At least hoped that all it was. "I don't remember the road name, Brad. I think it's...." Silence. "Jerry, Jerry, Jerryyyyyyyyyyyy! Damn it!" "What's wrong Brad," asked Laura. "Nothing!" I snipped back. Not a good move, but I was pissed. I dialed Jerry's number again and again with the same results of a pre-recorded message that stated "your number cannot be completed as dialed". Fine. On to Steve. "Hey Brad, what's going on? I haven't seen your truck in my mirror for a long while. Hahahaha." Then all went silent again. This wasn't our day. I called Steve's phone back and received the same damn pre-recorded crap. "What's really wrong, Honey?" asked Laura. Time to bite the bullet. "I have no freakin' idea where Jerry's short cut is! And we might not see him or Steve until we reach freakin' Canada, that is if we don't get lost first! So in laymen's terms, were screwed!"

The next one hundred forty miles were spent in total silence. It took some boggy, beaver-filled countryside to remind us we were all alone. If only we could reach Baudette, our gateway to the Promised Land. The home to maple syrup, ice hockey, and Brian Adams, well two out of the three ain't bad. We drove along, and I whisked off into my own little lustful musky daydream daze. Suddenly, I heard someone screaming my name. I snapped out of it into utter amazement as Jerry, Steve, Allen and Kenny were waving and yelling frantically as we flew by at seventy miles per hour. Deciphering how to get off the racetrack and whip back around to the boys, I spotted a dead end marked cul-de-sac only a hundred yards beyond the screaming baboons we'd just passed. It was the first side road I had seen in the last half hour, so maybe luck was changing for the better. We pulled up behind Jerry and I glanced over at my wife. I think she was happier to see those idiots than she was to be riding with me.

"Did you think we had left you for dead?" Jerry snickered. "You know Jerry, I was starting to wonder." "Well, enough screwing around. Let's get to Canada!" barked Steve. Back in the trucks we went and off to the races. This time, I followed very closely to Jerry for the next thirty miles as we drove an old country road that ran parallel to a raging river, which flowed out of Lake of the Woods. Unto itself, Lake of the Woods was home to a very impressive walleye population, I was soon to find out. That meant a healthy food source for our prey.

We strolled into the small town of Baudette, Minnesota. As we lugged in, we were greeted by a sign that read, "Walleye Capital of the World, and home to World's Largest Walleye named Willy." Willy was probably the biggest fiberglass walleye I had ever seen. Nothing but a sure-fire tourist trap begging to have you snap your picture in front of it. So, I did. Like any Wisconsinite that's working to fit in with the locals, I pulled over, grabbed the first Minnesotan we could find, and forced our camera onto them. "Cheese."

After a quick good-bye to the giant walleye, we headed to the gas station were Jerry and the boys were filling up while we played with our Willy. At this point, I could smell it. Canada. And up ahead, the border crossing awaited. To tell you the truth, I was pretty nervous. I hadn't been outside of the U.S. before, so I needed to chat with Jerry for some reassurance.

Let's backtrack. This whole fear thing stemmed back to a friend who had a very bad experience back in 2002. He and some of his college buddies decided on a whim to go camping for a couple of days in the great woods of Canada. The problem was they brought no supplies, unless you count beer, chips, cheese and a few blankets. As they were going to sleep under the stars, wolves began singing them to sleep, so they said. Personally, I think they blacked out from all the booze. Anyway, once at the U.S. and Canadian border, they were questioned how long they planned to stay, and what they had planned to do in Canada. Being college students, their smart-ass answer was, "get drunk and bang some Canadian broads!" For some strange reason, that didn't sit too well with the female guard. After a few hundred more questions, they were notified they'd be watched, but sent on their way.

Not thirty miles out of town, they pulled onto a logging road and set up camp. As the night wore on and alcohol was consumed, one of the kids started screaming about a bright, blinding light bouncing down the road towards them. The border patrol car stopped in front of them. Emerging from the squad, stepped their new friend from earlier in the day. She explained to them, or screamed at them, that someone had reported a forest fire coming from their location. She mentioned that burning was illegal right now due to the severely dry conditions. She labeled them as, "only a bunch of dumb Americans that would try to burn down thousands of acres of Crown Land." To boot, they were also illegally trespassing and in no procession of a camping permit. In very colorful language, they were told pick up first thing in the morning and leave Canada.

BY **BRAD MATHEWSON**

When early morning arrived, they scooped up the beer bottles and blankets and made a run for the border. Once at the border, Security was waiting for them. They were 'requested' to pull over to have their vehicle inspected. As they began, one of the armed guards picked up a duffle bag. Just as he was about to open it, one of the idiots thought it would be funny to scream "NO! NOT THAT BAG!" In a flash, three border guards drew their side arms and ordered all four college boys to the ground and not to move, or they were libel to be shot. The now pants-soaked boys dropped to the ground. They were immediately handcuffed and taken to a holding cell. From there, each one was interrogated for one hour each. After five hours, the Canadian's figured out that they were indeed just dealing with a group of very stupid college dipshits. They were all freed, and told to NEVER return to Canada. This story will forever teach me two things: Be cautious at all border crossings, and Mounties have zero sense of humor.

"So, Jerry. What should Laura and I to expect at the border crossing?" I hesitantly asked. "Well, they're gonna ask you a series of pretty basic questions. Just be honest and polite with them and you'll have no problems," said Jerry. "What about strip searches, water boarding, or the interrogation room?" I asked. "You've seen too many damn movies," Jerry laughed. I chuckled back, more out of embarrassment and relief than thinking any of this was all too funny.

Once we're back to our trucks, Laura and I take up the rear of the convoy to Canada. Steve's truck pulled up to the guard house. Not even a minute later, it's Jerry's turn. Again, in less than a minute, he crossed and sped away. "Oh no. Now where are they going? Hope they didn't just ditch us at the border expecting us to find our way to the resort. Nice friends you have there, Brad." Laura proclaimed. Again, I chuckled, but more out of nervousness that Laura managed to expedite.

It was the moment of truth. Mere feet from crossing into a land I had dreamed about since I was a little pup. My first Canadian Shield musky I wanted so badly was closer than ever. "Sir? Sir! Please shut off your vehicle." Snapped from yet another awesome daydream, this time by a Mountie that was none too pleased I was ignoring her request. "Sorry, I just thinking about the nice honeymoon me and my beautiful bride are gonna enjoy in your country." I'm thinking that was a winner on many levels. "What are you going to be doing in Canada? Where will you be staying? When will you to be returning," said the nice Mountie lady. I explained to the nice Mountie lady where we were going for our week long honeymoon. "You're taking your wife musky fishing for your honeymoon?" She laughed a bit too deeply for my taste. "Why not? It will be fun, right honey?" Laura gave me the first of a great many fake smiles. For the first time, I realized she really wasn't too excited to be going to Canada with four dudes she didn't know and her new husband for her honeymoon. I started to wonder if my dream was going to become a nightmare. As I pondered, the gate arm went up in front of my truck. "Welcome to Canada," said the guard. "Good luck." Somehow, I don't think she was referencing my fishing trip. This may have been confirmed when I drove past the guardhouse. I could hear the loud cackling inside. They all knew what a mistake I had made. They knew I would pay for it for years to come. Starting to realize this, I wasn't going to let them ruin my, err our, trip. I was going to show Laura that you didn't need sandy beaches, overpriced meals, hotels with pools, and swim up bars. This was Canada, and fun was what you made of it. I was going to catch my first Shield musky and have my wife score her first musky ever on this trip if it killed me. Or, she killed me, whichever came first.

A half mile from the border, we found the band of misfits entering the local grocery store. Since you cannot bring fresh fruit or vegetables into Canada, we followed them inside to pick up some produce. Trouble was, you could buy those same fruits and veggies at home for half the price. So my advice is, get real used to fresh fish fries, and eat everything else out of a can while in Canada. There was a bag of Idaho potatoes that literally made my wife gasp. They were three times the price as store bought in the U.S. While on the subject, you're only allowed one bottle of booze OR one case of beer, per person. With that, a 1.75 liter bottle was a tad too much volume and they might make you pay a duty tax. If you're from Wisconsin, bring a smaller bottle and buy a case of beer at the liquor store when you cross the border. Labatt Blue and a fish fry is nearly heaven on Earth.

Once back on the road, we had about one and a half hours to drive to the lodge. But this wasn't any normal drive. Much of it was the pure beauty of land untouched by modern civilization. It was what I had always imagined. But as we motored on, all that enthusiasm screamed to a halt. I had an earlier conversation with Jerry when he told me there were only two classes of people in this area of Ontario: very rich and very poor. We found the latter. This area was not well off by any means. Tar-papered shacks every few miles, many of the front yards resembled salvage yards stuffed with junked cars and trash. The infrastructure of Ontario wasn't much better. The roads were cracked and littered with small potholes. Telephone poles were leaning so far, some had large piles of rocks around them just to keep them upright. The single wires that hung from them were no more than ten feet off the ground because tree branches laid across them. All this was a very disheartening sight in a very beautiful setting. I took some encouragement in that I was there to put some money back into the local economy. Who's pocket that ultimately would end up in was out of my control.

BY BRAD MATHEWSON

CHAPTER III

OUR FIRST CANADIAN VOYAGE

As we drove further down a winding road, the first image of the resort brought an even worse feeling to my already heavy heart. I truly was hoping we had driven to the wrong resort by accident. My fears were realized when I found a sign that read "White Birch Lodge." I started thinking about the pictures of the cute, home-like cottages we saw in the brochure, and determined they must have been taken about fifty years ago. I was afraid to even glance over to the seat next to me. My unhappy wife simply uttered, "Guess we aren't staying at the Hilton." No. It was Shantytown. "How Romantic." I sensed some sarcasm, with a twinge of fury.

I assured my wife that the owners of this fine establishment promised me the finest of Canadian accommodations in a cabin that would be turned into a virtual honeymoon suite prior to our arrival. As we strolled up to the main lodge, the boys were already slipping their boats into the water and unpacking their musky gear. "Only got three hours of fishing. And that's if we hurry," Jerry said in an excitable teenage voice. "Where do we go?" I questioned. "Side door of the main lodge. Meet with Ben so he can get your fishing licenses in order. Get moving! We have hungry muskies waiting for us out there!"

As the wife and I rounded the corner of the lodge, an extremely large man, with a cigarette drooping from his lips, zoomed up in a golf cart and stared at us for an uncomfortably long period of time. We introduced ourselves, and he blurted out, "WHAT DA YA WANT????" I explained we had a reservation for this week. He offered an, "I don't know who the hell you guys are" expression, and strolled into the lodge. Laura and I look at one another, shrugged our shoulders, and followed him inside. We found the tubby Canadian in his office, rummaging through paperwork and grumbling something to himself about, "damn people." I rapped on the door and he glanced up for a brief moment to notify us to come back in a few minutes, as he was busy. So much for that friendly Canadian greeting! Not even some small talk that all Lodge owners give to their new customers whom are about to spend big bucks for a week's vacation they've been looking forward to all year. After waiting the mandatory ten minutes, I nervously knock on his door once more. This time, we're permitted to enter. Hallelujah! This time he was all business. Licenses were bought and filled out. Basic fishing regulations were explained. Then he notified us about the additional fees for the putting in and removing of our boat, daily docking fees, and the fact that he didn't like people bringing in their own gas. He wanted us to buy only his gasoline. Of course, it was at three times the price it should be, even back then. I politely told him we already brought enough fuel for the trip.

I quickly laid blame on the Hoelzel boys, as they told us to. That lit a fire under Ben's already scorched Canadian rear. "I'll be out in a couple of minutes to back your boat in with my tractor," muttered Ben. I quickly volunteered to back in the boat myself, something that must have been an oddity to Ben. "If your boat hits any rocks, I'm not liable for it. If you hit any of my posts or buildings, you'll find it on your bill."

The reason he wanted to back in our boat with his tractor was to charge an extra fee for it. His boat landing was beyond poor, and consisted of a very narrow gravel path between the lodge, a fish-cleaning house, and a large tree. You have to back your trailer between all that and down the face of solid rock to get into the water. Once you get there, to your left is a large pile of rocks hidden in the water, while to your right a giant boulder awaited. All this led to you having to start your motor the moment it hits the water to back straight out. Accomplish this and you shouldn't have any problem. Anyone with half-way decent boat skills can do this, you just have to stay focused. So I quickly backed in my boat, hopped out of the truck, and jumped in the boat as it's came off the rail. I fired up the motor, with old Ben eyeballing the whole situation from his office window. I can sense the hope in his glare for a mistake, but I nailed it, and in record time, if I do say so myself. I offered Ben a 'tip of the hat' as he threw the curtains shut. I hauled the boat up to the dock and tied it off. Finally, feeling in my element and in control, I sprang back in the truck and scooted up to meet Laura at our Honeymoon suite.

"Well baby, are you ready for your romantic cottage by the lake we've been dreaming about for the last six months?" Ever the optimist, Laura offered her first smile in some time. As I opened the door to our home away from home, I was transported back in time to around 1950. Laura said nothing as she went from room to room. The only clue of her disappointment was the slight shaking of her head. The floors were an orange and black shag carpet. The stove and refrigerator looked as if they were stolen from the Smithsonian.

Dark brown paneling covered the walls, while yellow stained ceiling tiles caked from the hundreds of indoor fish fries and bacon festivals hung above us. The strong smell of mildew lofted in the air. To top it all off, in the bedroom were two single beds. Not a king-sized love mattress, or even a double cuddle cushion.

Two single kiddie beds stared at us. As I looked over at my unimpressed wife, I thought she was going to cry. Somehow, she held it together and proceeded to open windows. She barked out orders to find some cleaning products so she could make this dump livable. I shut my mouth and did what I was told. I knew this was going to be a long, cold honeymoon and if I was lucky, I would get to sleep in the single bed next to my beautiful new bride and not in the boat.

After I finished hauling everything in from the truck, I begun casing the joint. My awesome wife had really cleaned the place up well and even pushed together the two beds. "Nice job! Now let's go fishing! The boys are waiting for us at the docks." Laura peered out the greased window. "It looks kind of choppy out there. You sure we should go?" I calmed Laura with the assurance that in a boat, on a lake, I'm in my zone. To ease her mind further, I had Jerry back that up. "Everything's gonna be fine. Just follow us. We're just going outside the bay three miles or so to a group of islands where we'll fish till dark. Then we'll all head back," explained Jerry. As we motored out of the protection of the bay, I realized the waves were much larger than I had thought. Once you left the bay, there was a large pipeline where wind and the building waves from the large open basin were free to smash you at full force. The worst part was when it hit you from the side, not allowing you to angle or cut into the waves. Instead, the waves picked you up and you're left with this almost weightless feeling with virtually no control of your boat. With a modified V, we were like a surf board hanging ten on top of three foot waves. Jerry's deep V's cut into the wave like a hot butter knife.

Once we managed to make it to the islands, Jerry yelled over the wind gusts for us to start fishing and watch out for rocks. I hoisted my rod, snapped on a bucktail and started working the windblown point. I gazed over at my wife with exuberance. She sat there, gripping her seat and with pale skin.

"What's wrong, Laura?" I asked, as if I didn't already know. "I don't like this, the wind and waves are getting larger and the sky to the North is growing darker by the minute," explained Laura. "This is what they call rock'n and rolling! You pound the windblown structure and hold on so you don't fall out of the boat." I encouraged her to hold tight, and I kept on fishing for another ten minutes without incident. Suddenly, a large wave crashed over the side of the boat, drenching us both. It was time to admit something big was brewing in the Canadian sky. "Put your life jacket on!" I screamed to my now petrified wife. I struggled to crank on the motor, but it wouldn't start. I glance over and find we were headed dangerously close to a pile of boulders. "COME ON YOU SON OF A BITCH, START!" Finally, the little Sixty Yamaha roared to life and I took note of our location. With me in full-blown fishing mode for the last twenty minutes, we had somehow drifted a good quarter mile from Jerry and Kenny without even realizing it. One way or another, I had to get back to them because my GPS had unexpectedly quit working, and this storm was going to be on us fast. As we made our way toward Jerry, the rain began spraying us in sheets, and the wind cranked up with at least fifty mph gusts. We slowly rode out each wave as it hammered our little craft. After twenty hair-raising minutes, we managed to make it back to Jerry and the crew. "Let's get to cover," I bark to the guys, but my voice was drowned out by the howling winds. I started waving my arms frantically until they saw me and scurried over. "We have to get to that next group of islands for safety," said Jerry. "I don't think my boat can make it through all that open water. Those islands have to be a mile away." "I'll lead the way breaking the waves, you stay close behind and ride in my wake. We'll make it there just fine." Jerry was well experienced in this type of setting, and though I had years of boating practice under my belt, I still felt unsure of trusting his experience. Either way, we really didn't have any other option.

This plan started off on a good note, as we cruised behind them without incident for at least a couple of minutes. Then Jerry's stronger, faster yacht started pulling away from our dinghy. Quickly, we were out of the safety zone of his wake. I tried shouting at the top of my lungs, but it was to no avail. None of the guys could hear us and were getting further away by the second. Soon, they were a full football field away. At that moment, the storm hit us with all she had. The three-foot waves turned in to five footers that splashed over the front of our little boat. Within two minutes, we had at least six inches of water on the floor of the boat. The bilge pump worked overtime but couldn't keep up. It was raining so hard and fast that I could barely keep my eyes open before stinging rain would pound them shut. I would wipe my eyes with the back of my hand, take a quick look in the direction of travel, and repeat this occurrence thousands of times over the next thirty minutes. Our little boat was riding up and down on the waves instead of cutting through them. Each time we would go up, I thought the boat was going to flip over. That's when I would unleash a little throttle and power over the waves until we'd head back down the other side. I scanned over at my bride and told her I loved her and I wouldn't let anything happen to her. The face she gave me I will never forget. It was of pure, unrelenting fear.

"We're gonna make it! We just started our lives together. We're gonna grow old and watch our grandchildren grow up!" My words left little impression. Now I'm not much of a religious person, but at that moment, I said a little prayer to the good Lord for some help.

I was sorry for bringing my wife to Canada. She was more than I deserved, and if we got through this, I would spend the rest of my life showing her how much I loved her. At that moment, and maybe for the first time in my life, death didn't scare me. Nor did Mother Nature. I had the one person I loved more than anything in the world sitting next to me, and I couldn't let her down. I was going to kick Mother Nature in the face and knock out anything in my path. I had learned long ago, you can do all the praying and wishing you want, but if you don't help yourself, no one else will.

As we rode out each wave, the rain felt like burning acid in my eyes. Fear turned into anger, and then pure rage, for we were going to win and live a long happy life together. Just then, as quickly as it had all began, the winds died. The black clouds eased into a smoky gray and the most intense double rainbow I have ever seen, colors so vibrant even Hollywood couldn't replicate it, morphed above our heads. We had made it to the islands. To this day, I'm still not sure how. I couldn't see Jerry or the Islands for almost a half an hour, but there we were. Laura appeared as if she had seen a ghost. That said, she was more than willing to make the two mile boat ride back.

"What did you think of that?" Jerry spoke with a smile on his face. "I think we had enough for today, Jerry. We're headin' back to the cabin and having a drink or ten." "Do you want us to lead the way?" Jerry asked. Laura shot Jerry a look that would scare the Devil. "No, it's safer for everyone if we go this alone," I replied. "Okay. Suit yourself."

After a relatively uneventful return trip back to the dock, Laura leapt out and bee-lined it to the cabin to relax and take a much needed hot shower. I wondered if she would ever get back into a boat again after that fiasco. I recognized that I had scared the hell out of her, and to be honest, I have been in some rough waters before, but nothing quite like what we had just been through. For a second, the fear almost took us both to an early meeting with our maker. As I was getting everything buttoned down for the night, I surveyed the bay and viewed white caps rolling in, each one a little larger than the next. I glanced down at my craft and I knew I had brought a rubber chicken to a gunfight. I vowed, then and there, to sell my Modified V as soon as we returned home.

A couple of hours passed. Suddenly I heard the war cries of our victorious crew as Jerry had netted a small musky and Steve and Allen each had landed a few Northern Pike. Not too bad for a few hours of fishing through a big storm. "How scary was that storm that moved in on us? How did you guys even make it through it with a boat whose gun wall sits maybe eight inches above the water?" Allen questioned. After having stewed on this for a few hours, I had pinned down the culprit of our adventure. "Allen. Your uncle told me that a Mod. V would work just fine for this trip. And now I know he was full of crap!" "No kidding. I stood in your boat on solid ground and I didn't feel safe!" joked Allen. I didn't find it funny. I peeked over at my wife and could tell this conversation was not helping my cause for getting her back into the boat the next morning. As with most disagreements, I tried smoothing things over with her by offering a cold beverage. "I'll take one, too!" said Allen. "Yeah. One for Steve and I," requested Jerry, as they strolled in through the clunky screen door.

With a freshly cracked Canadian brew, Jerry yanked up a folding chair at a table and plopped down. "Now let me show you guys where you can catch some fish without needing to go more than a couple of miles to do it. Where's your Sabaskong Bay map?" Jerry wondered.

After handing over the map to Jerry, he immediately began marking it up with a pencil, circling places to search for Muskies. Some he had taken fish at in the past, while others he thought always looked enticing but hadn't been to yet. A couple of hours and few beers later, we bid goodnight to our company to retire to our love nest. Well, the nest part, at least. I knew from that night on, any chance of romance was gonna be squashed by my friends stopping over and drinking up all our beer. But that's fishin', right?

CHAPTER IV

FIRST DAY, FIRST ENCOUNTER

It was now Saturday morning and I woke up stiff and sore as hell. Must have been that rusty spring buried in my back all night. I wandered into the bathroom for a drink of water, but instead of refreshing spring water, I'm treated to fish poop. Come to find out, all of the Lodge's water came straight from the lake, and the only water that's treated for drinking was the kitchen tap. Laura found that out the hard way. She brushed her teeth with fish poop. She was not amused by my nonstop giggling while she dry heaved into the sink after swallowing some of Canada's lake whiskey. Isn't that why we get married? Gotta have someone else to laugh at, right?

After a hearty breakfast of bacon, eggs and toast, it was time to hit the water. I could tell Laura was a little hesitant getting back into our dinghy. I assured her that the first sign of trouble and we would head back right away. She begrudgingly agreed, and we were on our way. We motored on out of the bay and stopped at a small group of oak covered islands. I started working double 10s over the rocky points. On my third cast, as I headed into the first turn of my figure eight, that's when she hit. The strike was so violent and unexpected that the rod nearly ripped away from my grasp. In a last ditch effort, I tried a short sweeping hook set, but it was to no avail. As I peered down into the frothy gin colored water, the giant and I locked eyes but for only a second. It really felt like a "nice try, Rookie. It's not going to be that easy," kind of look from the monster. With one flick of her deep finned tail, she was off like a torpedo and back to destroying anything she deemed edible.

I stood there for an thirty seconds, replaying the whole thing in my head. A new sense of confidence came over me. If we were on the water for this short amount of time and got to experience one giant fish, then L.O.T.W. must be teaming with hungry fifty inchers. What this young green horn was about to learn, one fish a pattern does not make. Four hours later, not another musky so much as raised. It was time to leave wind blown points and try a different pattern.

It was getting close to lunchtime and my stomach rumbled. I was getting a strong craving for my wife's Wisconsin famous pickles and bologna sandwiches. We decided to go on the backside of the island we were fishing and take a little break

BY **BRAD MATHEWSON**

from the wind and the waves and regroup. That's when I discovered something very interesting. My fish finder said it was sixty-four degrees - five degrees warmer than the water we had just been fishing. Inside the wind protected cove, the water was dead calm and the sun was beating on the sandy shore and wood strewn bottom. This was the perfect place for a musky to warm itself and not have to fight the pounding waves and heavy winds they had been having for the last four days. Before heading to shore, I had to drop a line. My first cast was just past two lone rocks with good reed cover. An all-around a great place for a musky to catch some rays and ambush its prey. As the DC-Ten hit the water, I was already engaging the reel to create that perfect bubble stream and create lift to bulge my bucktail past the rocks. Just as I did, WHAMMY! My line snagged tight. I set the hook hard and the fight was on.

Only one problem, as the fish neared the boat, I noticed it wasn't a musky. It was a very large northern pike. Laura was right on task, slipping the net under what would be my largest northern ever. As I unhooked the treble hooks from the corner of her mouth, (the fish, not Laura), I am stunned at how heavy and thick she was. Northern in Wisconsin, don't have the kind of thick shoulders that Canadian northern have. Once in the boat, we gave it a quick check of the tape and she measured out at forty-two inches. Where I'm from, that's a damn nice fish whether it's a musky or northern. I returned the northern quickly after a photo and she swam back to the same reed bed.

I tossed a few more casts and I see a familiar sight just two feet behind my bait. It was a musky! As it neared the boat, it knew something wasn't right and disappeared before I could even start my figure eight.

We angled the rest of the afternoon and only raised two more fish. We never really found a hot pattern to rely on. As the sun set, I convinced my wife to stop at one more spot. I explained that low light conditions are a great time to turn a follower into an eater. She agreed, but I could tell she was exhausted. And frankly, so was I. This was the longest I had ever had her in the boat and she fished almost cast for cast with me all day long. Just a reiteration of why I love her so much.

There were two islands connected by a sand bar and the sun was setting postcard perfect between them. Just as I made my last cast, out of the corner of my eye, I spot something black slinking slowly along the shoreline. "Oh, it's a baby bear!" My wife frantically scurried to remove the camera from the case. "Can we get closer?" Laura questioned. I eased on the trolling motor and we slowly creep up on the curious little bear. My wife snapped pictures faster than the paparazzi chasing Brittany Spears. WOOOF!!! I knew what that meant. Mama bear quickly made her way towards us. We weren't twenty-five feet from her cub. By the look she gave us city slickers, she was none too happy we hadn't asked her permission first. I jumped off the front deck and behind the wheel as Mama bear entered the water. Just like the movies, the motor picked the perfect moment to fail to turn over. The angry mother continued her approach. Luckily, a large cloud of smoke lofted into the air and the engine roared to life. Mama and baby bear had the tables turned on them, and they reversed course and took to the trees. That spelled just enough excitement for the day. We followed our plot line back to the dock. Time for two hots and double cot.

After our late meal, and just like clockwork, all the boys piled into are cabin and sat around the kitchen table to talk stupid, drink whiskey, and talk muskies lost and apprehended for the day. I did more listening than jabbering, which is a rarity for me. Of course, they all clutched massive fish. When you're telling fishing stories, guppies are massive fish. I'm sure my wife was in honeymoon heaven with five smelly dudes eating her snacks and drinking our booze. I might be lacking a little when it comes to the romance department. As the evening wore on, Laura retired to bed and my buddies retired to their fart sacks outside. My first full day of Canadian musky fishing was in the books. I was too excited for the next day to get to sleep anytime soon.

CHAPTER V

BEAR DUMPIN'

We woke up to driving rain slapping our roof and winds blowing like crazy, with gust of 40 mph. I looked over to Hoelzel's tent city, half expecting it to be floating in the lake, and here they're up and almost ready to go fishing. I peeped at the clock and it read seven o'clock. I may not know much, but I knew better than to wake my bride this early on our vacation.

I mean, there's a reason I gave her the nickname 'Baby Grizz'. Instead, I made up some instant coffee and witnessed my crazy friends dress in full rain gear and head for the docks, lunch pails in hand. Out on the bay, I observe a minimum of three foot swells roll in. At that moment, I decided that it would be better for us to stay on shore. I'm pretty confident that Laura would be relieved. I, on the other hand, was a bit bummed out. To keep perspective, Jenny had told me over the phone that there was plenty to do on a rainy day. And every other aspect of what she told me was dead-on accurate... this wasn't gonna be good.

At nine o'clock, Laura finally rolled out of bed. I filled her in on the weather and I could tell she was not upset in the least. After a quick breakfast, we headed for the main lodge for our day's list of fun activities. We strolled into the lodge, and the entire family stared at us like we had missing lips. I uncomfortably waddled over to Jenny and told her we wouldn't be fishing. I quizzed her on what events were going on that day. She gave me this empty stare, the kind where she might not understand English. "Well, you can go for a stroll. Or you can fish off the docks for walleye, crappie, and small mouth bass. There's leeches in the dock house. Just write down what you use." Laura and I glance at each other in dismay. "We could do that at home. Isn't there a place to shoot pool or at minimum watch some sports or movies?" "All we get is the weather channel and a few French speaking TV shows. I'm using the pool table as a make shift desk, so maybe you guys can play cards back at your cabin or something," offered Jenny. She had somehow made me even more peeved. "That sounds like a blast!" I replied, with my most sarcastic tone possible. With nothing else to do, I thought I'd keep up the banter. I conjured up my best John Candy thought. "I say, how's the bear dump situation here?" Surprised and upbeat by the question, Jenny jumped all over it. "We have a pretty good one! Make sure to go two hours before dark and park by the gate. Unfortunately, you ain't allowed to drive into the dump anymore." Somewhat optimistically, I got the distance to the dump. "Just five miles from the lodge. Dead Fall Road. You can't miss it!" cheered Jenny. I almost thought she was gonna tag along by her enthusiasm.

Since we had most the day to kill, Laura and I chose to try fishing off the docks. I'm not real thrilled about this, especially when I have a boat feet away. But it was better to be safe than to drown in your dinghy. My hopes were Laura would get the itch to give it another try after catching a few dock fish. I gave Laura a leech & slip bobber set up. Obviously, this is the simplest way for her to catch a ton of fish and have fun. I use a 1/8 ounce jig, tipped with a leech. If you have ever been to L.O.T.W., you will notice there are literally leeches swimming everywhere. Everything from crappie to musky feed heavily on them.

My jig barely touched the water and I heard my wife yelling she had one on the line. I see a handsome bronze back jump a foot out of the water and dive under the dock. Laura steered her out and into my thumb clamp. After a picture and quick measurement of eighteen inches, we released her. Laura genuinely smiled ear to ear. I realized that my time today was better spent helping her catch as many fish as possible, my first Shield musky will just have to wait. So I put my rod back in my boat and told her to cast back to the same broken rocks. The second the float splashed water, it sunk down again with another smallie. This one measured seventeen inches. The next couple of hours are a mixed bag of crappie, small-mouth, and walleyes.

We kept enough paper mouths and walleye for a fish fry that night, and my wife was beaming with excitement. She provided all the fish for our supper and I had more fun watching her than I ever could have had fishing myself.

I don't know if any of you have ever done a fish fry in a cast iron skillet, inside a cabin with all the windows and doors closed, but it's not something I would recommend doing unless you like smelling like a McDonald's fish fillet and your cabin looking like a bad Cheech and Chong movie. We did discover one nice thing. Those pesky smoke alarms wouldn't be waking us up in the middle of our Backdraft dreams. No batteries. I guess dead guests couldn't sue tight-assed Lodge owners. Something told me this wasn't an accident.

After our smoky supper, we decided to give the bear dump a try. We followed Jenny's directions and surprisingly, they brought us right there. This, by far, was the most shocking thing to happen all trip. We pulled over next to the large cyclone fence blocking us from driving down into the dump. From where we parked, you could see only about a third of the landfill. I withdrew my binoculars and sure enough, I noticed a small black bear. In its mouth appeared to be a well-used diaper. "Oh my God! That's totally disgusting!" hurled Laura. "Baby, Canadian's waste nothing!" I joked.

Just then, something seized my eye. A huge boar crossed the road not ten feet in front of the truck. His nose sniffed the ground as if he tracked something. As the large bear entered the dump, the other bears did a quick double take and high-tailed. Apparently, this was his dump. Once the monster black bear wandered off, we watched other bears come and go from the dump for the next few hours. I peered over at Laura and noticed she was having a good time. How many girls get to go to a literal dump on their honeymoon?

As we were about to leave, a black SUV pulled up alongside us and asked if we had seen any bears. I told them if they turned off their truck and sat still, they'd see a parade of trash bag totting bears in due time. They sat in their vehicle for maybe ten minutes before they did probably the stupidest thing my wife and I had ever seen. A dad and two young boys exited their SUV, while the smarter sex stayed inside. To up the ante just a bit, good old dad carried a white bag full of garbage to feed hungry Yogi and Boo-boo. They sauntered past the cyclone fence and disappeared into the dump. A few minutes later, I watched a large bear appear on the other side of the road. It crossed between our vehicles and entered the dump down the same path the father of the year had just led his kids. I couldn't take it anymore. I honked my horn in hopes of scaring the bear before it could do any harm to this idiot and his family. Seconds after blowing my warning, we witnessed dad and his boys running for the SUV and jumping in. They pulled up alongside us with their window down. The guy was in full panic mode while his boys are balling in the back seat. The story, as he told it, was they were strolling down into the dump with the bag when they heard a noise behind them. They whirled around to find a large bear not fifteen feet away, trailing them like a pet dog. That's when they heard my horn and the bear bolted into the woods carrying their dropped trash bag.

I listened to their whole story and told them to stay the hell out of the dump. People, bears are not cute cuddly pets! They are large predators that could have easily eliminated his whole family if it felt the need to. I felt sorry for the kids to have to grow up with a father who probably had grown up watching Gentle Ben and hugging bunnies. Bears are to be respected. His wife, now very angry, thanked us and sped off spitting gravel as they darted away. I noticed that they sported a southern U.S. license plate from a state I was pretty certain didn't carry many bears. (No, not Florida). "I think it's time for us to go, too," decided Laura. "Yup, time to hit the old fart sack," I pronounced. "You're gross, Brad."

CHAPTER VI

DEJA VU AGAIN

The next morning, I awoke to the sun shining on my wife's face. She was more beautiful now than I remember on our wedding day. I contemplated just how much she must really love me. Who else would agree to go on this memorable fishing trip instead of Florida for a honeymoon? Either that, or I was a pretty good salesman in that I had made Canada sound better than Disneyland. The third option was I didn't care what she thought, and would have gone without her, and she just tagged along so we would spend our honeymoon together. After some real serious debating, I decided it was one of the first two.

After another quick breakfast, Laura agreed to give it another shot. We hit the lake to find that musky that graced our presence days earlier. Though sunny, the winds weren't completely dead. I ignored it as I was thinking about our big fish spot from the other day and wondered if she was still in the area. I hoped she didn't move to another, more complex spot. We pulled up to the same reeds with the large rock and I let my wife have the first cast with her spinner bait. I watched behind her bait all the way back to the boat. Nothing. My turn. I bomb casted my Buchertail tight against the rock and reeled as fast as I could. I then reduced speed just a bit and repeated this all the way back to the boat. As I watched, a large musky followed my line. I thrust my rod deep into the lake and started whipping large figure eights, ripping my bait deep on the inside turns and high on the outside turns. I studied how the fish reacted to my bait. This went on for maybe a minute and until she disappeared into the deep. I kept it up for a while longer, knowing that sometimes a fish will break off and sit right under your boat to check things out. This wasn't the case. As I was ready motor up and head towards a new hot spot (or presumed hot spot), the skies commenced to darken again. Quickly, things took a turn for the all too familiar worse. The wind whipped to thirty plus mph The clouds rushed in at an alarming rate. I didn't even need to look. I could sense the tension swell in my wife from the other side of the boat. Time for the life vests, as it was gonna be a bumpy ride. "I think I can outrun the storm and make it back to the docks before it hits us. We're only two miles out." I worked hard to convince Laura, and maybe myself a bit. But I didn't want to go through the do-or-die experience we went through only days earlier, either. I turned over the little Sixty HP Yamaha and she actually started right up. I slammed down the throttle and the bow shot right up. I trimmed her down just a bit and we're on full plane. It was an all-out drag race against Mother Nature, and I was gonna hand her a pink slip.

The waves built to a height of three feet in the shallow bay. It was slightly more than a little chop and we bounced around the boat like two drunken pin balls. Every wave we broke made my head and ass feel like they were directly connected. We trudged through it, and miraculously, reached the docks in one piece. This had earned Laura hatred of this boat as much as I did. The only question was, did she hate me? After securing our boat to the docks, I stare out over the bay. A white wall of rain headed our way in break neck speed. I couldn't help but wonder how the boys were handling this storm. "I think your friends must have a few screws loose to want to fish in this crap every day," Laura said. I agreed with her, but deep inside, I really wished I was out there with them.

We dashed inside as the rain poured down in buckets. Only one thing newlywed couples could do to pass the time in Canada...play cards and drink beer! Nothing more romantic than a dirty, smelly, outdated fishing cabin. Technically, that really didn't matter to me or any other guy. Hell, we'd get it on in a horse stall if the opportunity presented itself.

After an early supper, I discovered an old radio in the closet. This was unexpected pay dirt. We rattled through the entire dial, and barely found a few stations. On one, I could hear a man's voice, but it was clearly French along with the every other damn station we could get any voices on. There we sat. No TV, no Internet and no radio station we could understand.

I officially proclaimed it was starting to suck. I threw the old relic back into the closet. Now what were we gonna do?

"I was thinking about the bear dump," said Laura. Honestly, I had other husband and wife things in mind. Those damn bears were always stealing my picnic basket! Seeing bears wasn't a bad alternative. I'd have preferred 'bares', but this would do. We hopped into the truck and were off to the only form of entertainment we would get on this trip. As we pulled in, there were three other cars watching. How sad is it when the only fun you can find in God's country is staring at black bears eating dirty diapers? The rain let up, but the winds were still quite strong. I was skeptical if a bear would even show up.

We waited a long half hour until Laura spotted a mom with two cubs headed our way. They parked right in front of our truck as if waiting for handouts. Then, a man in a red ranger started chucking large marshmallows at the bears. This idiot started yelling, "Come hear little bears! I have all kinds of goodies for you!" Moron. We watched this guy emerge from the passenger seat with the bag of marshmallows and started pelting the young cubs repeatedly like he's Randy Johnson tossing at doves.

The cubs began to whine and the game was over. Mama's gonna charge the mound and go Mike Tyson on him. We watched in excitement and fear as the man dropped the marshmallows, but instead of jumping into the ranger, the idiot took off screaming and slipping in his own shit back down the gravel road. The bluff charge had me convinced that we were both going to witness an awesome, and well-deserved, bear attack.

The idiot had it coming. Instead, old mama bear and her two cubs enjoyed a more-deserved bounty of marshmallows, and let the fast-baller stumble into the night.

BY **BRAD MATHEWSON**

CHAPTER VII

DUMB OR TOUGH

The next morning, the weather presented us more of the same. Sunny skies, but blustery wind with gusts up to forty mph. Laura immediately suggested to fish off the dock again that morning, but I was at that point where we came to fish musky, and needed to at least try to boat out into the bay to have any chance. She reluctantly tagged along, on the condition that she got to do some more walleye fishing for another fish fry that night. Didn't have to twist my arm to eat fish. Sounded like a win-win.

We motored over to a promising weed bed. I set Laura up with the old stand-by slip bobber with a leech. The bait no more than hit the water and the bobber was yanked under. She reeled in a nice eater walleye, and continued this trend. Within the next ten minutes, we had our limit of four walleyes that were ready for the skillet. That's one reason why I loved Canada so much. So many fish, they almost jumped into your deep fryer direct from the lake. That behind us, I was anxious to get out there and try a little musky fishing. We spent the next three hours working the bay, all while getting beat to hell in the pounding waves. I was determined to tough this day out, but Laura had quite enough.

We scoot the boat back into the shoreline to the dock. Once there, I caught a peek at the owner's wife and teenage daughter sunbathing in the sweltering 60 degree sun. I had to think, it was a beautiful July day if you grew up in Canada, thirty plus mph winds aside.

As we pulled up to the bathing ladies, I asked how the swimming was in the lake. I understood that the water temperature on my graph read sixty-two degrees, and personally, I didn't think any sane person would swim in water that cold. But in Canada, maybe sixty-two is balmy?

"Why don't you tell me. I thought you Wisconsinites did your polar bear swimming in the winter. This should be like a hot bath for you," said Jenny. To me, that sounded like a challenge. And being a representative of the Badger state and never been known to take being called chicken very well (see Marty McFly), I stripped down to my boxers and dove into the water. This was where the 'sane' reference above would have done me well to think about moments before diving in. The water was so cold that my manhood retreated into my body so fast, it was like having an 'iney' instead of a large 'outy'. (This is a fishing story, isn't it?) Jenny's teenage daughter dove in and joined me.

Very cool on one hand, and very uncomfortable on the other, considering my newlywed wife was feet away. I asked Laura to strip down and come on in. Again, her reluctance was apparent, and she wasn't insane and stayed ashore. For me, after mere minutes, I was shivering so bad my muscles began to ache. I glanced up and Laura and Jenny were already hiking away. I was alone with an eighteen year old girl...on my honeymoon... in a lake. Better get out of the water before my wife started wondering what was going on down here. As I began my exit, the ice cold water had zapped away my strength in the few short minutes I had been in. Trudging myself back onto the dock, while keeping my boxers from falling off, turned out to be quite the chore. Jenny's daughter, Becky, had a good laugh as my boxers slide half off my ass. Once on the dock, I was pretty embarrassed (not a-bare-assed), so I sprinted back to the cabin and into a hot shower. Quickly, I was reminded that this was the same water I had just came out of. Damn it.

"What the hell were you thinking? Stripping down and going for a swim in water that cold? Are you insane?" questioned Laura. I quickly defended myself and that I did it for the people of Wisconsin, to show that we were just as tough as our northern neighbors. "I think all you proved is you're not very bright," Laura ventured. Maybe, but it's like that song goes "if you're gonna be dumb, you gotta be tough". I think I proved my point.

After I got dressed, I did my standard bay review and see the familiar wall of demon water about to ruin yet another day. It rained cats and dogs the rest of the day, with the occasional crack of lighting. We were trapped in our small, one bedroom cabin with only beer and the occasional game of cards to keep us entertained. Again. Not exactly the pinnacle of romance and relaxation you think you're gonna get when you're on your honeymoon. I was just hoping Laura wasn't going to file divorce papers or have me committed to a mental institution when we arrived back in the states. At this point in the trip, I wouldn't have blamed her for either.

CHAPTER VIII

END OF A RELUCTANT JOURNEY

I was not shocked to see it still raining when I woke in the early morning, but what I was surprised to see was Steve and Allen breaking up camp and packing everything into the truck. Steve was a die hard Musky hunter, and neither rain nor snow nor wind would keep him off the water. His (PMA) Positive Musky Attitude is stronger than anyone I had ever fished with. I dressed quickly and darted out to see what was going on.

As I approached camp, I questioned, "Hey, you girls giving up already? It's just a little wind and rain." "Brad, you don't know how bad it is out there. Every damn day we've been pounded by rain and wind something awful. We're wet and cold and I can't take this shit anymore. It's getting to where we can only fish the back side of islands and we have to plan our route all day. Ducking behind islands because the waves are getting too large. Bullshit. We're getting the hell beat out of us every time we have to cross open water with no wind protection. There's gonna be an accident out here and someone's going to drown. No fish is worth a life. We're going home." Steve wasn't giving in, he was being smart.

"Steve. All you have to do is duck behind the islands and you'll be just fine," joked Jerry. That apparently didn't sit well with Steve, who truly did feel like he was letting his son down by giving in. "Jerry, you're f****** stupid if you go back out there again! The wind is blowing nonstop, with thirty-five mph gusts. Plus, it's raining all the time. Don't expect me to go looking for your body!" warned Steve. "I'll be fine. We'll hang around camp for a while and let things simmer down a bit," said Jerry. Steve shuffled away from Jerry. "Well, Allen and I are leaving. We just have to load the boat and settle up with Ben." As Steve approached me, he uttered, "So how's the honeymoon going, Brad? Everything you thought it would be? Betcha didn't think you were gonna be stuck in this crappy little cabin because you can't get on the lake."

I agreed with Steve. "Damn weather sucks and my wife is wondering how this adventure could possibly be better than Florida. I hope she doesn't try to kill me in my sleep."

"Well good luck with that," Steve chuckled. I think he actually meant that.

With that, Steve and Allen loaded up their boat and left for the dairy state. Part of me wanted to leave with them and forget this nightmare ever happened. I just wanted my wife to experience my childhood dream of going fishing in Canada, and if we spent some time hunting musky, that would be ok, too. Who was I kidding here. I wanted my first Canadian Shield musky more than anything in the world. Giving up was not an option. The wife and I would just have to fish smarter next time we could get back on the lake, I told myself.

Later that morning, the wind 'died down' to the mid-twenty mph. I noticed Jerry and Kenny making their way down to the docks. I wished we could go out too, but the lake was still too angry for our little dinghy. I grabbed my rod and a bucktail and headed down to the docks to shore cast for musky. Laura and I had overheard the lodge owner telling another guest that there have been a few nice musky taken off the docks, including a forty-five incher. One guest even claimed to have had a nice fifty-inch fish sweep at his crank bait while casting for small-mouths. This time, I went down alone and spent the next three hours casting every dock and piece of structure I could find, though the cold rain was destroying my PMA. Just as I was picking up, a group of walleye anglers from the cabin next door were gearing up to head out in there twenty foot bath tub Lund, when one of the younger guys started screaming. "I think I hooked a Musky!" Just then, a mid-forty inch fish launched itself like a rocket from the water. The inexperienced walleye fisherman dropped his rod too much, giving Mr. Musky just enough room to do what he does best: the old 'head shake and gone' trick. Before you knew it, he's gone in a matter of seconds. The surprised teenager just stared blankly at his little jig that had swung back and landed with a loud thump on the dock. I looked over at him from across the dock with a huge smile and said, "that's musky fishing for you." I don't think he took my observation well. He threw his rod in the boat and slumped himself into a seat. I shouted over to him, "don't feel bad, I haven't caught a musky and I've been here for going on six days now." With that, I could see his mood change and he smiled back at this sorry musky hunter.

I knew my time here in Canada was coming to an end. The forecast was predicting more rain with even stronger winds, and I had overheard Jerry tell Kenny if this weather didn't change soon, they would also be leaving. Back at the cabin, I retold my musky story to Laura. She felt bad that it wasn't me on the other end of that rod, but that's fishing. As the day went on, the wind picked up even more than any other day so far, and I knew Jerry and Kenny would be leaving the next morning. We would be left all alone, without really knowing our way back to Wisconsin.

Later in the day, I noticed Jerry climb into his truck and head for the boat landing. Kenny headed down to the docks on foot. I put on my rain gear and head for the boat landing to find out what was going on. After a quick conversation, my thoughts were proven correct. They were heading home in the morning, and I was concerned with staying behind. "We are leaving in the morning. If you want to come, you are welcome to follow us home," said Jerry. Poor Laura, I thought.

The weather had been horrible and we were pretty much stuck in the cabin at Thunderstorm Alley. Not to mention, I nearly drowned us on this trip. I had to decide whether to push forward and stay the distance, or cut our loses and head home. Neither option sounded pleasant.

Back at the cabin, I broached the subject with Laura. To my surprise, her little eyes light up knowing she was about to be freed from this well-intended disaster. But she was so kind, she still offered to stay it out because she knew it was my dream to catch my first shield musky. I smile and tell her it's time to go. She gives me a heartfelt hug that reminds me why I married her in the first place. "I'll start packing!" With that, Laura's off to getting the hell out of here.

The number one thing on my list was getting the boat on the trailer and store away all our gear for the long ride home. I reversed the boat trailer down the Mother Nature made rock face, strewn with loose rocks and cracks, otherwise known as the boat landing. (I use those terms very loosely). I ran back to the docks and started the boat. The bay's waves were cranking four footers, and I knew I'd only have one shot at riding one of those waves onto the trailer. If I was off even a little, I'd be trapped on the shallow rocks with no way to run my motor. So just like the surfers do in Hawaii, I motored out a ways and watched the waves as they built and broke on shore. When I thought my timing is right, I drilled the throttle and rode my little dinghy into shore like the Big Kahuna. With perfection, it's up onto the trail so Laura could latch the winch hook to the bow. "That was just like Greg Brady on the Hawaii episode of the Brady Bunch. Only you didn't eat the surf, like that wussy!" Laura giggled. By supper time, we were all packed and ready to go for the morning departure. I had talked to Jerry and told him we had planned on leaving in the morning, too. He and Kenny had already settled-up with Ben by this point.

I went down to the lodge to settle up our end of the bill so we could depart nice and early Thursday morning. At the lodge, Ben's daughter informed me her dad had gone to town, but she would have him stop by our cabin that night when he got back. A little annoyed that this was gonna linger over us until Ben's arrival, I went down to the docks. My annoyance was quickly dissipated. That lake seized me with total awe. The sheer, untamed wilderness that depends on her for life was astounding. Even more so, I found her unbridled beauty in everything she touches to be invigorating. Her face in the setting sun would make a supermodel jealous with envy. She had taken a part of me now, and I knew I would return year after year. Not just for the toothy beast I had dreamed about, but to fill my soul with the wholeness I had been looking for all my life. My eyes dampened as the sky fell to black.

Back at the cabin, Laura and I waited up that night until eleven with no sign of Ben. We headed to bed in hopes of getting up bright and early to catch up with him.

CHAPTER IX

HOMEWARD BOUND

The alarm blared out its wake-up call at a nice early six o'clock. I stretched, meandered over to the front window, and see Jerry and Kenny driving down the road for home. Unreal. I snatched my cell phone and called Jerry to ask him why the hell he was ditching us. Of course, I got the favorite "your call can not be completed as dialed" signal. I stomped back to the bedroom and whipped on clothes. "What's wrong?" I heard Laura ask. "I'm going to kick Jerry in the nuts when I see him next." Laura, the ever calm presence (when not having her life threatened with drowning), reminded me that we had a GPS now and would make it home just fine. This appeased me a little, though my fumes were still smoldering.

After ten minutes, we finished loading the rest of the stuff in the truck. Time to find out where the hell Ben was. I marched up to Ben's house and pounded on the door. All seems lifeless inside. I knocked again and this time could hear a voice bellow out, "Who the f*** is it?" A pissed off, half-naked, potbellied man, sporting tighty-whiteys marched to the door. "What da ya want?" I enlightened Ben, stating I had spoken to his daughter the night before, and she informed me he would stop by our cabin so we could settle up. Half asleep, he muttered to us, "I'm a very busy man and I didn't feel like stopping by last night. I haven't had my coffee yet, so I can't function. I'll be down at the lodge in an hour or so." Immediately, without a chance to reply, the door slammed.

Not that I was keeping a stop watch, but over an hour and a half later, Ben and his wife finally exited their cabin and hopped in their golf cart for the sixty yard ride to the lodge. They had to be extra careful not to burn off all those much earned calories. That damn golf cart carried them everywhere.

Once they reached the lodge, I'm handed an itemized bill that showed every little thing they could charge for. I mean "everything." Such as: boat launch, boat landing (back on trailers), bait, dock fee per day, lodging, towels, cabin cleaning & tip for housekeeping, ice (after their fridge wasn't working) and licenses. Oh, and of course, no money back for leaving early Thursday instead of Saturday. To boot, they lumped in taxes onto the end of it all. The only thing we didn't get charged for was the amount of flushes the toilet made. Thank God for that, after those greasy fish fries, I would have had to give them my boat. After I reluctantly handed the man in the red suit and horns our money, there was an awkward silence in the room.

Ben turned from us, never thanking us for coming or offering us a farewell, and retreated to his office to count his bounty. I was so mad, I wanted to barge right in there and punch him in his jelly belly. I glanced over at Laura, and she tossed me the 'let's go' look. Against my better judgment, I agreed and we stomped out.

We hopped in the truck, and I sped out with gravel flying and my temper flaring. I studied our trusty GPS system for the first time. After twenty minutes, the stupid satellite wouldn't connect and we're shit out of luck. I suddenly remembered a small pamphlet from another lodge I had thought about checking out while were up here. On the backside, a basic map showed how to get back to the border. We drove around for a half hour before we found the highway on our little map. That little piece of luck helped us make it back to the Canada/U.S. border.

Our luck continued, as there were no lines at the border. I pulled up to the gate and shut off my motor. A no-nonsense looking guard glared back at us through the window. He slid open the window in a pure business tone. He demanded where we had gone in Canada, what we did, if we kept any fish or game, and if we had any items to declare. We answered all his questions to his liking, but then he asked me if there were any bodies in our truck or boat. I couldn't help it. I stupidly answered, "You mean dead bodies?" He examined me with steel-cold eyes and ordered, "Pull over to the side sir, and remove your boat cover."

"Nice going, Brad! Now they'll probably tear our truck and boat apart looking for dead bodies," blamed Laura.

A short moment later, Mr. Border Patrol Guy rummaged through our boat and quickly inspected our coolers. Upon further examination, we were given the nod, and would be on our way. "By the way, I was looking for aliens," stated Mr. Border Patrol Guy. "You guys have aliens here, too?!" I asked. My wife gave me the classic 'shut the hell up' glare. I quickly revved the truck and headed for Wisconsin.

Still quite a bit agitated by Jerry's ditching of us, I tried to give him a call. To my astonishment, he picked up. "What can I do for you, Brad?" Jerry answered. I'm a bit dumbfounded that there was absolutely no clue as to why I would be calling, or pissed off. I barked at him, demanding to know why he ditched us. From his point of view, he didn't. "I went up to your cabin and noticed you guys weren't up yet, so I didn't want to disturb a newlywed couple so early in the morning," Jerry said. "That was very considerate of you, but because of that, Laura and I had to drive all over God's green earth to get back to the border. Remember, we followed you here and have never been to Canada before!" "Yeah, but you must have made it back into the United States. So you got to see a little more of the country on the way out. I had to look at the same scenery on the way out as when I came in. Very boring, let me tell you," Jerry explained. I knew he meant well, or at least thought he did. Still, it was amazing how oblivious he could be. "Well, if you two need directions getting back to Wisconsin from Minnesota, you just give me a call and I'll help you out." Smart ass.

After hanging up the cell, Laura tried calming me down. "I'm really sorry you didn't get your first Canadian Musky on our trip. And that everything went bad while we were there. Are you always this lucky on fishing trips?" Somehow, that didn't calm me. Now that she mentioned it, I started thinking about the first time I went musky fishing in the states, and that trip, too, was a total disaster. Maybe this was a very common thing for me. You start wondering if it's destined to be a long life of fishing trip mishaps. At least I had someone to share them with now.

CHAPTER X

FIRST TIMER

A man will always remember his "firsts" in life. His first kiss, touchdown, home run, and his first time in the woods alone. He also will never forget his first musky trip, when he'll spend hour upon hour casting for "Old Toothy." May even convince himself that there isn't a damn fish in the whole lake because he's covered every square inch! But if he's truly lucky, he might catch a glimpse of one as it swipes at his lure. You know they call muskies "the fish of a thousand casts". There's good reason for it.

I think it's more like ten thousand casts, and the one thousand number is just a fish story.

The man to baptize me into the exciting and very expensive sport of musky hunting was my good friend, Jason. We were still in high school at the time, and every month or so would come up with something we hadn't tried before. It just so happened that we would be making this trip in late October when the fishing was supposed to be really hot, but the temperatures were not. According to the local weatherman, who made a living telling half-truths, there was a Canadian screamer headed our way. My grandfather once told me that if you want to know what the weather is going to be like, get a rock and hang it from a tree with a piece of rope. Then look out your window at the rock. If it's wet, it's raining, if it's swinging side to side, it's windy and if it's white it's snowing or a large flock of seagulls just flew by. In other words, just look out your damn window, you lazy bastard.

The trophy lake my soon to be ex-friend was taking me to was called Lake Du Bay in central Wisconsin. Before we went there, I explained to my friend that I would like to fish on a nice quiet lake where I could relax and collect my thoughts a bit. He assured me we were going to just such a place.

Upon arrival, I rediscovered why my buddy was an idiot with no comprehension of numbers. I say this, because I was staring at a lake that was a sixty-seven HUNDRED acres of flowage that appeared to be the size of Lake Superior. He wasn't lying about being the only ones there, because no one would be stupid enough to go fishing in those blustery conditions on this large of a lake. Like clockwork, the heavens burst open with an assault of snow, wind and freezing rain. "Well, let's go fishing," Jason said. Like I said, he's an idiot. Not sure what that says about me, because I went along.

We launched the boat and started exploring possible fishing spots we'd hit first thing the next morning. The whole time out there, I found myself keeping a lookout for massive sea going vessels so we wouldn't get run over and killed. We drove around the flowage for two straight hours marking possible fish holding areas on our map. My buddy's demeanor was that of being possessed by the fishing Gods. He acted like we were cruising around the sea looking for lost treasure. He never even noticed we were being bombarded by three-foot waves as they came crashing over the side of the boat. I felt like we were in a bad episode of Gilligan's Island without Ginger or Marian. That's just my luck ship wrecked with no women, just my buddy's ugly mug for company. "Let's go back," I screamed in my pubescent voice, sounding more like Mike Tyson than Mike Ditka. "Fine," yelled Jason, "Um, where did I put that map"? We scattered about the boat searching for our directions home. We quickly realized that it was as lost at sea as the Titanic.

With the map swallowed up by the Bermuda Triangle and nightfall approaching fast, we knew we were pretty screwed. All we could see were a few scattered lights around the shoreline and we had about as much of a chance at finding the landing as the Milwaukee Brewers would have winning the pennant. The only viable option was to head for shore and drive around the whole flowage until we found the boat landing. We soon discovered that when you have an extremely large body of water, there tends to be more than one boat landing. This particular flowage had eight. We motored along the shoreline, passing up dock after dock. Three hours later, we made it back to the correct landing. I might add that we had passed this particular landing two times before and good old Jason swore it couldn't be the right one each time we passed it.

We finally arrived back at our camp, which was conveniently next to the lake. Once again, not thinking, we were perched right in the line of the high winds screaming off the lake. We were easily soul-pierced with brain-freezing Arctic air. Setting up a tent felt more like flying a kite on a chilly late autumn afternoon. Once we managed to get camp fully erected, we jumped into our delicious and highly nutritious meal of potato chips, Oreo cookies, and Mountain Dew. Ah, to be a teenager again. After supper, we crawled into our snowsuits and winter boots in an attempt to keep warm. We realized that sharing a sleeping bag to keep from freezing was the only other step we had available to us. If that weren't bad enough, we had to endure all this in a tiny, two-man pup tent that may as well been a coffin. The reason they call it a pup tent is when two guys squeeze inside, all you'll hear that night is whining. My teeth were chattering so much during that night, I think I swallowed a couple of fillings.

The next morning, I unzipped the door and stepped out into a whole new world. Everything was fully covered with a fresh layer of fresh snow. Snow made everything pure again, if only for a little while. It covered up all that's ugly and turned everything beautiful. I love snow. Unfortunately, the picturesque morning was to be the only highlight that day. As we hit all the hot spots in the flowage, old Mother Nature had another stormy and miserable day in store for us. Even worse was the fact that we hadn't boated any trophy muskies. I knew

I had cast my bait at least a thousand times with nothing to show for it. The local warden sure got an ear full when we got back to town. I told him that it was illegal to spout false propaganda and blatant lies about catching muskies.

Jason and I located a local diner to wolf down cheeseburgers and take advantage of some much needed heat. With our faces stuffed with beef patties, an old man wandered over and sat next to us at the counter. His weathered face and shabby appearance was making us youngsters a little nervous. He stared through us and knew what was bothering us. "You boys ain't having any luck catching muskies, are you?," asked the old man. "No sir," I mumbled. The whole time, I'm thinking this crazy old man has been stalking us, waiting for the right time to slaughter us in our sleep. "You boys should make your way over to the far west side of the flowage. There's some deep water over there, with plenty of suckers schooled up. Old toothy won't be too far from his food source. But you gotta be careful when you motor over there. There be lots of stumps and shallow water if you don't stay in the old river channel," the old man explained.

We thanked the old musky hunter and literally ran out of the dinner, jumped into the car, and flew back to the landing. Our PMA (Positive Musky Attitude) was reinvigorated by our encounter with the wise hunter. A newfound passion for the flowage began to return and we were soon back on the hunt for the fearless, toothy beast that prowled these stump laden waters. As we started across the flowage, I kept a watchful eye on our new map we had purchased to keep us in the channel and out of harm's way. For GPS (Global Positioning System) hadn't been invented yet so a good map and looking at your depth finder was the only way to navigate.

I'm not positive if simply thinking something can cause a jinx, because as soon as I thought we were into a lucky streak, my friend found his old companion, trouble. Jason insisted that we take a short cut across the lake instead of following some stupid old man's warning. I pleaded with him, but it was his father's boat and not mine, so I only had limited pull on this decision. We were now on course with fate, and it obtained us only minutes after leaving the river channel. In an instant, a loud 'whack' echoed, and the motor leapt from the water. The whole boat suddenly hurdled forward, catapulting us through the air and onto the front deck. After a quick count of arms, legs fingers and toes we realized we were alright. We started examining what transpired, we quickly found that the blades on the prop where gravely damaged, and the lower unit was extremely dented. The power trim and tilt also had seen better days. Other than that, all was peachy. I could just picture Jason's dad beating him with the shaft of the fishing net when we got home. Frankly, he deserved it. Hell, I wanted to beat him with the shaft of the fishing net, and it wasn't my boat. Fortunately, we were lucky enough to get the boat started and back to the landing and on to the trailer by nightfall.

Back at camp, another disaster awaited us. While we were out fishing, the wind had ripped our camp apart. Our belongings were scattered into the next three campsites. It looked like a tornado had gone through a trailer park. This was more insult than injury. We quickly dashed through the campsites to collect our junk. By this point, I had had enough of this fun. It was time to pack up and get the hell out of dodge.

It may have been the quietest ride in a car I had ever experienced. Usually, Jason was well known for his diarrhea of the mouth. On this particular ride, he never said a word. I think I could feel his sweat dripping, knowing his dad was going to carve him a new asshole when we got home. This wasn't something I wanted to be a part of, because I wasn't overly sure if he'd carve me one, too. When we arrived back to his house, I collected my things as fast as I could and dashed off. I wasn't even a few yards down the road and I could I hear Jason's dad explode into a sea of obscenities that would make a teamster blush.

The next day at school, I saw Jason in first period class limping into the room. When the teacher told him to quit standing and take a seat, he declared, "I think I'll just stand, if you don't mind." Musky fishing sure takes a toll on your body. If you don't believe me, just ask Jason...

By **BRAD MATHEWSON**

CHAPTER XI

RESOLUTION

The day after our long excursion back to Wisconsin from our wonderful Canadian honeymoon, I wandered into the garage to survey my boat. I was in deep contemplation on what to do with my Modified V Aluminum boat. I wondered if I could take it to the recycling center where we drop off empty beer cans. I spent the next few hours cleaning out all the fishing gear and wrenching off my newly installed Lowrance GPS. Once the clutter was removed, I gave the old boat one last wash and wax. When I was done primping it as much as you can doll up an aluminum can, I lugged it out to my family's business and parked it on the front lawn with a sign. About a week later, it was gone. My wife was about as happy as our wedding day.

For me, it was a bittersweet moment. Sure, she almost wrecked like the S.S. Minnow, but I had grabbed many fish in that can. Life is all about the next step. You'll only fall backward if you don't press forward. I concentrated on what lie ahead, and that brought a smile to my mug. It was time to go shopping for a new boat! There it was: the silver lining on a Canadian Honeymoon Musky Hunt.

MUSKY TALE OF THE TAPE – JUNE 2009
BRAD - 0"
LAURA - 0"
STEVE - 37" 39" 44" 36"
JERRY - 35" 36" 38" 40.5" 43" 39.25" 40.25" 45"
ALLEN - 36" 39" 30"
KENNY - 32" 35" 37" 22"

I understand that fishing can be just as much luck as it is skill. But the man who is mentally strong even in times of defeat is going to win the battle in the long run. The old adage "Not dead, can't quit". For me pushes me to fish longer and harder even when those around me want to give up, you have to want it more than the next guy on the water.

BY **BRAD MATHEWSON**

MUSKY HUNT – AUGUST 2009

CHAPTER XII

CHANCE FOR REDEMPTION

As the summer wore on, the constant reminder of my epic failure of not catching my first shield musky weighed on me day and night. In the book "MUSKIE MANIA", Ron Schara wrote his entire first chapter to "The Mystique' of the musky: "Perhaps, above all else, it is the musky's elusiveness, the close follows, the near misses, the massive sizes that make musky fishing for most addicts. But whatever the ingredients, the musky mystique is real. It exists in the mind of the muskies' adversaries, the fishermen. And it will continue to exist far beyond the day when each angler has made his own last cast, beyond the day when the smartest musky falls to a hook."

One late summer evening, I was on the my laptop gazing at pictures of giant L.O.T.W. muskies when fate started ringing in my ears. I knew it was only a matter of time before I would be reunited with my watery mistress. As I awoke from my daydream, I realized my cell was blowing up and my fellow musky nut, Steve, was on the other line.

"Hey Brad. Would you like to go to Canada musky fishing?" asked Steve. I was so ecstatic, I almost dropped my cell. "You looking at next July or August?" Steve started chuckling on the other end. "Hell no. We're going in two weeks." It was my turn to start laughing. I quickly found he was dead serious. Steve explained that they had an opening because his son, Allen, couldn't go due to school starting up during the eight day trip. An opportunity to spend eight days in Canada made me soil my shorts again. I told Steve I'd check with the bosses and let him know ASAP. There was nothing better than a spontaneous road trip to go musky hunting.

I made a quick phone call over to my parent's house to speak with my old man about the opportunity to go back to Canada for the second time in a year. I work in the family business as a cabinetmaker. There's tons of long hours, some paid and some not, but the trade-off is I can usually get off of work if something important comes up, even if it is last minute. It's a trade-off I can live with.

After a short conversation and obtaining my father's approval (which led to lots of FAVORS throughout the coming year), I had to call the second, and REAL boss, my wife. She was already disappointed in my sorry excuse for a honeymoon.

BY **BRAD MATHEWSON**

I was lucky to be married to such a beautiful and understanding wife. Most women, after taking them to the great north woods with four other guys for a musky/honeymoon/almost drowning retreat, would file for divorce the second we returned to the states. But not my wife. She was more upset I didn't succeed in catching a Canadian musky. At least, to my face she was more upset about that. Lord knows how she really felt about the matter. Just reiterated what a special person she truly is.

All that said, I knew this wouldn't be an easy conversation. I had spent a ton of cash for our first trip, and was concerned with dropping even more coin only months later. I carefully broached the subject to her at dinner that night. Though I could sense the hesitation in her demeanor, I was surprised when she told me if L.O.T.W. and muskies were that important to me, then I should jump at the chance to go again.

I dashed to my cell and gave Steve a jingle. Time to have some fun with this. "Hey Steve, I don't think I can go." Steve gasped on the other end, with a bit of a grumble. "If you can't go than I can't. That really f***in' sucks!" Steve complained. I couldn't keep from laughing. "I'm just screwing with you. I wouldn't miss a chance to redeem myself!" Steve burst out. "You little shit!" We were both on cloud-freaking-nine. "What kind of weather should I be prepared for the last week of August?" I questioned Steve. "That's the thing you have to know about Canada. It could snow or it could be ninety degrees. You just don't know. It's the time of year fall is about to begin. That transition period where I've literally seen it all in my twenty plus years of fishing L.O.T.W. I'd pack some cold weather gear and some warm weather gear and make sure you have sunscreen, because the UV rating can be as high as Florida with the amount of water reflecting light. You'll get hit in both directions. Also, those damn thunderstorms can perk up as quickly as you saw in July." Steve also informed me that it would be pretty much the same crew as the first trip, with Jerry, Kenny, and himself along for the ride. This made me pause, because normally they have up to ten guys that made this trip on a regular basis. For some reason, nobody else really wanted to go. I knew this would up the ante, because fewer wallets meant less splitting of costs. Less splitting of costs meant more coin to drop by each of us, most importantly, me. This was something that required me to think about it as little as possible.

I knew this would be my best chance yet at scoring my first shield musky. I was going to be guided around the lake by a guy who was probably the biggest bullshitter this side of the Mississippi, but had the catch rate to prove it. Steve had caught more muskies in his lifetime than I could ever dream of, and you know I daydream quite a bit. Steve had been fishing muskies for over thirty years, while I was still a green horn with few fish under my belt, and no Canadian muskies. The plan to hold that first fish was to shadow Steve all week, cast for cast, and watch him like a hawk. Doing that, I could learn the finer details of being a great musky hunter. This advice was given to me by Jerry, Steve's older brother, and main rival when it came to who caught the most fish and who seized the largest fish of the week each year. Those two were always in a pissing match of some kind.

BY **BRAD MATHEWSON**

Some trek up to the north woods of Wisconsin or Minnesota as their annually 'Rights of Passage' to hunt deer, drink beer, and downright act stupid, otherwise known as 'DEER CAMP'. The Hoelzel brothers take it to a whole new level, in what is known as 'MUSKY CAMP'. Every year, during the last week of August, they form a train of five trucks hauling boats up to Lake Of The Woods in an attempt to outdo one another in an all-out musky battle royale. Each guy tossed ten bucks into a pot for largest musky. These days are thirteen hour marathons of endurance, with no man allowed to sit unless traveling to the next honey hole. If you do take a break, you will be severely ridiculed for being a puss and not giving it your all in the name of the mighty musky.

I quietly wondered if I could keep up with the brothers. I was young enough to be one of their kids, but these guys had stamina that was legendary. Steven once told me they were on L.O.T.W. one day, and Jerry went out fishing with a new guy who was under the weather with the flu and didn't want to leave his bed. Jerry made the poor sap come along because he needed a net man. He insisted that the guy was bound by his word to follow the golden rule when fishing with the Hoelzel clan, which was "always have two men in the boat, no matter what."

This poor son of a bitch had to endure thirteen hours of ninety degree heat while alternating from the floor to hanging over the gunwale chumming for muskies. Needless to say, that was the last time he ever went on the Hoelzel musky hunt. Their list of green horns tagging along to Canada was quite long, and a good many have been one-and-done trips. Those poor souls were probably anticipating a nice, leisurely vacation basking in the fresh forest air and soaking a bait, while having a few cold ones at day's end. Those stupid suckers never had a chance.

BY BRAD MATHEWSON

CHAPTER XIII

ROAD TO REDEMPTION

We met at our usual gas station to fuel up on coffee and bullshit. All yapping about who was going to catch what, and who was going to finally catch a fifty incher. Once in the truck, I asked Steve how many fifty-inch fish he had nabbed on L.O.T.W. He presented me a nasty look. "None. I haven't landed a single musky that has taped out at fifty or more inches," Steve disclosed. I voiced my concern that I thought there were tons of fifty plus inch fish swimming around L.O.T.W. "They don't get that big being stupid. A fifty incher is one hell of a musky. They don't come easy. I have put in my time and even some overtime on that lake, but the fifty-inch fish have been a sore in my side for years. Not saying I haven't hooked a fifty inch fish before, but landing one is the hard part. I've lost a lot of big fish up there. Just can't seem to get them in the net.

Call it bad luck, I guess. I had on a fifty inch northern I fought for a long minute only to have it throw the damn bait during mid-air back flip right next to the boat. Son of a bitch," Steve growled. I quietly hoped that I'd get one on my first trip with him, just to spite him. Steve beat me to the punch on that one. "I've seen guys get that old fifty incher already. Friend of mine, Bucky. We were fishing this little mucked up bay with a real slue hole and a couple of little lily pads here and there.

I was not impressed at all. In fact, I didn't even want to fish it. Well, Bucky throws his one and only bait, a Cowgirl, to the far back of this little cove. As the bait nears the boat, I peep over, and here this huge musky is right behind his bait. Old Bucky never looks down nor does a figure eight. He simply yanks his bait out of the water, and this fish launches itself like a rocket at Bucky's double 10. The fish misses, and Bucky is screaming like a girl, "Did you see that huge musky, Steve!" Steve started shaking his head. Even the thought still chapped his ass. He continued, "I'm like, 'you stupid f***, he's still there next to the damn boat! Put your damn bait back in the water! Dumb old Bucky swings his rod like he's trying to split firewood and slams his Cowgirl right on top of this musky's head and sure if she doesn't hit it. He's got her on for probably five seconds before I get her in the net. I unhook this green monster, and put a tape to her. She is just over fifty inches. I practically poop my pants, Brad. I don't know who was dumber, the fish or Bucky. Guess it doesn't take skill to get a fifty incher. Sometimes, it's just a really stupid fish and the fisherman to match." This bode well for me. I'm not one to lack confidence in pretty much any situation, but that story practically rubbed me a boner. I KNEW I was gonna land one, and land one on that trip. "I have a lot of Bucky stories. He sure is special. Glad as hell they only made one," said Steve.

Just after supper, we arrived at my not so favorite White Birch Lodge. Sure enough, my fat Canadian buddy was sitting by the boat landing. Take a wild guess what his ass was parked in... his golf cart. Some things never change, just like his chipper attitude. No hugs or handshakes or happy to see you again for his paying guests, but I was shocked that he actually greeted all of us by name. I bet his wife forced him to at least say that.

"Well, enough small talk. Which docks can we have, and which cabin are we in? I want to get on the water," ordered Steve. Steve was always business, but he seemed more focused than usual for this hunt. After we put the boats in the water and got settled in our cabin, we had a good three hours of fishing light left. As we eased away from the docks, I turned to Steve, "Let's go see if that big musky Laura and I were after is still living in that sandy cove. It's less than a mile away." Steve offered me some slack. "We can give it a try, but don't hold your breath. That was six weeks ago. She may have moved to the other side of the Island or slide out into the main basin." Sure, or she could have died of old age, but we couldn't just drive by the spot without checking it out.

Once we reached a destination and the motor unwound, I was up and made a long bomb cast instantly. "Easy there, Brad. I wanna slowly move in with the trolling motor before we let her know we're here," explained Steve. Slightly embarrassed, but still jacked up, I settled myself down by remembering what I had told myself about shadowing Steve and listening to what he offered.

Steve eased on the troll and snatched up his rod. On Steve's first cast to a lone patch of reeds, he has a fellow stalking his rainbow colored double 10. "Nice fish right behind my bait. Probably forty-two to forty-four incher," whispered Steve. I examined as Steve went into his figure eight with dynamic skill. I thought this guy was a musky magnet. After he went around twice in an eight, the fish vanished. "That's not the same fish," I uttered. It was nice, but nothing like that behemoth we saw weeks earlier.

I made my first real cast into the cove. Of course, I mistakenly let my bucktail sink for a second before engaging the reel. I commenced cranking and found myself snagged to something on the bottom. "How can you be snagged already? It's all sand bottom in here. Just heave harder," Steve chortled. My rod was doubled over, but I couldn't free the Cowgirl. I panicked because I didn't want to lose a twenty-five dollar bait minutes into the trip. Steve led the boat right over top my line. We peered down into six feet of water, and here we found my bait hooked into an old anchor rope. What were the freaking odds. "Now what are you gonna do? You jerk any harder you're gonna have a two piece rod," Steve exclaimed. I glanced to the back of the boat. "Start the big motor. I'm gonna wrap my line around the transom cleat and I want you to slowly put it into gear and give her a little gas." Steve was skeptical, but went along with it. He cranked on the motor and slipped it into gear with a touch of gas. Sure enough, that old rope severed in two and I was reunited with my bait. Ten minutes in, and I was already having better luck than my honeymoon.

Steve didn't share my enthusiasm, and instead shifted into Professor Musky mode. "This is going to be a long week. We haven't even started to fish any rock yet. Hope you brought a lot of Cowgirls," Steve sighed. I glimpsed down into the deep. "All I see is rock," I questioned. "Exactly. This lake should be called Lake Of The Rock. You're gonna be surrounded by it all week, so you'll need to learn about the different rock structures this lake has to offer. Musky, unlike the Northern Pike, prefers to be in warmer water to help metabolize or in laymen's terms, digest there food. The warmer the water, the higher he metabolizes, meaning they have to eat more. The huge fishery is in the heart of the Canadian Shield, which means the bed of the lake and the lake shore, along with all the islands, is rock. Rock absorbs a lot of heat. So even on a cool day, these fish will still be fairly shallow to take advantage of the sun's life-giving rays. This lake has the highest concentrations of muskies in the world because these fish spend a good bit of their time in shallow water. You have a much better chance of contacting one or a dozen in a week."

Steve tossed his line out as he gave a college level thesis on the basic types of rock structures we would be encountering:

Rubble Rock - Remember what you see on shore continues out into the lake, so piles of small rocks on shore will continue out into a lake. If you see this between two islands, it creates a saddle. A good spot to find muskies.

Split or Cracked Rock - this too, could be seen on shore and would extended almost like a solid field on flat rock into the lake. Hundreds of cracks could be on its surface, with many deep enough to hide Mr. Musky. They're likely to appear out of nowhere and pounce on your bait. I have even seen them lying on top of these shallow, or what I prefer to call them, rock flats.

Shear Rock – Steep, cliff-like walls that may rise fifty feet and usually are accompanied by deep water. Muskies like to feed on the black crappies that school up around these deep rock faces.

Shelves or Garages – Looks like someone took a saw and removed a giant square block out of the face of a shear rock wall, creating a shelve wear musky like to hang out. Many of these garages are large enough to park an automobile. It's very important that you don't short your cast on such places, for a full cast to the back of this structure is where they will be found, if anyone is home. If there seems to be a smaller garage inside, that tends to be the proverbial hot spot within the spot.

Reefs – Ridges of rock at or near the surface. If you find a reef next to deep water, (main basin), you have found yourself a big fish spot where the hogs will sun themselves. Safety and food are just two flicks of the tail away.

Boulders and Reeds - I will just say this, if you go find a sandy cove and out in front are reeds and a couple of boulders, then that's where the fish will be.

I know, that's a lot about rock. But all of this was from decades of experience from a guy that lived it, breathed it, and took the brunt of hell from it all. You don't get this type of schooling from a schmuck behind a desk. Example, my brother-in-law had to take a Geology class to earn his Bachelor's degree. Every damn class, he told me he'd zonk out in. One day, he decided to sit in the front row in a feeble attempt to pay attention in class. No such luck. Dumb bastard fell asleep right in front of the Professor. Somehow, he managed to pass the class and earned his degree. But to this day, he couldn't tell you the difference between sandstone and magma. Steve described attributes that mattered to a musky fisherman. I mentally took notes.

"Those are just some of the basics I have found fishing up here. You'll learn more as the week goes on," said Steve. "It's probably time to go in and have a few drinks, have some supper, and then off to the old fart sack," I declared. "Sounds good. Tomorrow, the real work, I mean fun, begins," Steve replied. Somehow, I didn't think he actually meant fun. I had the feeling I was about to lose my ass, because it was gonna be worked off.

CHAPTER XIV

DREAMS REALIZED

For our first full day of fishing, we were in the boat and ready to leave by 8 Am As always, Jerry and Kenny beat us out and were departing for parts unknown by the time we arrived. Steve yelled out to Jerry, "Where's your other splash guard?" Jerry flipped him the bird as they motored off. I looked over to see Kenny smiling ear to ear. He offered us a big thumbs up. I was a bit perplexed at this apparent inside story. Come to find out, on Friday morning at our place of departure, Steve had asked Jerry why the hell he still had his splash guards on his boat from back trolling for walleyes on Lake Winnebago. Steve razzed Jerry about how was Kenny supposed to figure eight off the back deck with them in the way. Jerry explained to us that they were a "pain in the ass to remove and reinstall." He stated Kenny would just have to fish around them. Well, I guess the fish Gods were shining down on Kenny, because somewhere between our departure spot and Canada, Jerry had lost the left splash guard along the highway. Kenny had at least half a chance on his figure eight.

After retying our leaders on all our rods, we journeyed out. I can't stress how important this is on any body of water, but it's paramount that you keep in the habit of checking your line for any signs of fraying. You will be working a lot of rocks and super tough reeds that will make short work of any braid throughout a long day. I recommend taking off three feet from the leader whenever the need arises to re-tie. We owe it to ourselves and especially to the muskies we hunt. Many a great beast have been lost due to negligence of line or poorly tied knots. While on the subject of must-do's, make sure to sharpen those hooks. I check them after I have made any contact with rock or those tough fibrous reeds, which I swear are tougher in Canada than in Wisconsin. I keep a file in my pocket for those little touch-ups you need throughout the day. Anytime you become hooked on a rock the hook is usually in need of major repair. When time is of the essence, I replace the hook and sharpen the beat up one back at home.

Our first stop was to Raspberry Island. We worked the rubble rock along it's south shore for an hour, pounding our double 10's every ten feet. That's the way Steve instructed me to fish as it had worked well for him in the past. We covered every inch of productive water. An hour later, with only a couple northern in the slot, twenty-seven and half to thirty-five and a half inch ranges, we moved on to the classic sandy cove of Three Pine Island. On Steve's first cast, he tucked his bait tight to the lone reedy boulder. Suddenly, a huge swirl appeared next to his bait. As his double 10s near the boat, I witnessed a nice torpedo closing in.

Steve led his fish into a figure eight by ripping it deep from the start, then ripped it up on the outside turn, and then back down deep on the inside turn. This gave his bait a little different appearance than most guys that figure eight. On his second time around, she struck it. I was quick on the net and had her within the boat in mere seconds of Steve hooking her. Personally, I would rather net a super green fish than have someone take her for a long fight and have lactic acid build up from her over exerting herself. I'd worry she'd die of delayed mortality, which happens more than one thinks. Steve and I are of the same belief on this. That's why you have huge nets with fin saver bags, which are basically like a kid's padded play pen.

Once in the boat, I took a moment to soak it in. There was the first Canadian Shield within my boat. Maybe I wasn't the one to hook it, but I did play a part in its capture. This type of moment couldn't be ignored. Musky fishing is a team sport, and is always an accomplishment. I knew it would be only a matter of time before I was on the rod end of a great feat.

"Now that's how we catch them up here! Almost seventy percent of my fish come in the figure eights, so do them correctly, and you will be rewarded," said Steve. We whipped out the measurements and came up with thirty-nine inches. Even Steve, a wily veteran of Canadian Musky, was tickled with this fish. "It's only nine in the morning and we have our first contact. There's so much more to come!"

A quick pic was snapped, a traditional slimy hand shake for the net man, and we're back to fishing. We worked our way around Three Pine with not even a looker, so we motored over to Mather's Reef. Leave it to me to hook my Cowgirl right on top of the reef. Steve had to move us onto the reef, with our keel rubbing rock, so I could jerk my double 10 out of a crack and not scare any muskies in the area. Little did I know, a lot of rocks were going to be reaching out and grabbing my bait that day, and a lot of good hooks would be ruined in the process.

After fishing Mather's Reef and Mamiou Point, and me getting stuck on the rocks a couple more times, we head over to Lowes Island. Once again, Steve nabbed a fat, forty-two and a half inch musky on a rainbow colored double 10 in a figure eight once again. We continued to work the area for a few more hours, and then decided a change was essential. Steve intended to show me something he had discovered ten years ago. As we motored down toward Big Marsh Narrows, we made a sharp turn back to the northeast. Suddenly, Steve turned the boat off.

"Take a look out in front of the boat and tell me what you see," said Steve. I surveyed the area and noticed water breaking. That told me a reef was near the surface. I reviewed the map, but didn't see anything that resembled any sort of reef. To a map-reader, it just appeared like a wide open basin. "I have that marked on my Lowrance. Named it 'Dinner Table'. We've had multiple fish taken off of this gem. There's always hungry fish waiting to eat. Best thing is, nobody knows it's here except the occasional poor bastard with his boat," explained

Steve. "Found it by accident one day. Saw a pelican standing on it during a low water year. Been a hot spot for us ever since." Hard to believe its not marked on the map, the track line is so close by. My heart started racing. This just felt like a winner. I immediately set up my rod to cast. "Remember, it's really shallow on top for a stretch before she drops off into a series of deep cracks," Steve preached.

Unfortunately, I'm barely listening, and as you can probably guess, I cast right on top of the damn reef, didn't engage my reel fast enough, and managed to get snagged once again. I raised my rod tip high in the air and gave it quick snaps in hopes of getting off before Steve would start scolding me. Failure. "Don't tell me you're fu**ing stuck again!" howled Steve. "I'm not stuck. I'm hooked into a prehistoric rock fish," I bantered back. Steve grumbled, and heaved out his rod. "I don't want another spot to go to waste," proclaimed Steve. He unleashes a mighty cast, and not even a minute later, he worked a figure eight at a musky hunting his bait. "Get the net! Got a nice one here!" Steve barked. I lay my rod down and engaged my reel so line could freely extend out as we drift away from the reef. I snatched the net under the beast as quickly as possible. She was a nice forty-three incher, a quick pic and off she swims. At this point of the morning, the count is Steve three, Brad zero. Dammit. "You got to get some of this action, Brad. It's only eleven in the morning. Plenty of time," Steve declared.

Well first I have to retrieve my bait from the reef as I'm into my mono-filament backing on my reel and can see my metal spool. We slowly use the trolling motor to get on top of the reef which is strewn with prop ears and metal parts. In the very center, my double 10 was hooked onto a piece of rope that probably was used for a marker buoy at one time. I reached my hand in and worked my barbs free of the rope. "Nice. You weren't hooked on the rocks this time! Good job," Steve joked. Funny guy. With the only further action being my first follow from a 20 inch musky with what looked to have a broken mandible (jaw), it was off to the next spot. This would be Steve's favorite spot on the lake, and would quickly become mine as well.

"Now Brad, everyone in our group knows about this spot, but I never see anyone else fishing it. There are always nice forty inch fish on it, so be ready. Cast where I tell you to and don't hook any rocks this time," Steve ordered. As we pulled up, Steve shut down the big motor and let the wind push us in like a sneak attack. I observed a truck-sized boulder that has broken off the island, with a four foot by sixteen foot wide slot of water between shore and the boulder. This was a perfect hiding place for any giant. The water off the face side of the boulder dropped into thirty feet of water, making this the optimal feeding shelf for any hungry muskies. "Cast right down the slot when we are parallel with shore," instructed Steve. I made my first textbook cast of the trip, right down the old shoot.

Not even halfway back to the boat, I saw Mr. Musky following my blue with silver blades Bucher double 10. I hastily rush into my figure eight as my bait reached the boat. The fish broke off on my second turn, but I keep figure eighting the bait. Meanwhile, Steve had already made his own perfect cast and low and behold I'm not surprised to see who's following his rainbow double 10. With a nice turn on his eight, Steve hooked up with fish number four. Another short battle ensued, and a forty-three incher was in the net. After yet another epic pic, Steve slides her back to her home. "Enjoying the show? I think I'm going to hire you as my full time net man," Steve gagged. "Blow me!" I barked back. "That fish wasn't the same one you had going. I know there's another fish in there. We'll keep working that slot for a while," Steve assured me. With that, we tossed dozens of casts back into the slot, but nobody else seemed to be home.

Annoyed, Steve thought he should try the front side thinking the musky might have re-positioned it's self there. On my second cast, Steve hollered, "she's coming hot on your bait! Be ready!" As my double 10 approached the side of the boat, I went into my figure eight. The fish trailed tightly behind my bait, nipping and speeding up on every turn. What seemed like ten minutes later, she smashed my bucktail as I hung my bait on a outside turn. I quickly depressed the thumb bar and thumb my spool in a twenty second battle within a mere 3 feet of line out. She got up on top the water and sprayed like a wet dog coming in after a long swim. That fish was baptizing me into the Canadian Musky Club. A flood of emotions came over me at once. That had me yelling at Steve to get the net, and in the same sentence screaming, "she's barely hooked." Something many a net men have heard from there partners even when the fish has three treble hooks in her. Steve slid the net under her like a pro's pro. "Nice fish, Brad!" Steve cheered.

I unhooked her and held her up for the pictures, its a dream fulfilled. Finally, this green horn from Wisconsin had succeeded in catching his first Shield Musky. I had spent many hours on her surface, gazing at her elegance and dreaming of the amazing world beneath. Lake Of The Woods is a lot like a woman, beautiful on the outside, but even more so in her deep watery soul. It had taken two trips, the first one being mostly chalked full of heartache and disappointment, but I was finally embracing a forty-three inch musky. She was my personal best. I had succeeded in my hunt and its time for her to hunt again and me to try and fool her once again. A CPR (catch picture release) ritual is complete and my trip had only just begun. In that moment, it could have ended right there and then and I would have been the happiest man in Canada.

That would be the last fish Steve and I caught that day. The temperature was eighty-five degrees Fahrenheit with only a paltry five mph wind blowing out of the south. The sky was clear blue all day. We did happen to raise 30 muskies all on double 10s but most were lazy follows. All I knew was, I had made my dream come true that afternoon, and my personal sky was cloudless.

CHAPTER XV

GLIMPSE OF A GHOST

Dead calm. The kind of calm that made you question what the hell is going on. Eeriness aside, we ventured toward the dock that morning with a brand new battle plan. A plan born the previous night, while having a few cocktails during our late night supper. Steve shared stories of the monster muskies his friend Tom had caught only a few years earlier. These Goliaths were captured out in the main basin, west of Blue Island, by fishing small islands and reefs that are surrounded by deep water, with no other structures around for miles. These smaller structures were magnets for fifty inch fish that could follow around schools of fish and feed at will. If not feeding, they could slide up on a protected rock shelf and sun themselves with nobody harassing them with buck tails all day. Tom spent all his time fishing big water muskies and he might not see but one or two fish all day. However the ones he did see were huge. He collected a fifty-one incher just a few years prior, and raised a good many more. The reason everyone and their brother wasn't out there hunting for hogs was it was too dangerous most days. We all fish out of our standard sixteen and a half foot Lunds or Alumcraft deep V walleye boats, the water is just too rough most days to brave long runs over open water to access these spots. Lake Of The Woods is a fairly shallow fishery with over 14,000 islands to hide behind when it's windy. But if you're in Sabaskong Bay with a west wind, things can get pretty hairy. The wind has such a huge open basin to blow across, even in a fifteen mph wind by the time you get out past Blue Island to the south and Manitou Island to the north. Those waves have traveled all the way from Painted Rock Island which is many miles away and they were 3 footers already. Just think what happens when that wind goes up five or ten mph. It can get downright suicidal, unless you're in a heavy fiberglass Ranger. So to get to this fishing vortex, you need a day of flat, calm winds, which doesn't happen very often in Canada.

Even if it does, you best be careful you don't get stuck when the wind picks up.

"See you girls later. You can waste your time chasing after all the muskies you want in the nursery, but Brad and I are chasin' the big girls," Steve jabbed at Jerry and Kenny. Steve called the area we fished in Sabaskong Bay 'the nursery' because it's a relatively shallow structure with many small reefs and oodles of islands between, with no real deep basin. We did see some nice fish from time to time, but most fish were in the high thirty inch to low forty inch range. Nice fish, and I'm more than happy to catch them all day long, but sometimes you need to challenge yourself with new water and bigger prey.

As we headed west toward the basin, we could see our first little rocky island. I'm geeked and eager to start fishing any minute. Steve chuckled. "Brad, you know that island you see is probably fifteen to twenty minutes away, don't you?" I'm skeptical, but after ten minutes of continuous motor boating, we didn't seem any closer. I also noticed we had dead calm water in our protected bay, but the wind and chop had picked up a little. Steve had taken notice, too. "This is how it usually starts. It keeps building as you get further into the basin," said Steve. As Steve predicted, that little chop turned into two footers not twenty minutes out. "What do you want to do?" yelled Steve. Without Laura with me, I was a bit more risk-tolerant than the first trip to Canada. "Well, we made it this far. May as well try it for a little while. Who knows when we'll make it back out here again." Steve smirked. "Okay. But if it picks up any more, we're gonna have three footers in a blink of an eye. It'll be a long, rough ride back to the bay," Steve warned. Remembering the chop we survived in our little dinghy a few months earlier, and now sitting in a much better prepared boat, I was cautiously confident we could handle whatever Mother Nature tossed at us.

That confidence took a quick punch to the biscuits, not five minutes after my internal proclamation. The wind had picked up even more. You could see the waves building in the west and headed our way. Thankfully, we had made it to a small rocky island covered in Canadian white paint, otherwise known as pelican shit. Word to the wise, don't get downwind of these white rocks. You'll be treated to the most vile smell on the planet. This particular island held one Charlie Brown Christmas tree and was scattered with years of driftwood and pelican feathers.

As I'm scouting the desolate island, I noticed that somehow a lone pocket gopher was happily making a new home under the little tree. How that poor bastard got stranded way out there, I'll never know. Couldn't help but wish he had a little Ginger or Maryanne gopher to keep him warm. Though, he could live in comfort without being told what to do twenty-four, seven. Anyway, there was a small reef just to the right of the island where Steve and I made multiple casts to. Steve was having a hard time keeping the boat in position for us to make accurate casts. The waves started to break over the front of the boat, making it look like our little trip was gonna be cut short. That was until Steve had a nice mid-forty inch musky give chase to his bait. That convinced us to stop being babies and tough it out in an attempt to hit the reef from every direction. We successfully worked a circle around the reef, but nothing else showed. I advised Steve that we should motor up and cast the wind blown point to see if any hogs were in a great ambush spot. "I'll try, but I don't think any muskies will be off the points. Too windy. But we'll make one drift through, just in case," said Steve.

Steve shut his hefty motor down, causing it to feel like we were on a never-ending roller-coaster. The boat then headed for the jagged rocky point faster than his trolling motor could control. We had one quick cast each and were long past the point.

We came into what looked like a small eddy that had formed when the wind and wave action forced water to break on the front side, and spun around the corner into a cove. This cove consisted of jagged broken rock, but also a nice shelf and the water dropped off sharply to twenty-five feet. Steve and I silently acknowledged our findings with a nod of the head. This was the spot within the spot we'd been searching for. I unleashed a cast but came up empty handed. By the time I wound it in, the wind had pushed us faster than the trolling motor could keep up. Steve had only one shot on this run. That's when Steve's day changed in the blink of an eye.

Halfway back to the boat, I see what appeared to be a log in the water following Steve's double 10. That log was quickly confirmed to be a shockingly large fish. I jumped down from my casting deck in the back of the boat and grabbed the net. I knew if Steve hooked up with this beast, I was going to have to net her pronto. As Steve went into a figure eight, she broke off and headed back to her home. I squinted at Steve. He was as white as a ghost and literally shaking. He plopped down in the chair, attempting to control his jitters.

"Brad, I'm thinking that was probably a mid-fifty inch class musky," proclaimed Steve. "Let's make another drift and catch her. Just give me a minute. Legs feel weak." I hadn't seen this side of Steve before. Even with all his years of Musky experience, he was still awestruck by the fish. It oddly gave me both a sense of encouragement (that I wasn't the only one that felt that way), but also a feeling of sheer terror, because if a man that had achieved as many musky hauls as Steve had and gets weak-kneed, what the hell did that mean for me?

A few moments passed, we fired up the big motor and headed up for another drift by. This time, our building waves were now three footers breaking violently on to the front deck and we were getting wet. We pressed on, and during the second drift, I casted from a crouched position in hopes that my bent knees would act like tiny shock absorbers. Unfortunately, my body was contorting with every roll and bounce of the boat. This water was suitable for a Ranger, not an Aluminum pop can. There were a few times it felt like I was gonna be thrown into the surf. I couldn't imagine being able to doggy paddle very well after being slammed into a sharp algae-slicked rock. We were so focused on making pin point casts, we didn't realize the danger that the wind was brewing.

By the time we noticed the chaos on the lake, I fell down off the elevated casting deck Steve had built out of treated plywood and carpeting. This deck was built between the gun wall and over the transom a few feet higher than the front deck. It offered an awesome view into the water below. Thankfully, my slip was into the boat, and not an even better view underwater. Dusting myself off, we agreed it was time to get the hell out of Dodge. Steve, with his new story about the one that slipped away in hand, cranked down on the engine to get us home. We only hoped we would make it back to our protected bay in one piece.

The ride back was one of the roughest I had ever been on. The bow would cut through one wave and then be raised up seconds later by another larger wave. We'd then be dropped back onto the surface like we were body slammed by Hulk Hogan over and over again. To top it all off, the spray from the broken wave soaked us thoroughly, and the sixty-five degree temperature made our wet clothes feel like we were standing out in the cold November rain that Axl Rose whined about. After a hair-raising thirty minute boat ride, we finally made it back to our dock. We were in a desperate need of a change of clothes and a new pair of unsoiled underoos. As we pulled up, what little joy we had left was quickly dowsed when we found our host's three hundred pound wife sunbathing, in the nude, next to the dock. I guess Canadians are open to just about anything. I knew I'd have issues sleeping that night.

Back in the boat and the day not off to a good start. I really wanted to go exploring in the big water to catch my first fifty-inch musky, my new Canadian goal. It was time to catch a musky so we made a long run down to the King Island area. This was another one of Steve's favorites. But first, we had to make a quick stop at a spot Steve had named 'Split Rock,' where I had caught my first Canadian musky the day prior. We used the same sneak up method to the spot, and Steve tagged a thirty-six inch musky on only his third cast. I couldn't believe my eyes and it was on the same rainbow double 10 bucktail. Our next four hours were spent fishing around the tiny islands in front of King Island, with only two exceptionally small fish raised.

BY **BRAD MATHEWSON**

Being unfulfilled by the day's offering, we decided to see if we could get through the shortcut between Blueberry Island and Little Blueberry Island. This was a narrow, weedy channel and sometimes when the water was low, it grew extremely weed choked you couldn't pass through. As luck would have it, the water was deep enough to provide safe passage on this day. With all the handsome weed growth, I suggested that we do a little fishing and see what turned up. "This is the first nice looking weed growth I have seen all trip. I thought this lake had descent weed cover," I questioned. "You should have been up here twenty years ago. You could have renamed this Lake Of The Weeds. Everywhere you went, there was nice looking weeds that would hold fish," said Steve. So what happened to all the weeds in the lake? Come to find out, invasive species called rusty crayfish decimated the weeds. Some of the bays that were full of coontail, cabbage, and lily pads, now have nothing. Anytime we got in shallow areas, you could gaze on the rocky bottom of the lake and see rusty crayfish skeletons everywhere. Make's me sick.

Getting into the weeds for the first time on this lake, I pitched out my black and silver double 10, while Steve utilized a little spinner bait. As we worked the large weed bed, I searched for isolated weeds or channels within the weeds, anything that stands out. Suddenly, Steve cried out, "Brad! You got a nice musky behind your bait! I think she's going to eat it! AH!!! I think she has it in her mouth!" I searched for my bait but I can't find it and I don't feel any resistance. "Set the damn hook! She has it!" yodeled Steve. Without thought, I did what any former bass fisherman trying to be musky hunter would do, if you guessed screw up then you would be right. In my excitement, I set the hooks without the straight upward swing one would do if a fish were swimming toward you with your bait in its mouth. Nope, not me. That would have been the smart way. Instead, I set the hooks with a hard sweep to the right, jerking the bait, and probably some of its teeth, right from the musky's mouth. To top it off, the fish was in the forty-five inch range and would have been a new personal best.

Steve just shook his head in dismay. "Brad, Brad, what more do you need the musky to do for you? Do you expect them to jump in the boat? You should have crossed that musky's eyes." I sulked back in my seat. It was a bad blow to my ego to have quality musky wander away because of my own doing. Thankfully, not ten minutes later on the same weed bed, I would have my chance to redeem myself with an even greater musky.

The weed flat we were fishing was about the size of a football field with open water behind weeds that bumped shore. It was time to dig deep into the bottom of my tackle box and give the local muskies something they haven't seen yet, my oil colored Lindy Tiger Tube. Using all my pent up frustration, I made a long bomb cast about sixty yards out. The instant my bait dabbed the water, a large swirl materialized, followed by a hefty mass on my rod. I reeled down and slammed it to him with a devastating hook set that would make Joe Bucher proud. In an instant, an upper-forty inch pig was dancing for its freedom in the shallow water only a foot deep. Doing head shakes and gill flares in an attempt to throw my tube bait. Anyone who is familiar with the old Lindy Tiger Tubes, you already know how this will end. All too often, this fight is won by the musky. I'd say probably seventy-five percent of the time, from my experience. I don't think I stayed hooked up with this bull for the full eight second ride. After the complete musky victory, little did I realize this was the beginning of the 'Brad and Steve Fishing Tiger Tubes' drama-fest.

After a few hours of getting bucked off a number of times, and getting very pissed off, Steve and I did manage to raise nine fish. Steve hooked up and lost four fish, himself. The one fish I did catch was a nice thirty-nine inch northern pike. What I learned on this adventure was that the biggest problem with the small tubes was getting the hooks buried into a musky's hard mouth. The giant bastards are so mighty, their teeth sink into the soft rubber body. It felt so much like real prey to them, they'd hammer on it as hard as they could. Somehow, you have to break their strong grip and slide the hooks into their jaw. Most times, it's a surprise when they hit it. You fight them all the way to the boat, and all they do is open their mouth and they're gone.

We experimented the rest of the day with smaller stinger hooks attached to the back of the tube with absolutely no luck. Steve and I had a strong love-hate relationship with the Tiger Tubes. They gave you a lot of action and heartbreak, but we kept coming back for more. In fact, anytime we see them at discount stores, we still buy all they have. To me, it's a shame they quit making them a few years back. I have tried most of the other tube baits on the market, and they do catch fish, but not like the action you get from a Tiger Tube. I hope Lindy starts making them again. Great bait, no matter what Steve thinks.

What really seemed to get the muskies going were tube baits being ripped back to the boat, as fast as we could reel. We tried to go slower and let them just hang there, but these fish were super aggressive. The hot and humid temperatures had the fish metabolism at its highest of the entire season, meaning they were on a feeding binge. Contrary to popular belief, they feed more often in the summer than they do in the fall. We had temps in the upper eighties, with humidity making it feel triple digits. The wind howled out of the west to southwest, and the dreaded bluebird skies kept our PMA very low for the rest of the day.

BY BRAD MATHEWSON

CHAPTER XVI

BROMANCE

It was a brand new day, and Steve and I made our run to the King Island area where we had most of our action the previous afternoon. I also convinced Steve that since the Tiger Tube showed us so many fish in this locale, we were both going to fish it for the morning, then make the switch to any other lure.

Almost twenty minutes from the time we left the dock, we were back at Split Rock and balls deep in action. I quickly acquired a follower as I started my figure eight back towards the boat. The fish suddenly disappeared just as Steve's tube neared the boat and seconds latter reappears with Steve's tube gobbled in its mouth. A befuddled Steve sets the hook and blasted that porker into my awaiting net, and it stretched out to be a nice thirty-eight incher. "You stole my fish!" I jabbed at Steve. "I guess they just think I'm better looking," joked Steve. "No.

I think it's because you smell like fish and you have a small dick", Steve chortled loudly on that one. "Funny guy! It's nice having someone do nothing but net my fish for me. When are you gonna start fishing?" Steve blasted back. Having my nuts handed to me on that one, and unable to come up with a proper rebuttal, I prodded that we go fish Whale Rock since we're in the area.

Whale Rock is a large rock that's, well, the size and shape of a whale. It's got two garages on the front side and a sandy, protected cove on the back side. We tried the backside first, and of course Steve raised a nice upper-forty inch fish. I made a cast toward a small patch of reeds, and almost immediately, a nice low-forty incher comes boat side. I figure eight three times, but she was gone as quickly as she had appeared. Without a ton of other action after 30 back casts. Steve gets on the trolling motor and moves us to the front side to see if our luck would be any better. We started casting into the garages and Steve hooks up on his first cast with a beautiful forty-two incher that he steered right into my waiting net. I'll be honest, I became very talented at that netting gig. Too good. I started thinking I had so much practice that I was developing tennis elbow. I should have started charging cash for my netting services. I could have paid for my fishing trip with net fees. Now I know how Joe Bucher's fishing partners must feel. "Hey, jerk. Why don't you leave some muskies for me?" I ribbed at Steve "I might need to buy another chip for my camera. This one will be full by day's end. Maybe I should fish left handed and give the muskies a fighting chance," Steve boasted. Looking back, I'm not sure

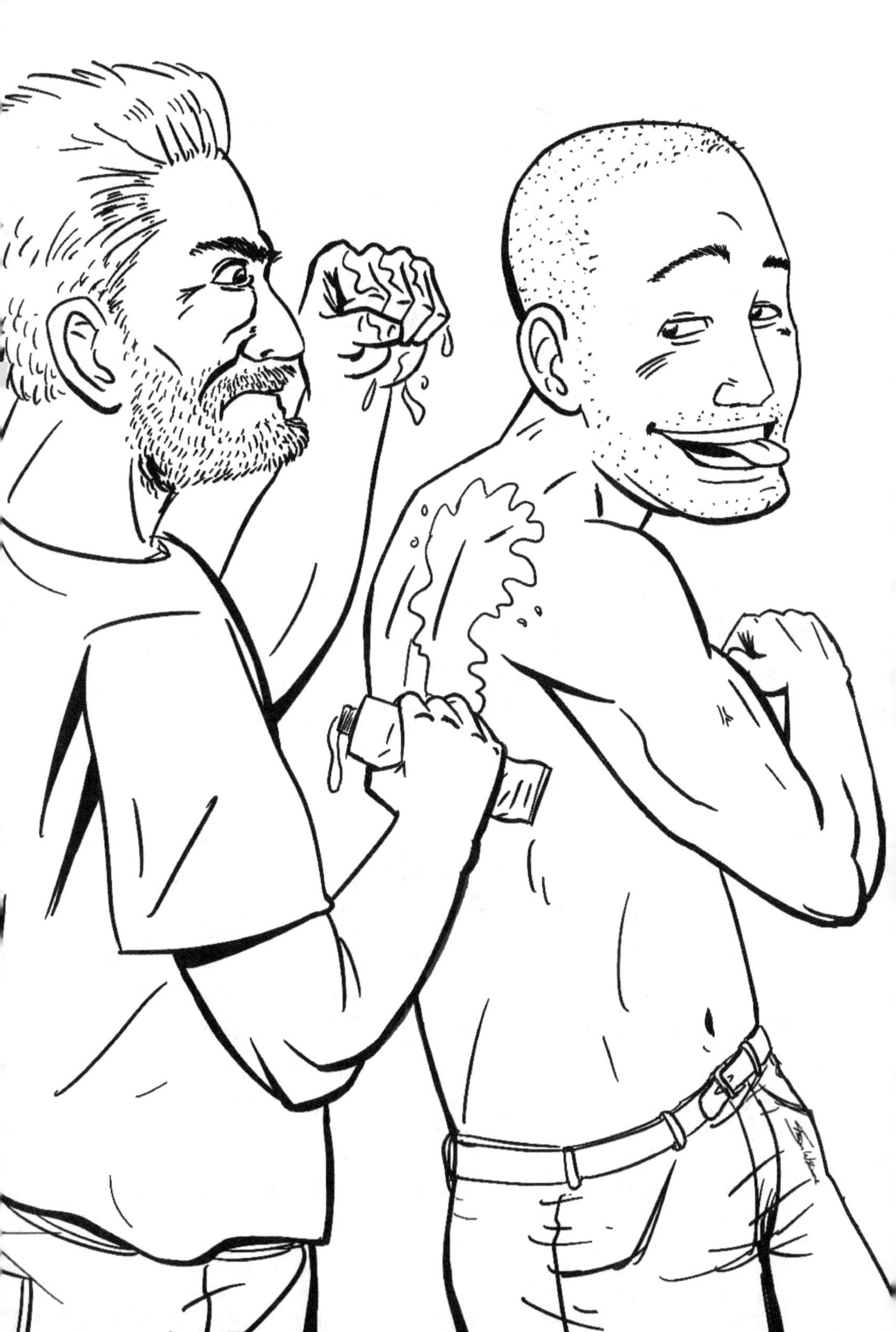

if it was Steve that was so good, or me that was so bad that was making things appear better than they really were for him. "I'm happy to see none of this good fortune has gone to your head." Steve let out a belly laugh that probably spooked any fish remaining in the area to deeper waters.

As we fished around King Island, the wind remained dead calm. The lake was glass and the heat was stupid hot and moronically humid my boat thermometer read 90, that's Fahrenheit for you Canadians.

With these awesome fishing conditions, we managed to see zip the next three hours. Noon hit, and we noticed the water had turned pea green. This was a sign of an algae bloom that hindered any chance of observing a fish, even if it followed bait right back to the boat. Damn thing would need to jump up and slap us across the nose to know it was there.

"We need to get the heck out of here and find clearer water," Steve complained. He paused and lifted his sunglasses just above his peepers. His eyes bugged open like saucers. "Hey Brad, you are looking beet red across your back. You'd better get some sunscreen on," warned Steve. "How am I going to put lotion on my back?" I tossed puppy dog eyes at Steve, who nearly choked on his tongue. "Oh, hell no. I'm not rubbing any lotion on your back. I don't swing that way," Steve barked. "I know it's against the guy code to put lotion on another man, but I think I have a solution." I grabbed the bottle of lotion and worked my way over to Steve. "Put lotion on your fist and start punching me in the back until I am fully covered," I ordered Steve, in the straightest possible voice I could muster. "That is the dumbest idea I have ever heard," insisted Steve. Striving not to burst my own gut, I gestured the bottle toward Steve. "No, it's perfect. My 'Casper the Friendly Back' will thank you for it!" Steve glared daggers through me. "If you tell anyone about this, I'm going to kick your ass," said Steve. I snickered to myself, but he actually started putting lotion on his knuckles. Figuring I'd not only get a great story to tell his brothers, but much needed lotion on my scorched back, I let Steve start punching my back until it was completely covered. Having gotten what I needed, and to poke the bear, just as he finished up, I started yelling out "harder, harder!" Steve jumped back. "Fuck you, Brad! I'm done!" I barrel rolled back to my seat, laughing beyond control. "Piss off, let's go find some new water to fish," Steve muttered. He leapt to the drivers seat and fired up the E-Tec.

Having had my fun, we took off and left the King Island area. Steve took the short cut by Little Blueberry Island and headed north toward Hay Island. When we arrived, the water was much clearer with only a slight tinge of green. The wind finally picked up to 10-15 mph and so did the fishing. Steve and I both made the switch from tube bait to double 10 bucktails for the afternoon. We concentrate on working sandy coves in this new area and in the next 2 hours managed to raise seven fish. Steve stuck another forty-two incher on the old figure eight. Then like clockwork, the action stopped like someone flipped a switch. We gave it hell until dark with no more fish.

On the boat ride back to the lodge, the coolest full moon I ever witnessed in my life hung high in the Canadian wilderness skyline. "Steve, stop the boat and get your camera out," I requested. We both gaze up into the night sky at the message straight from Mother Nature. What we saw was a beautiful full moon with wispy cloud cover, but the shape of the cloud resembled that of a giant musky head. You could clearly see an eye, with its mouth wide open with two large teeth gnawing as it engulfed the moon within its massive jaws. The whole scene lasted maybe thirty seconds. We had just enough time to snap a few pictures of this majestic view. It was one of those experiences you could only have on Lake Of The Woods, and it's one of the reasons I keep coming back. I truly love Ontario. That single moment ensured that this location would forever be a part of my soul.

"That was the most amazing moon I have ever seen. If it wasn't for the camera, no one would believe us," said Steve. We both sat in eerie silence for a moment. Then we realized the picture we were painting. Where else could you have two dudes parked in a boat, gazing lustfully at romantic moon above the Canadian wilderness? We both came to the same conclusion: get the hell back to camp before someone saw us out there and got the wrong idea.

BY **BRAD MATHEWSON**

CHAPTER XVII

THE MORE THINGS CHANGE

"See you boys later," Jerry yelled, as he and Kenny sped off bright and early the next morning. You would think that we might run into one another out on the lake, but that pretty much never happened. We would discuss the day's events over a few cocktails while making a late supper, but that usually would be the extent of our daily meetings.

During one of these 'discussions', the reference to 'Musky Alley' was made on several occasions. This tweaked my interest. I was itching to check out what made this spot so special. "I think it would be much easier to just show you than explain it to you. I'll warn you ahead of time, so you won't be disappointed, it's not like it used to be," Steve warned. Truly, is anything like it used to be?

With Musky Alley being our destination, we hopped into the boat and made off like the wind. As we approached this gem of a locale, I thought it was more of a place to call in a moose than catch a musky. "Used to be a lot of moose around here years ago. They'd moose hunt the crap out of this area," said Steve. As I gandered around I saw a vast area which almost felt marsh like, but with crystal-clear water that was nearly six feet. This back water had basketball-sized lily pads, wild rice, large reed beds, beautiful looking cabbage and a spiral weed that grew in tight bunches we called wild celery. Once this took over an area it would grow so thick I don't believe a fish could swim through it. There is a channel that cuts through the center of "Musky Alley"which weaves along for what seemed like a half mile.

Before disappearing around some jagged cliffs. The channel bottom is muck with coon-tail growing up three to four feet, the water has current you can see by the slightly bent over weeds, the alley varies in width from 10 yards wide to 60 yards wide. To the right of the channel of weeds is a large bog that is bermed up along the shoreline. If you stood on your tiptoes, you could see over the berm into the bog which appears immense and had a very 'moosey' feel to it.

As we slowly motored down the channel, you could see cabbage kicked up and dirt clouds from where some fish had been lying. We make our way at a snails pace as to not spook any, as we hope to try and catch some as we float our way out.

After what seemed like an eternity of putting along, the area opened up into something I'd never seen on L.O.T.W. It was such a vast area of cabbage, lily pads, and those damn curly cue celery weeds, casting around them would be impossible to do without fouling up your bait.

"Imagine fifty-inch fish appearing out of these weeds, in water this clear and shallow, on a regular basis. Or, fighting a musky in here with nowhere to go but deep into the weeds. The whole area was fish-able with a spinner bait or a buck-tail burned high. It was crazy in here. For two years, you could spend you whole week at a time fishing just this little area and catch tons of musky. They'd just be stacked in here like a deck of cards. Suddenly, with a snap of the fingers, they were gone. There are still some nice fish in here, but it ain't like it used to be. Damn rice beds are missing, too. The lake really changes from year to year," moped Steve. "My theory is the curly cue celery weeds are out-competing against the native weeds. They grow so dense in here it inhibits muskies from freely going where they want to, also it has slowed water flow enough that the oxygen level was lowered. This makes the water temperature much higher, thus not an ideal place for large predatory fish," explained Steve. Once again, it felt like I was in Musky 101 with Professor Hoelzel.

Having to at least give it a college try, we wasted the next three-plus hours casting around the endless weeds as we floated along the slow channel that looked text book perfect when it came to musky habitat. But nothing to show but a decent forty-two incher seen by Steve, and two small northern caught on my spinner bait. "We should get going there's no reason to waste anymore time in here when we have other places we know that will produce fish," said Steve. By this time, I too was amped to try something different. "How about you and I take a short jaunt over to the Split Rock again, it's only a couple minute ride," said Steve.

This time we came at Split Rock from the backside and with a well placed cast of my silver and blue Cowgirl into the crack where the large Volkswagen sized boulder had broken off from shore, I felt a thump. It was about damn time. I'd been working on a personal three-day drought that was starting to remind me of my sex life. And with a few space shuttle thrust's it was over and a 35 incher was in the net, no record breaker but a monkey off my back.

"Don't ever tell anybody about this honey hole. It's closest to a sure thing as I have ever fished before. When one fish moves out, another one takes its place," said Steve. We pounded the spot hard from every angle for the next twenty minutes. Suddenly, I heard Steve yelp out, "Here she comes! Eat it, damn it!" Just like a dog wanting to please its master, the musky sucked Steve's Tiger Tube in. Chalk another thirty-nine incher on the old bumper board.

After a few hours of moderate success, we ventured off to fish around Blueberry Island. As drops of sweat pearled up on my bald, I peeped at my temperature gauge. It read an agonizing air temperature of ninety degrees Fahrenheit, and just a 'touch' of humidity.

When I say touch, it was feeling me up pretty damn good. I ripped off my shirt in a feeble attempt to cool down. I winked over at Steve, "I need some lotion on my back." "You're gonna burn to a crisp before I fall for that again!" Steve gasped. I blurted out with laughter. Sometimes it's just too easy to rib him a good one.

Here is a little trick I learned years ago when I spent my summer bass fishing and actually catching fish instead of wasting my future retirement money chasing muskies. Instead of taking off your shirt and having all the string-bikini babes interfering with your musky fishing, quickly remove your shirt and dunk the whole thing right into the lake. This completes Part I of this insanely complicated procedure. To keep Part II simple for my fellow A.D.D. (Attention, Deficit, Disorder) readers, put the now waterlogged shirt back on. As the water evaporates, it will create a personal air conditioner for you. This keeps you cool, and most importantly, focused on catching muskies. Even the slightest breeze will make you think you're home watching a ballgame, sucking down a brewsky. Just make sure you do this during the heat of the day and not as evening descends upon you.

That nice air conditioning during the day will make you feel like you're locked in an ice box drinking cooled cat piss if you do it too late in the day. That's a long ride back to camp when the temperatures drop twenty degrees and your nipples shoot off. Speaking of which, on the cold ride back to the cabin that night, I didn't follow my own advice. I dunked my shirt at 6 pm, and paid the price for it with razor-sharp nips, that surely would have sliced right through Janet Jackson's pasties. (Super Bowl XXXVIII)

On the cold ride back to the cabin, Steve decided we should make a stop at Mather's Reef and give the night bite a chance to make up for our slow day. Watching my hands turn blue, I chose to fish my Top Raider in baby loon, while Steve went for a Cisco Topper. We quickly work the reef, the sound of plop, plop, plop filled the still dusk air. A sharp downward rip into a figure eight accompanied an enticing bubble trail. Then, in motion reel up, engaged the thumb bar and fired at another fish holding target. With a plop, plop, splash, thump I set the hook, but nothing was there. Another plop, plop, plop, splash, a quick hook set, and still nothing. I get waaay too excited fishing top water in the evening, and I have a tendency to set the hook before I feel the weight of the fish. I tend to do the same thing when I'm chasing bass.

"What the hell are you doing over there? Let them have it! Don't pull it away from them. Musky fishing is hard enough without you making it harder!" woofed Steve. I hate to say it, but he was right. Chasing muskies wasn't rocket science, even if most of us make it out that way. They don't hold any magical powers. All they want to do is eat, reproduce, and feel safe. Their brain is the same size as most people who spend all their time and money chasing them. Shouldn't be so hard, right? Somehow, I think I've just insulted myself. Damn it.

BY **BRAD MATHEWSON**

CHAPTER XVIII

OPPORTUNITY MISSED

As I made my way down to the boat landing the following morning, I heard Kenny holler out my name. "You wouldn't want to switch partners, would you? I'm getting sick of trying to fish around that damn splash guard on Jerry's boat," said Kenny. Not one word of that sounded like any fun, so I blurted out "I'd like to help you out, but I've been hired on as Steve's full time net man and photographer. Why don't you just remove Jerry's splash guard before he gets down to the dock and throw it in the woods? Just blame a bear." Kenny debated a moment too long, as Jerry made his appearance before the incident could occur. "Nice splash guard, Jerry."

You know we're chasing musky, not walleye, right?" Steve blasted him again. "Thanks for noticing," grumbled Jerry.

I felt rather full of myself that morning, and notified Steve that it was the day I was gonna be catching my first fifty-inch musky. Maybe I didn't have the time on the water as Steve did, but that's why there's a thing called luck. Steve did not share my enthusiasm on this subject. "I'm gonna start calling you Charlie Brown, cause the only thing you've been catching are rocks. I have the worn out file to prove it."

His logic was sound, and hard to argue against. I hadn't done much to that point in my musky fishing career. There was just this feeling in my gut that told me my luck was about to change. Either that, or I ate a rotten egg for breakfast. It was too soon to tell.

"Wanna try a new place, or continue to hit our milk run and see what happens? We've been seeing a lot of fish, and one of these days they have to turn on," said Steve. I can be a stubborn bastard, so we're off to the old haunts to try to turn those followers into eaters.

Our first stop, of course, is back to good old Split Rock. It's pretty much impossible to drive by without giving it a cast or ten. Problem with this morning was the wind was howling out of the southwest at a decent clip. So we started by fishing the windblown side, as muskies like to have their nose into the current as a general feeding pattern. My first cast sailed past the point, directly in the spot I aimed for. Within moments, a shadow followed deep behind my double 10, but veered off not ten feet from the boat. I whipped out a text book figure eight not once, but twice with no avail. Steve then cast to the exact same spot with his rainbow trout colored double 10, and low and behold, he had a follow right up to the boat. On his first turn of his eight, he drove the hooks home. By now, I'm a trained zombie and knew my roll. I dropped my rod, jumped down off my platform and scooped up the net. With a quick thrust into the water with perfect timing, I might add, Mr. Musky comes to the realization he was hooked and makes his first run alongside the boat right into my waiting picture booth. The whole procedure took less than fifteen seconds. I was definitely a pro at netting muskies and deserved to be paid union wages. Now, if I could just get as good at the catching part. Look out Jim Saric!

"She tapes out at forty-three inches," said Steve. With that being our fourth musky to hit the forty-three inch mark we were averaging in the low forty inch mark per fish. That's a pretty lofty average that we were eager to maintain the rest of the trip. To perhaps help us with that, the weather forecast said we would hit near ninety degrees with a decent opportunity for a thunderstorm early in the afternoon. We hoped that would be the weather change we needed to turn those passive fish into aggressive monsters and start them crushing our baits away from the boat instead of trying to make something happen in the figure eight every time.

As Steve and I were taking an actual break and relaxing for lunch, which rarely happens, usually its a quick sandwich as we drive to the next spot. Things were agonizingly slow that morning, outside the forty-three incher a few hours before. We had been bobbing around out in the King Island area, when a condition change I had recently learned while reading "Musky

Hunter Magazine" seemed to be coming. In the magazine, Steve Heiting spoke about how stable weather patterns that last more than a few days can really put the fish in a lock-jaw mode. But a quick change in the weather can turn those lazy followers into an absolute feeding frenzy, if you're in a prime spot when it occurs. The bluebird skies that we had all week long were now forming high clouds quite rapidly. There was a high static feeling in the air, like you would have before any large thunderstorm, the wind had also picked up from nothing, to I guessed, 20 mph. "Lunch time is over. Let's stick some pigs. I know the perfect spot that really turns on with a strong southwest wind. It's only a quarter mile away," stated Steve.

We pulled up to two islands with a twenty-yard wide channel running between them. The water is ten feet all the way around both islands, except in the channel where it dropped off sharply into twenty-five feet of water. With one shoreline being sheer rock sporting two nice garages, and the other side being a sand-flat covered in reeds, with a steep drop off. This was an ideal location anytime, but even more so in a condition change. As we moved toward our spot with the trolling motor, you could visibly see the current created by the wind, the channel itself is only forty yards long. I could hardly control my excitement knowing what could lie ahead. When I think feeding frenzy, I picture fifty-inch hogs vaulting from the abyss like a pack of snarling piranhas. Think about it too much, I'd get a turtle-head and have to dash to the shitter as fast as possible.

"I'm going to fight the current and keep us in position as long as I can. Remember to cast off both sides of the boat and make accurate casts to everything that looks fishy. I don't know how long we'll have before the storm hits and we're running for cover," expressed Steve. With that, I started making alternating casts toward each shoreline and able to cover each side on our first drift through. As I reeled in on the sandy reed side, I peered over and witnessed a Goliath giving chase to Steve's double 10. That mule was all of fifty inches, and everything kicked into slow motion like a bad kung-fu movie. Instinctively, I flew off the perch. Steve and I locked eyes. I snagged the net as Steve frantically wheeled into his figure eight. "He's all yours!" I declared to Steve. The massive jaws opened up revealing razor sharp teeth. As it crunched down on Steve's bucktail, his rod bowed with the power of the beast's weight. I now had the net in the water as the musky dove straight under the boat. Steve, somehow, managed to stop her dive and brought her back toward the surface. During a brief moment of victory, the behemoth decided she had other plans. With one gill-flare and head shake, Steve's left holding a limp rod and shattered dream of landing his first fifty incher.

"Son of a bitch. I thought I had her for sure. Guess that's the way it goes sometimes," moaned Steve. I am genuinely surprised at his calmness. He has experienced more 'big one that got away' misadventures than anyone I knew. Adding another to his belt, he took it with astounding grace. "Let's not stand around with our dick's in our hand. There's more fish in here than that tubby bitch," Steve commanded.

On my next cast, I promptly roared out to Steve that I had one. He quickly returned the netting favor. Steve bent over the boat edge and chuckled. "You don't have a musky, Brad. You got a big northern pike on the line." Damn it. "This one is big! We'll have to get a picture after I net her," said Steve. After a nice back and forth fight, we landed the northern in the net. I was truly shocked at its girth. (That's what she said). It's a forty-one incher, which was my personal best for a northern. After a quick pic with both our cameras, I returned her back to her watery home. "That was a really nice pike, Brad. Haven't seen a real big one in a while. A few years ago, Allen and I were fishing this same spot, in very similar conditions, when I hooked what I thought was a big musky. When I got it near the boat, I was surprised to see a true fifty inch northern pike. But like all big fish I catch, they have a tendency to get away. She gave a couple of big head shakes, threw the spinner bait, flipped me the fin and was gone," said Steve.

Suddenly, out of nowhere, a large explosion rocked us. Lighting struck a tree on the other side of the bay, nearly a half mile away, that sent tremors through our souls. The black clouds trained in on us furiously, with wind pulsating rapidly to over 40 mph.

You could literally see the wall of rain headed right for us. We quickly threw on our rain gear as Steve fired up the big motor. "I'm going to try and outrun it! We'll head north by northwest. Get into a protected bay I know on Big Marsh Island 'til things blow over," barked Steve.

We managed to hit the bay without getting too wet, and sat as the storm passed in front of our face a quarter mile away. It was like being at home watching a storm unfold from behind a storm chasers lens, only we were powerless to change the channel. It was a site to behold. The storm blew over almost as quickly as it blew in. Within twenty minutes, it was over. Curious, we journeyed back to our hot spot to find out if the fish were still biting. Unfortunately, they weren't because of another "condition change." Due to this short storm, the wind had stopped blowing and our once strong current had disappeared, taking the muskies with it.

Upon our return, the bay was littered with small, leafy branches and debris. A few of the islands had trees completely broken off. I couldn't help but wonder what we would have done if we were trapped in the storm. On Lake of the Woods, the weather can turn in the blink of an eye, so it's a good idea to carry a weather band radio to keep abreast of potential storms popping up. It's big water and you are in a wilderness setting miles away from your resort. When a storm does conjure up, you're pretty much on your own and should head for nearby cover. Don't even think about attempting to fish through a lighting storm with eight foot rods. You'll be the one getting grounded. At camp that night, Jerry told us he never even saw the storm. Tells you how quickly storms can appear and disappear up there. L.O.T.W. has its own weather making ability. You have to roll with whatever she decides to throw at you. Mother Nature: the toughest S.O.B. out there. Beautiful, relentless and unbiased. She'll mess you up without thinking twice.

CHAPTER XIX

SUN AND SAND

The next morning, Mr. Weatherman stated we were in for partly cloudy skies and temps in the nineties once again. I was starting to wonder if we were in Florida rather than Canada. If only my wife could have come up here this time of the year instead of early July, she would have had the best honeymoon ever. Florida would have been a fart in the wind, in comparison. (Which, to be fair, it always is anyway).

"Today is the day when the fish really turn on!" declared Steve. I was skeptical. "Brad, you and I are going to put a lot of muskies in the boat today, dammit. We should concentrate our efforts fishing the ten or so islands on the north side of Blueberry Island." "You're the guide, so just guide. Just lead the way to that Musky Honey Hole, and we'll beat the water to a froth!" Steve had an extra get-up in his step that morning.

Whether that meant we would catch jack-shit or not, I was unsure. But it was a bit contagious. Let's fish!!!!

It was to be a day of rock garages and cracked rock reefs. It was amazing how the muskies would hold on the shelves of these garages. Sometimes in really skinny water, too. The day started out with me catching a fat thirty-eight incher at the first spot we stopped at. Good start. It came out of a garage and ate my black nickel bladed double 10 the instant it splashed into the water. Not twenty minutes later, on the same island complex, I had the same result. Only this time, it was a plump thirty-nine incher. Definitely heading in the right direction.

Feeling pretty sure by this point, I declared, "It's my day today, Steve! I'm gonna catch a dozen muskies. Feel free to assume the role of net boy today! Might as well just hold on to the net all day and dip it into the water every twenty minutes so I can take pics of my latest catch." Steve merely chuckled, either out of amusement or annoyance. Frankly, I didn't care. Too bad this dream scenario wouldn't last. Turned out, those would be the only two fish I would enjoy catching this day. In fact, I gained the nickname 'Sir Nets-a-Lot' that morning.

The rock bite petered out by noon, even "Master-Guide," Steve couldn't make anything happen. So it was time to try a new tactic that we hadn't deployed yet. To do so, we needed a good north wind, which had been blowing all night long for us and continued yet today. At a meager fifteen miles per hour, it was nothing that would stack up water, but it would move some bait fish into the wind blown sandy bays. Now, that's my kind of fishing. No rocks to get hung up on. Only hidden branches and downed trees to snag up in. If nothing else, it would be a welcome change of pace. It was Tiger Tube time, our secret weapon of hardship, sorry Linde boys.

The plan of attack was to work the smaller isolated sandy bays and coves, targeting the shallow reed pockets, isolated wood and lone boulders. When I say 'shallows', I mean cankle-deep shallow. We would cast our tubes up on the sandy shore and rip them back with short snaps of the rod, reeling with our high-speed reels as fast as we could crank them. When we tried fishing the larger expansive sand flats, it seemed like a waste of our time. On our first sandy cove, we knew we were onto something. I raised a mid-forty inch hog. And only seconds after I raised one, Steve uttered out "Holy crap! I have a nice one here! Get the net!" As I slid the net under Steve's forty-six inch musky, we both gawked at each other. Finally, the Tiger Tube had produced a fish that was in the net, and even Steve couldn't deny it's awesomeness. This was not one those 'she got away' stories, as we had become famous for on our trip. And so the tube bite was on for Steve, in the very next cove, I put the net under yet another forty inch musky. Which just so happened to be the same musky that hit my Tiger Tube, I set the hook and the bait came sailing out of the water. Thankfully Steve's tube came flying by her face only seconds after my swing and a miss hook set, insert horse shoe into butt hole. With his kind of luck, some was bound to rub off on me, right?! We fished two more sandy coves. Steve nabbed a thirty-eight and a thirty-four and a half inch musky before things turned back to the way of old. I at least managed to hook (and lose) three muskies in the low-to-mid forty inch range. Steve lost four in that same range, too. To say we were disgusted by that would be an understatement. I subsequently threw my tube bait on the floor and went to my Top Raider.

Overall, the day wasn't too bad. Six fish, with numerous close calls, is a good day. After seven straight days of temps in the nineties, my white, pasty Wisconsin body could have been brought to the local burn center. Either that, or a nice jug of Canadian Whiskey to ease the pain. At minimum, it at least made me forget about the burn.

CHAPTER XX

END OF THE LINE

Dawn crested over the Eastern skyline. It was our last day of fishing on Lake of the Woods for this trip. We were scheduled to high-tail it out bright and early the next morning. It was now-or-never, where I had to leave it all out on the lake in hopes of catching that fifty-incher. Truthfully, I wanted a shot at the big fish money pot that was brewing. Can't lie, that was definitely in the back of my mind the entire trip. I had to pay for this trip in some way, shape, or form. Trying to sell my used underwear on Craigslist hadn't panned out like I had hoped, though it seems to work for the ladies. So the Coup de Gras would be the look on Steve's face when I caught the winning fish. I also needed to make sure I at least tried to take a long look around and enjoy the sights and sounds I had been missing all week. Sometimes that one-track musky mindset could get the best of me. The beauty this lake has was almost heaven on Earth. The one thing missing was my one true love stuck back in Wisconsin. She only experienced a small sampling of what this great country had to offer. Oh, Canada, I will be back in you, for you are forever in my heart.

"What are you doing down here so early? We don't usually get on the lake until eight o'clock," uttered Steve. I admired the beautiful morning sunrise and pretended I didn't hear him. It was our last fishing day, which was always hard to say good-bye to. After you get into that routine of waking up, fishing all day, coming back in dog tired, chowing on a late supper while bullshitting over a glass of whiskey, it's a good life that's tough to let go. Why would anyone want anything more?

"This would be the perfect place to retire. Once this lake gets into your head, you'll do just about anything to return," proclaimed Steve. Didn't have to say much else to convince me of that. "Let's say you and I stick a couple of fifty inchers, finish off the rest of that whiskey and we'll call it a trip," I replied. "Sounds good, Brad. Now you know why we always come back to Canada." Yes, Steve, that was without question.

After a brief discussion of the last day's plan of action, we decide to march out and attack every spot we had seen muskies, but we didn't connect. It was basically a long milk run. No time for new spots, just nail the good ones and leave the rest for next year. Steve planned to utilize the good old Tiger Tube, while I would dabble with the double 10 until my arm fell off. With a jump-heel kick, we were off to King Island to catch a fat bastard.

We pull up to Split Rock, and I'm still amazed at this locale. I swear Split Rock is just a large boulder that has broken off the mainland. A six-foot channel of water resides between it and shore, and the face side drops down to thirty-feet. This spot is unlike any I have ever seen. I know you shouldn't say "always" in musky hunting, or anywhere else for that matter, but I'm gonna say it: in regard to this spot, you will "always" see muskies. After a couple of casts into the pocket, sure enough, here comes a nice musky. It took a lunge at Steve's tube bait, but muffed. Steve starts ripping it even faster, which excites the hell out of this musky. I watch as she lines up and just crushes Steve's lime green Tiger Tube and makes a mad dash for deeper water as if she'd just stolen a candy bar from a gas station. Steve set the hook and the fight ensued. As it neared the net, the line suddenly went limp. "Damn tube bait!" announced Steve. Just as quick as the musky dropped the bait, Steve reeled up for another cast. As he tried to reel in, the bait stopped cold. Here, that same musky reappeared seemingly out of nowhere, which means she was probably there the whole time just deeper than what we could see. And engulfed the bait just as Steve lifted it out of the water.

I stood with the net, reached over and we have her in the net only a second after she got hooked again. "I can't believe what just happened! That is one stupid fish," Steve joked. Only then did I realize that Steve had a horseshoe permanently embedded in his ass.

I yanked the tape measure out and determined we got another thirty-nine incher. We kept on pounding the water around the boulder until it looked like a frothy head on a freshly tapped beer. A quick glance at Steve bait as I'm reeling in mine I recognize an all to familiar shape, and I see him set the hook. My rod is quickly laid down and my all too mind numbing routine begins as I net a little thirty and half incher, "Brad. I mean this from the bottom of my heart, don't ever fucking tell anyone about this spot. It is a musky magnet," ordered Steve. I'd never share this, unless you count writing it in a documentary for the world to read. But that's only a matter of perspective, really. Right?

We fished Split Rock for another half hour and until we were certain we had pounded her sufficiently. We found fish every single time we stopped by, so it was time to give her a rest until next year. Our next spot was only a short boat ride away. This spot was named the "Whale Rock". We had caught a few fish off it, but had been seeing nice mid-to-upper forty-inch fish on it all week, that would give us one lazy follow back to the boat each day we worked it. First, we fished the sandy cove on the left side of Whale Rock. I have a small musky come out of the shallow reed bed, but nothing more. We worked our way around Whale Rock and casted into two garages on the front side hoping for better luck, but nobody was home. "Maybe that fish slid off back into the main basin," said Steve. I was skeptical. We had seen that fish on four consecutive days. I knew there was a reason she'd lay up there. Being the ever-persistent bastard, I tried one more cast into the garage and hook up on the first rip of my black tube bait and a healthy forty incher is in the net in a matter of seconds. "That's not the fish were after but I'll take it," I said.

There was another sandy cove similar to the left one, only this time it's the color of pea soup from the algae bloom that had blown in. Steve's nose twinged from the goopy water. "There ain't gonna be nothing in this snot hole. Let's move along." Once again, my stubborn butt begged to differ. After a brief complaint, Steve agreed to change to his rainbow trout double 10, and gave the snot a shot. While I kept firing my blue double 10 into every nook and cranny in the small cove. Each cast I pulled back with not even a sniff from a fish. After a minute, Steve finished his bait switch and launched it right next to the reeds where I had just cast a minute earlier. The water exploded with split pea soup everywhere. With the water being only two feet deep, the fish had nowhere to go but up. "I got him! Get the net! Get the net!" bellowed Steve. I would hear that in my dreams for the next few months. "I'm already standing next to you, dumb-ass! Keep your damn rod tip down so she doesn't jump!" I reminded Steve. Some people like to see a big musky dancing on the water and head shaking with its gills flaring. I admit, it's an awesome sight, but I do all I can to keep it from happening. Most of the time if that happens, the fish can wrench itself loose from your hooks or cut your 100 lb line with it's gill rakers. I've seen it too many times to count. With nowhere else to go in the shallow cove, Steve's fish decided to make a bee-line out of the cove and right for the boat, where she believed the safety of the deep basin awaited. Unfortunately for her, she swam into my waiting net. A few high fives and war cries were exchanged. We had put in quite a bit of time on this particular musky all week, so it was a bittersweet moment. We would stop two times a day vowing to nab this fish. We knew there was another, even larger one that we had seen early in the week, too, but that was just a one-time encounter. This forty-six inch heifer had taunted us on a daily basis and became a personal target.

I think the algae that had covered the cove helped in fooling this fish into reaction, striking on Steve's bait, instead of getting a good long look at it back to the boat and then probably being spooked by it. We also believed that timing was a major factor. A quick peek at my lunar charts later revealed we had just entered into a major period when that fish was caught.

Steve leaned back in his boat chair and contemplated. "You know what? If nobody gets a larger musky at this point, then I won the big fish of the week money." Having not learned my lesson yet, I responded with the smug "The day isn't over yet. I still have a chance." Yup, still cocky, even though my week in comparison to his wasn't going quite as planned. It only took that one lucky cast to change everything, and I was counting on that cast to hit before the end of the day. Steve acknowledged the possibility remained, but the likelihood was minuscule.

We fished until our agreed upon time of six o'clock. At that point, we'd all get off the water to trailer our boats and get some packing done while we still had a dash of light. As luck would have it, I never saw another musky after the forty-sixer Steve held. But overall, I was pleased to have had such a good trip and learned a ton about muskies from Steve. I may have only caught five muskies myself, but I reeled in so much information that only experience on the water could give you. Experience I would use on future musky adventures. That was just as valuable to me as taking a picture with a Canadian Shield musky. The one skill I no doubt mastered was the art of netting musky. I racked up a perfect record of seventeen consecutive muskies netted with no botched net jobs, which was Steve's best year ever. Apparently, I was Steve's lucky charm.

Later that night, after all the stories were told and the whiskey was consumed, I laid in bed listening to my fellow fishermen saw logs. An old quote from my old high school teacher, Mr. Steinhorst, came to mind that summed up my last two musky trips to Canada: "Failure isn't always a bad thing, if it's what's needed to motivate one to succeed." It may have taken me two trips before I was able to catch my first Canadian Shield musky, but I never gave up. Even after Mother Nature had kicked me in the nuts on my first trip, I was determined to achieve my goal. And achieve it, I did. Next year, I would set my bar even higher. Next year, the goal was to CPR a fifty-inch Canadian Shield Musky.

BY **BRAD MATHEWSON**

CHAPTER XXI

HEADING HOME

The next morning came too quickly. It was an early wake-up call for the day I had been dreading all week. It meant the fun was over and time to return to our jobs, wives, kids, and other adult responsibilities we managed to forget about over the last eight days. Not to say we didn't miss our loved ones, but the spirit of Canada consumes your mind and body. All you think about is hunting muskies, with the occasional notion of getting the mandatory sleep required to live. I've never in my life thought a week of absolute punishment on your body could feel so good for your soul. It was like a rebirth. As we finished packing, I came to the realization of having to wait a year before I could feel this soul rebirth again. It was so pure and complete, if felt like all my problems I had before the trip had somehow vanished. It had given me an entirely new perspective on life, and showed me what was truly important.

"Let's get going, boys. We have a long trip home ahead of us, and I have a lonely wife waiting for me," announced Steve. "Oh, I'm sure she had some company while we were gone," I jabbed at Steve. "Screw you," Steve chuckled. We jumped into the truck and led the way home. Jerry and Kenny followed us the whole way.

It took almost two hours to reach the border in Baudette, MN. Steve and I went through the border crossing first. This time, I managed to keep the funny business in check and were free to enter back into the United States without incident. Unfortunately, I scanned back to see Jerry go through, and witnessed him step out of his truck and head back towards his boat with a border agent in tow. Thankfully, only a couple of minutes later, Jerry and the border agent reappeared with Jerry quickly jumping back into the truck and driving off. Apparently, he kept his shenanigans in check as well. Though deep down we were secretly hoping for a full body cavity search.

Jerry trailed us to our prearranged meeting place in town to buy gas and take a leak before the long trek back to Wisconsin. Steve and I went in to use the restroom, while Jerry lugged up to the gas pumps to fuel up. While draining the main vein, Kenny came in with a tinge of restlessness. "Why did Jerry have to get out of his truck at the border?" I asked Kenny. "I don't know if he wants me to tell you guys, but he is really pissed off," mentioned Kenny. "His trolling motor wasn't locked in place and it deployed sometime during the two hour drive.

He hadn't noticed the gravel and smoke that accompanied the front of his boat," said Kenny. "How much damage did it do?" asked Steve. Kenny pursed his lips. "The skeg is gone. The prop is gone. It looks like you took a saw to his motor housing and cut it in half, length-wise," gestured Kenny. My wallet had sympathy pains for Jerry. Steve and I glanced at each other, and couldn't help ourselves. We started to crack up slowly, and it eventually turned into full out laughter. I even had tears in my eyes. "We have got to see this in-person. Bring the camera," I said, still giggling to myself. "Try to hold it in when we see the carnage. Jerry will really be pissed," said Steve.

As we get to the boat to witness the destruction in-person, I blurted out to Jerry, "Oh my God! What the hell happen to your trolling motor?" I admit, I'm not the best actor in the world, and did this while struggling to keep a straight face. Not sure if I succeeded in that or not, considering I was smiling the whole time. "Jerry, we mainly drove on gravel roads. Didn't you notice a giant dust cloud when you looked in your rear view mirror? There must have been gravel flying everywhere as you were trolling down the road," said Steve. Snickering to myself, I couldn't help but stare, "I always wanted to see what the inside of a trolling motor looked like." Steve looked over at me and smiled. I couldn't contain myself. I burst out in an uncontrollable gut-busting laughter. In an attempt to escape Jerry's wrath, I ran for the truck, with Steve not far behind. Once inside, the tears returned and we both laughed for the next ten miles. I could just imagine Jerry's fumes filling up the cab of his truck.

BY **BRAD MATHEWSON**

As we cruised down the road home, Steve told me an even more hilarious tale that had happened to Jerry years earlier. A story that had given him a nickname that stuck for many years. Apparently, Jerry was up in Boulder Junction, WI, where he and a buddy had been out musky fishing. His friend had to leave at noon that day, so they loaded up and headed back to the cabin after fishing hard that morning. After lunch, Jerry decided to do a little musky fishing by myself, so he headed for his favorite lake. While going around a corner, his fiberglass tri-hull flew off the trailer and went rolling down a ditch somewhere. Meanwhile, the ever non-observant Jerry kept driving to the boat landing, without a boat.

He didn't even notice his boat was missing until he started backing the now empty trailer down the boat landing only to discover that the boat was long gone. He started back-tracking his route and found a guy waving his arms frantically a few miles down the road. Next to him, down in the ditch, was Jerry's boat. The guy had seen the whole thing happen and had pulled over to gather up all of Jerry's fishing gear into a pile. He was nice enough to wait guard until someone returned searching for it. Lucky for Jerry, only one rod had broken, and his boat got beat up, but was still seaworthy, somehow. A short time later, they managed to winch the boat back onto the trailer. According to Jerry, the reason for the accident was his buddy didn't hook the chain to the front, and he forgot to tighten the hull strap. Personally, these are all things the owner of the boat should be doing, not a passenger. By the time Steve finished telling me this new story, we both were in belly rolls and started crying once again. Jerry a great fisherman, but lousy hauler. At least we got a ton of good laughs at his expense. The Hoelzel boys make me feel like a part of their dysfunctional family, and I wouldn't have it any other way. Lesson learned: Always check your rear-view mirror to make sure your boat is still there and not in a ditch miles behind you.

MUSKY TALE OF THE TAPE - AUGUST 2009
BRAD - 43" 35" 38" 39"40"
STEVE - 39" 42.5" 43" 43" 36" 38" 42" 42" 38" 43" 34.5" 38" 40" 46" 30.5" 39" 45"
KENNY - 39" 39" 41" 42" 38" 39.5"
JERRY - 29" 33" 37" 38" 39" 40.25" 41" 41.25" 33" 34" 36" 42.25"

I felt that I had made incredible strides from my first Canadian Shield hunt. Fish were raised, even caught, and pictures snapped, proving I was on the right trail to track down that elusive fifty-incher. It wasn't meant to be in 2009, but it only takes a little success to feel like you know what you're doing. Being that I had finally gained some hard-earned success led me to believe that my next visit to Lake of the Woods would be one for the books. I just hoped they weren't comic books.

BY **BRAD MATHEWSON**

MUSKY HUNT – AUGUST 2011

CHAPTER XXII

OVERDUE REUNION

It would be two full years before I would get to lay my eyes on one of the most beautiful ladies I had ever seen. (Lake of the Woods, that is. Not Steve's ugly mug). 2010 was not to be, as I wasn't able to find a partner in time to go on the annual August trip. I was heartbroken, to say the least. I vowed that summer that I would never miss a date with her again.

July of 2011 came around, and I was once again stuck in the predicament of not having a partner to go with. I was in full-blown panic mode when Jerry called me. He notified me that his brother, Stewart, didn't have a partner either that year and we should team up. I quickly took down Stewart's number and gave him a call. I had only met Stew briefly once before, and he was definitely a "Hoelzel," so I knew we would get along just fine.

Having groomed our return to Canada details, our departure from Wisconsin was determined to be a little different. Instead of leaving Friday morning and driving straight through to Canada to squeeze in a couple of hours of fishing, Jerry had decided we should leave Saturday morning instead, and to make it a shorter trip, we would travel to their family cabin in Boulder Junction, WI on Friday after work. Jerry's thought was this would save three hours on the trip. I have no idea where he went to school for math, or that he passed it at any level. The distance wasn't changing, so I wasn't sure which type of mathematical calculation he was conjuring up. Either way, it didn't add up. But, whatever.

Stewart arrived at my home around 6:00 pm Friday night. I could hear him before I could see him. He drove a musky man's dream rig: Large F–350 diesel with a very spacious super crew cab and eight foot capped box. On the way up to Boulder Junction, the cat was let out of the bag, so to speak, as he informed me his daughter was going to be a freshman in college that year. Freshman orientation was on the following Saturday, and he had to be back on Friday night, which would cut our trip one day short. That was a real kick in the Bucher-tail, if you know what I mean. Not that I could have changed anything, as I was in need of a partner, but when you dream about L.O.T.W. as often as I do, one day lost might as well be another week lost. He informed me I could stay another day if I wanted and he would come back alone, but I'd have to find someone that would be willing to fish three in a boat. I believe it's dangerous to musky fish three in a boat, especially when we fish out of

16.5 foot boats and I really didn't want to ruin someone's day on the water aiming to do so. Even if adding another day of musky fishing was pretty much the greatest thing in the world, I just couldn't do that, no matter how much I wanted to.

On the way up, we stopped at a Burger King for some dollar mini-burgers. What a freaking scam. You have to spend ten bucks just to fill up on those one dollar bites. Evil genius who thought of that crap probably got million-dollar raise. We arrived in Boulder Junction around 9:45 pm and as luck would have it, a Green Bay Packers preseason game was on. All eight fellas looked like they'd been enjoying happy hour for quite some time.

This year's crew and their boat partners were as follows: Jerry with Brian (Wolfe), Jan with Joe (JR), James with Danny (his son), Rodney with Bruce (Bucky), Me with Stewart (Stew), and last, but certainly the least, Steve with his son Allen (little Al). Steve was pie-eyed and poking and jabbing anyone who came near him. A little too touchy-feely, for my taste. The group of drunken musky men hit the old fart sack around 11:30 pm Being a very light sleeper, I listened to the sound of nine Harley Davidson's under one roof until the wee hours of the morning. Since I slept for crap that night, at least I could sleep on the way because Stew insisted on driving the whole trip. No skin off my nose.

I heard someone's alarm clock blast awake. I glanced over to my phone and read it was 5 am. I quickly dressed, made the bed, and loaded my stuff back into Stew's truck. By 5:30 am, everyone was packed up and ready to go. Just as the first rig trudged onto the road, all five trucks screamed to an abrupt halt. I watched Bucky leap from Rodney's giant carpet van, fling open the side doors and dive in. "What the hell is he up to?" questioned Stew. Apparently, everybody else had the same question. We all get out and walk on over to see what all the commotion was about.

"I can't find my passport!" Bucky whines. "Shit. Keep looking in the van and the rest of us will check the house," complained Jerry. I went downstairs and checked under his bed. I yanked off all the blankets and flung them aside, but still found no passport. The rest of the group was upstairs checking under the couch.

In between cushions, in the refrigerator, in the bathroom, in the garbage can, even in the shitter itself, but no luck. By the time we returned to Rodney's van, old Bucky had worked himself up a pretty good lather. He had torn Rod's van apart and still had no passport in hand. "Well, screw this. I'm leaving. Bucky, you're shit out of luck. You and Rodney will have to meet us up there once you get a new passport," proclaimed Steve.

"Bucky, did you happen to use your sleeping bag last night? I'll bet you twenty bucks your passport's jammed in there," I said. "That does sound like something Bucky would do," hinted Jerry. Bucky flung open his curled up bag and unzipped it. "I found it!" Bucky screamed. "Good! Now pry open that wallet of yours and withdraw the twenty bucks!" I joked. "Let's get the hellhound out of here. Wasted a half an hour looking for Bucky's damn passport," bitched Steve.

BY **BRAD MATHEWSON**

We all gathered up into our trucks, and hit the road. "Did Steve ever tell you the story on how Bucky shit in his boat," stated Stew. I burst into laughter, acknowledging I did hear about that story. A few years before I met the Hoelzels, they were in Canada on their annual musky trip, when Bucky paired up Steve for the day. It was late morning and Bucky had been drinking heavily the night before. He suddenly informed Steve he had to use the bear's outhouse onshore. (In other words, shit in the woods and wipe with leaves). Steve stowed his trolling motor and was about to drive over to shore when Bucky declared he couldn't hold it that long. "Ah, shit. Just use my five gallon bucket," Steve gestured.

Apparently, good old Bucky had piss poor aim, and emptied his bowels all over Steve's floor, casting deck, and inside the gun walls. Bucky peered up at Steve. "I'm so sorry, Steve. Guess I didn't know where my asshole was," alleged Bucky. Steve turned around and realized his boat was caked in Bucky dump. "How the fuck didn't you know where your fucking asshole was?! You've had it for fifty fucking years! You turned my boat into a shitter!" bawled Steve. "I have old rages in the side compartment. You better clean all this shit up. I want this boat to be so spotless, you'd lick the side of it," Steve hammered. Bucky looked around and puppy-eyed Steve. "Can I get a hand cleaning it?" requested Bucky. "Are you fucking kidding me right now?!?! It's your shit! You clean it up! And make sure wash the floor down with tons of water. Forgot where your asshole was. I'll give you a fucking mirror and show you an asshole!! Fucking kidding me," Steve grumbled. To top it all off,

the next day, Steve was fishing with his brother, John, whom is a neat freak. John started cleaning up Steve's boat that the morning using the same rags Bucky had forgotten to throw out the previous day. When Steve saw what John was doing with those rags, he went into full outrage all over again. John wasn't too pleased about handling shitty rags, either. Bucky is what we called 'special'. To this day, I'm surprised nobody has dumped him on a white pelican island and drove off.

Later that day, we finally made it back to White Birch Lodge. This time, though, we were in the big cabin on the point. That cabin can sleep up to eight guys, but somehow, we were gonna fit ten dudes in it. Once again, we aren't the best at basic mathematics. I glanced at my phone and saw it was only 2:30 pm We saved almost three hours by staying the night in Boulder Junction. (As in, we got there three hours earlier in the day when compared to driving straight through from home. We still were there a day later, and still took the exact same amount of driving time to get there, so it's really a matter of perception on whether we truly 'saved' any time, whatsoever).

Anyway, by the time Stew and I reached the cabin after buying our Canadian fishing license, we realized all the rooms had been spoken for. Not only that, all the beds except one cot was assigned. Being the youngest guy there, I was stuck sleeping on the dirty couch that looked liked it had been saved off the curb back in the fifties, it smelled of fish fries and moth balls. At least I was in Canada. Who needed a good night's sleep after thirteen hours on the water, anyway.

As I made up my bed – err, couch – err, fart seat, I noticed Wolfe waltz in. It looked as if he took a swim with all his cloths on, as water dripped from every inch of him. "You know, we're up here to fish, not swim," I jabbed at him. "Jerry forgot to tie a damn rope up to the boat. When he launched it, damn thing just floated away. I instinctively jumped in and swam out to get it and motored it over to the docks," cried Wolfe. "Why the hell would you risk your life for a stupid boat? Especially somebody else's boat. The next guy to launch his boat could have went out and brought it back to you," I said. "It was my fault that it floated away. I should have tied the rope to the cleat," explained Wolfe. I told him I'd have made Jerry swim his ass out a get it himself. Hell you could have drowned because Jerry forgot to take care of his property. In hindsight, Wolfe agreed. Damn lucky, if you ask me that nothing did go wrong. "Too many guys have been attacked by man eating muskies in these Canadian waters, you could have ended up as just another statistic," I laughed.

Over at the dock, I found Jerry fiddling around with his instruction book as he tried to figure out his ancient Eagle Fish Finder GPS unit. That piece of shit had to be one of the first ones off the assembly line. Every year, Jerry has to relearn how to pull up his Lake Of The Woods map on it. He usually wasted a good hour messing around with it before he'd inevitably give up and try again the next morning. For some reason, after he'd sleep on it, he'd always figure it out. Uncanny. I was in the process of launching my boat and trying not to make eye contact with Jerry as I motored over to the dock. For some reason

I had become the official "can you fix my electronic gadget" guy anytime Jerry, or anyone else, had a problem. It was a title I never wanted because it took me away from fishing time, but I always felt bad for someone when they had a problem, to the dismay of my fishing partner.

"Hey, Brad. Do you know how to pull up my L.O.T.W. map on here?" asked Jerry. "Jerry, it feels like I am reliving the movie "Ground Hog Day" didn't we have this same conversation last year? Thought you were going to buy a new unit?" I questioned. "There's nothing wrong with this one, just user error," said Jerry. "I won't argue with you on that one. I have a Lowrance, not a garage sale Eagle. This might be a case of the blind leading the blind." Stew convinced me to just let it be, as we could have easily wasted another half hour tinkering around with it.

Once out on the lake, we fished right up until the edge of darkness. I managed to get a nice forty inch musky to follow my black/orange double 10 to the boat, but she was just window shopping and never gave a strike at it. It was time to head back to the dock for supper, a stiff cocktail and some rest.

"Hey did you guys hear what Jerry did," asked Allen, as we hopped off the boat. "Now what," said Stew, as he tied up his rig. "He went out to his truck to put his windows up, and he thought he placed his keys back into his pocket. Apparently, he had them caught on the outside of his pocket. He went back down to get something out of his boat and spotted his keys hanging by a thread on his ratty jean shorts. When he went for them, they flopped off down between the cracks of the dock and sank into the lake," chuckled Allen. Stew, burst out into belly laughter. "You have to be shitting me! Nobody's that stupid," Steve asserted. "That's not even the funny part! Dumb bastard stripped down to his underwear and is diving under the dock looking for his keys as we speak," said Allen. As we look over we see Brian hanging over the side of the dock holding a flash light, while we see Jerry come up for a breath of air before disappearing back into the deep like Jacque Cousteau searching for Atlantis.

"Best part of it, he has no spare with him," laughed Allen. This would be classified as, 'Things that could only happen to Jerry.'

A half hour later, after Jerry's baptism in L.O.T.W. that would free him of all his sins, (but not from bad luck), he came strolling into the kitchen, wearing only his holey, whitey-tighties. It was the equivalent of a wet t-shirt contest that I did NOT want to be a part of. "Found my keys! Somehow must have slipped into the lake," said Jerry. "Good God, Jerry! Cover up! I can literally see everything," I winced. "I saw a nice mid-forty inch fish tonight on a reef hog. Couldn't figure eight her in," said Jerry. The whole time Jerry yakked, Steve had his back turned while making up a drink.

He had no idea Jerry's outfit consisted of see-through underwear and white tube socks stretched up to his kneecaps. Steve whirled around in complete horror. Jerry was no spring chicken. He's in his early sixties, and by that age, it didn't bother him to stand around wearing nothing. Sure lent the rest of us youngsters lifelong nightmares. "Jerry! What the fuck!? Put some damn cloths on."

BY **BRAD MATHEWSON**

Nobody wants to look at your old wrinkled ass," demanded Steve. "What? You don't like it," Jerry questioned. "I need a drink. I lost my appetite, Jerry please get dressed," Stew yelled. By that time, we all had lost our appetite. Nasty.

CHAPTER XXIII

NUTSACKED

The first full day of fishing on L.O.T.W. was something I waited all year for. It always seemed to set the tone for what the week would have to offer. On our first stop, we worked our way around the Island point when I heard branches crackling in the large oak tree. We gazed up to witness three bears growling and popping their teeth at us. "I don't think they want us to join them for breakfast. Better move elsewhere," I stated. Even before I finished my request, Stew was already steering us away.

By noon, not a single musky would join us. Not even a quick peep show. The day held high clouds and bluebird skies, with no wind and low eighty degree temps. Not the kind of day one hoped for, but we made the best of it. "Any ideas? I'm all out of go-to spots. Wanna go explore new ones?" inquired Stew. This was a slippery slope. We were so close to the King Island, and

BY **BRAD MATHEWSON**

Split Rock was a whisper away. As long as Steve hadn't hit it yet, I knew we would find a musky or three. Trouble was, I had promised never to expose anybody else to this treasure trove of Muskies. Weighing the pros and cons, and whether Steve would ever know, we trudged our way to the honey hole.

The most consistent spot on the whole lake didn't let me down. Stew had two different muskies follow his bait, but neither would convert with the figure eight. "Maybe our day is gonna turn around after all," said Stew, who seemed genuinely excited at our first real action of the trip. The sun began baking us in the afternoon heat, so I dug in and grabbed my lotion. "It sure is getting hot out. I should put on some suntan lotion," I gestured to Stew. "Forget it. Steve told me all about your perverted man-lotion requests," Stew chortled. I bust a gut, knowing full-well what Stew's reaction would be.

We spent the rest of the day sampling sand, shallow reefs, weeds, deep breaks, points, garages, and saddles, but still no fish. In fact, I didn't see a musky all day after that first cast at Split Rock. The day turned out to be one long, drawn-out kick to the nut-sack. My PMA (Positive Musky Attitude) needed an adult beverage or ten in order to drown the musky blues.

Before we move on to day two of my year three, a side-note to pass along. Reminder: any day fishing is better than any day at work. It was days like this that I had to appreciate all that I have, and the value, and the privilege it was to hunt for such a magnificent fish. If nothing else, the day was a learning experience, in that I could always take from it what didn't work and attack the water with a different tactic the subsequent day. The musky is said to be the fish of a thousand casts, but sometimes it can be just one cast. Whenever you think you have them figured out, they throw you a spitball, obligating you to learn the process all over again. Any time on the water is never wasted time, whether you catch a musky or not. So cowboy (or girl) up, and fish smart, long and hard, always keep a PMA. That's the only way a big musky will ever end up in your net.

BY **BRAD MATHEWSON**

CHAPTER XXIV

JERRY-RIGGING

"Morning, Brad. Looks like you'll be fishing with me today. Hope you've worked on your netting skills. You're gonna be liftin' my muskies all day long, takin' my picture, and shakin' my hand," Jerry declared. I rubbed the bald on my head and quizzically stared at him. "What time did you start drinking this morning? Damn hallucinating," I jabbed back. "Brad, when you're as good as I am, it's only a matter of time before they're jumping on your hook and begging for you to hold them!" Wow, shit was getting deep around here. I was starting to believe that the term 'fishing story' stemmed from the Hoelzel brothers' deep, deep vat of pure bullshit.

We each had been fishing with the guy we rode up with the first two days. It was then decided we'd swap partners every day until the last day, when we'd swap back to our driving partner.

I welcomed the change, and the chance to hear other perspectives on musky fished that I might not have been privy to.

Not all the guys were into swapping, a few of them would rather swap their wife for a new musky rig than part ways with their musky buddy. Once you've fishing with a guy long enough most communication is done with grunts or disapproving looks.

The morning started out slow as chilled Canadian molasses. Of course, I had to pull up Jerry's L.O.T.W. map on his old piece of crap Eagle locator again. Unlike old fart Jerry, I had a better memory and didn't waste half the morning figuring it out. Thankfully, the musky gods seemed to be shining down on me once we moved on to our next stop. Maybe it was karma for helping hapless Jerry.

We were fishing a shallow reef, enclosed by abysmal water, when a musky smashed my green reef hog and propelled itself nearly three feet in the air. The confrontation was on! The battle was a give-and-take effort. Jerry's adept boat-handling skills kept us out of harm's way while the behemoth hauled us around. I practically had a wet dream thinking about my name being etched in the Fresh Water Hall Of Fame with this fish. I wondered if they would even name a bait after me. At minimum, horny babes would embrace my powerful rod. I realized I needed to snap out of it and concentrate. She and I tussled for what felt like hours. Back and forth, splashing furiously, she strived to escape my clutches. To this day, I don't know how Jerry got her to slide into the net, but she put a hefty strain on his aged back as she thrashed for freedom. Not to digress, but I wonder if fish ever think "Oh No! I'm about to be clubbed and mounted on this guy's living room wall!" I know I think that when my wife is pissed at me. Anyway, I seized the net from Jerry, the great wanna-be musky guide, and unhooked her. Jerry grunted and nearly lost his balance as he withdrew her from the net. He plopped her on the bump board as my heart raced. I just knew it was gonna be a Canadian record. I could already imagine bikini-clad babes chanting my name as I brought this giant back to the boat landing.

"Oh! That's a nice fish, Brad," groaned Jerry. With the fish in hand, he turned his back to where I could barely make out its size. "Well? How big is she?" I asked, froth seeping from my maws. "You really want to know?" questioned Jerry. Holy shit. Canada, this bastard could be a World Record Musky! "YES!" I screamed out. Jerry slowly rotated, holding the fish as he revolved. "It's a whopping twenty-three inches. By far, the smallest musky that's ever been in my boat. That's how your day starts out, Brad! Congratulations are in order!" Jerry laughed. My heart sank, I really thought he was under twenty two inches that's my personal best for smallest musky. I guess my dreams of booze and bikini babes will have to wait for another day. I never had a success feel like such a defeat. You have to have a little fun in the boat each day otherwise it can be too much like work.

Barely being able to breathe from laughter, Jerry labored to hand off my freshly taken little shrimp back to its home. As he did so, the little bastard tried to free himself from Jerry's geriatric grip. In the process of fighting to get free, a tooth punctured a vein in Jerry's delicate tissue paper skin. I released the musky and whirled back. To see Jerry's arm was caked in blood. It was pouring out so fast, I thought about applying a tourniquet or activating Jerry's Life-Alert necklace. I dashed into Jerry's first aid kit and plucked out some iodine and gauze. I scurried over to Jerry and quickly bandaged his wound as best I could. The bandage was saturated in a deep crimson in a matter of seconds, and Jerry's eyes began to roll in the back of his head. I yelled, "Stay with me, Jerry! I'll save you!!!," but before I could crank the engine on to zoom to shore and get help, I watched Jerry bleed out and keel over. I analyzed the situation. We're alone in Canada with nobody within miles. After a good two seconds of internal debate, I threw the old dead bastard overboard and went back to fishing. I figured there was nothing else I could do for him at that point, no reason to cry over spilled milk. Might as while keep fishing. It's what he would have wanted.

The End.

OK, maybe I exaggerated that a tiny bit. This IS a fishing story, isn't it? Truth is, a little nick from a musky tooth is like being cut by a razor blade. Reminder: always carry a first-aid kit in your boat, and never wash out a bloody cut in lake water. There are worse things than a little cut, any of that nasty bacteria in warm lake water could ruin your day. I strongly recommend iodine or rubbing alcohol. Even clean bottled water will do just fine.

Once the ordeal was finally finished, I recommended that we fish only isolated reefs and see what ensued. I knew there were hogs in that reef to be clutched in my cold, sweaty palms. "You sure you haven't been drinking the lake water? That was a twenty-three inch fish. Unless you're like your wife and like'em small," prodded Jerry. "Off to the next spot, old man," I grumbled. I was too pissed to come up with some whimsical comeback.

We trolled up to the next reef, and sure enough, Jerry long-bombed a Reef Hawg the second it hit the water a very unhappy thirty-one inch musky crushed his bait, and darted straight into the net like a wet noodle. I used to be a hardcore bass fisherman, until I landed my first musky, which caused me to pretty much drop bass fishing all together. In order to spend all my free time chasing muskies. That said, there have been times when the mighty musky is a total pansy when compared pound-for-pound with a small mouth bass. As tough as it is for me to admit, bass are a much tougher fighting fish. The caveat to that is, bass are far easier to catch in large numbers versus musky. Truth be told, I'm in love with both. I used many of the same tactics I used when chasing bass when hunting musky. I'm a smarter, better musky hunter because of bass.

"Take a look at this fresh bite mark on its side. Must be a bigger musky living around this reef somewhere," said Jerry. Sure as shit, a nice, seemingly fresh chomp was removed from the side of Jerry's most recent haul. This would dictate a good portion of a hour, as we needed to spend quality time picking apart that reef for Mr. Big.

On back-to-back casts, I tagged thirty-seven and twenty-seven inch northern. This was something I had only previously done with bass. As the piss and vinegar began to foster in my veins, I analyzed the marine below. On the outer edge of the reef were those two car-sized boulders, maybe twenty or so yards apart, with a twenty-five foot drop off. Little did I know, that was the gateway to the fifty-inch musky heaven I was sleuthing for. I casted my green reef hog right down the middle of that corridor. It wasn't twenty feet from the boat and utter shock set in. It was reminiscent of sticking your finger in a socket. A minimum fifty-incher stalked my bait. The more I think about it, it could have been a sixty-incher. I accessed the situation, and discovered that I only had two feet of line left in front of my leader and she was slowing in her following, basically I had run out of real estate. I struggled to snap the bait into a figure eight to entice a strike, but anyone with this type of experience knows you're pretty much screwed blue. There was no way in hell to make a Reef Hawg figure eight to catch a fish, much less a two hundred incher. After thirty seconds of dicking around, the seven hundred and fifty inch Goliath had departed. I could hear my heart crack.

Jerry analyzed the situation, and considered getting us to the backside of the reef. He believed this would give her a chance to re-position and hit her from a different angle with a good cast. Before he began our move, he yelped "I got one!" I quickly secured the net, thinking this dirty bastard just stole my fish. I slipped the net under a nice thirty-nine inch musky and presented it to Jerry. He grinned ear to ear. "Thought I hooked your fish, didn't you?" queried Jerry. I smirked with relief. "Nope. You need skills to catch the big ones," I jested back. He admitted we were on to a nice musky fish complex, and I pushed to keep pounding those waters for that fat bastard. "Keep your granny panties on. I have to get a pic of this one first. Then we'll work our way around. Gotta be patient, young man," boasted Jerry. I knew he was right, but when you see an enormous fish, you just want to hammer the water to a froth to entice a reaction strike. Sometimes that tactic worked, but most times after raising a nice fish, your hundred back casts just cause that fish to swim elsewhere to find calmer waters. The only thing you're left with is another story.

Jerry and I ended up spending an hour laboring around the outside of the reef complex. Turned out, that fish haven was more complex then we first thought. There were several broken rock spines that we marked on our locator. We thoroughly fished each one, and found schools of walleye stacked up at the twenty-five foot mark where the spine ended. This answered why the muskies were hanging out there.

"Brad! Get the net! I got one," Jerry barked out. "You have to be kidding me! Leave some muskies for me!" I whined, as I whisked up the net once again.

This was starting to remind me of fishing with Steve, where I ended up spending the entire day maintaining the net. I slipped the net under yet another beautiful Canadian musky which measured out at thirty-seven inches. "I think you've spent enough time building up your ego for today, Jerry. It's time to go after that big slob," I declared. "OK. But don't get mad at me when she jumps on my hook. There's nothing I can do to stop her," bragged Jerry. I raised up Jerry's camera to snap the next picture and struggled to get the frame set up. "I don't think your big head will fit in the picture," I quipped.

As we headed to the front of the reef, I casted my Reef Hawg right between the same two boulders. Within seconds, the same Goliath fifty-incher made another boat side visit. Just like last time, I achieved the same results. Nothing I did could entice her to eat my Reef Hawg. In hindsight, I should have chosen another style of bait. We returned hours later, just as the sun was dipping below the horizon, for the evening hunt, but to no avail. She wouldn't be captured that day. The ever-optimist in me believed there was always tomorrow. I verbalized this on a daily basis even though my PMA was running low.

The last spot for the evening would be Mamiou Point to work bucktails down the shoreline. No takers. Having failed miserably, again, we gave one more shot not a hundred yards away, at a locale named Mather's Reef. Working the reef, we found Steve and Allen pulled up to Mamiou Point as well. We observed them working down the same shoreline we had just fished two minutes earlier. Apparently, the old horseshoe remained shoved thoroughly up Steve's ass, as he hooked and landed a forty-two inch musky on only his second cast. Dickhead.

When we arrived back to the docks that night, we found out that Allen had nabbed a nice thirty-eight inch northern that we had planned to have for supper, along with a mess of walleyes that James and Danny had gathered over the last couple of days. "Looks like we're going to have one hell of a fish fry," I pronounced with extreme joy. If I wasn't gonna have a full net, having a loaded gut was a satisfying alternative.

BY **BRAD MATHEWSON**

Fate has a funny way of messing with you if you ever, and I mean EVER, take her for granted. Just as the grease was warming in the kettle, the Pike must have had other plans. Allen strolled up the dock toward shore, toting the giant Northern that was freshly yanked from the live well. He suddenly tripped on an extension cord and collapsed flat on his belly. Allen tried crawling after the Pike as it flopped on the dock, but the slippery fish whisk through Allen's grasp and back into the lake. That fish rode around in the live well for nearly ten hours, only to be released ten minutes before it was to hit the spittin' grease.

"Thanks for throwing back our supper," laughed Jerry. Allen turned bright red. Alone that would be an embarrassing incident, but amongst a bunch of seasoned fish hunters, after a long day of grinding, Allen stood no chance. He would take a barrage of straight fire from us the rest of the trip.

Luckily that night, we had plenty of fish, French fries, and of course, whiskey to go around. There is nothing better than a Canadian fish fry and swapping fishing stories with good friends. That's what all this is really about, along with, and maybe most importantly, the bragging rights that come along with catching the largest musky. At that time, that honor usually went to Steve or Jerry. Maybe one day it would be me.

CHAPTER XXV

FOR THE RECORD

The next day I was back fishing with Steve. I went to sleep hoping some of his luck would rub off on me. Up to this point, if it weren't for bad luck, I wouldn't have any at all. I guess that's fishing. I always look forward to fishing with Steve, even if I spend most of it as his professional net man. The knowledge he has of L.O.T.W., combined with his ability to read the water and know where the spot, on the spot will be, is scary.

I happened to check the weather on my laptop before we left and the forecast called for mid-seventies with overcast skies. Of course, there was a ninety percent chance of rain that afternoon, too. At the very least, it would be a welcome change in the weather pattern that had been holding over the last five days. The constant mid-eighties with almost no wind and bluebird skies wasn't exactly what every musky hunter dreamed of. Any change in weather should get the fish popping, I hoped.

Up until noon, we hadn't even raised a single musky. It felt like they all had lockjaw. Either that, or the small cold front had shut them down more than I had anticipated. Either way, it sucked on toast. "I want to try that little spot nearby that I saw a big fish on a few years back," mentioned Steve. Steve and I motored over to a large rock island. Out from the west side were a series of tractor-tire sized boulders in ten feet of water. Just as we're setting up for our first drift, the wind picked up out of the south. That little condition change was all it took to turn things on. As we worked our way through the structure, I had a gut feeling we were going to catch one. This spot felt very fishy, in a good way. Inexplicably, we worked the whole area without so much as a single follow. It didn't take Steve long to want to call it and move along. Not me. I had to get one last cast out in a particular spot I hadn't dropped one into yet. I tossed a back cast, as we were completely clear of the Island now. I chucked it out to a lone boulder that I had already tried on one side, but had ignored the other. When my tiny, showgirl-sized crappie was no more than fifteen yards from the boat, I heard Steve holler, "HOLY SHIT, BRAD! YOU HAVE A GIANT BEHIND YOUR BAIT!!!!" As I was on the back casting deck, and the right hand side of the motor, I noticed the fish was too large to even think about a figure eight. I kept her coming along the boat, up to the steering wheel. Then, I reversed her out as wide as my stubby arms could reach with a eight foot rod.

As I came around the backside of the motor, she was down maybe three feet with her mouth slightly open.

Her color was a blackish gray, and she was really wide and deep. Now, I'm not going to bullshit you and say she was a fifty, sixty, or seventy pound fish, because I don't think anyone can judge a fish's weight by watching it in the water. What I am sure of was her length. This girl was clearly a mid-to-upper fifty-inch whopper, maybe bigger. I'm pretty damn sure of this, because as a professional cabinet maker by trade, and I read tape measurements all day, every day. When I'm fishing with other guys, I usually guesstimate their fish to within one inch a majority of the time. Admittedly, that's on thirty and forty inch fish. When you jump up into the fifty-inch class, they get much thicker and deeper, making judging a tad bit more difficult. I will stick with my guess. I did stay at a Holiday Inn Express once years back, I think, so I know what I'm talking about.

I got her following around the left side of the motor, where I decided to speed up my bait. As I did, everything morphs into slow-motion. It felt like a climax to a Die Hard movie or something. The musky kicked into high gear and opened her enormous mouth. I could see my dreams down her throat. My little bucktail resembled a tadpole to this behemoth. She started closing her mouth with my bait just barely inside the tip of her jaws. In my head, I'm screaming "EAT IT, EAT THE FUCKING BAIT!!!!" By the time she closed her massive jaws down, I barely had her hooked in the corner of her mouth. "STEVE!! GET THE GODDAMN NET SHE'S BARELY HOOKED, I'M GOING TO LOSE HER!!!" I cried out.

Steve leapt down from the front deck and grabbed the net. He strikes a full swipe at the fish, but it swam just far enough away from the boat to evade Steve's wingspan. I questioned if the tubby fish even knew if it was hooked, so I free spooled and gave it a little pressure in hopes of turning it back. It's immediate reaction was to toss two open-mouth head-shakes. With that, I witnessed my dream evaporate, and my line go limp. That fish could have easy crushed my bait and given me the perfect hook set. Instead, she toyed with my bucktail, merely using it to scratch an itch.

"NOOOOOOOOOOOOOOOOOOOOOOOOOOOOOOOOOOOOOOOOOOOOOOOOOOOOOOOO, I CAN'T EVEN FUCKING BELIEVE IT!"

I stood devastated, contorted with questions and no answers. "I can't believe that just happened! Why didn't she just eat the bait?! Her mouth was wide open! Why just nip the bucktail?! DOESN'T MAKE SENSE!!!" Steve swiped his hat from his head and scratched his head. "That's the way it goes with the big ones. You rarely get to see one, and if you do, something will inevitably go wrong. I know how you feel, Brad. That, with no doubt, was the biggest musky I have ever seen. A mid-to-upper fifty-inch leviathan for sure. That was your once in a lifetime fish, Brad." declared Steve. I wobbled to the nearest seat I could find. "I feel sick to my stomach," I winced. "You look a little pale," noticed Steve. I ran the scenario through my brain over and over again. We HAD to take another shot at that fish. I had to take another shot, or my sanity would pay the price. "I don't think she'll bite again. I think it's best if we come back later to try again," Steve determined. I reluctantly agreed. The odds of that caliber fish striking bait twice in minutes seemed infinitesimal to me.

It didn't take long for the dreaded, 'biggest mistake I could have ever made' feeling to kick in. I concluded that not going back on that fish immediately sealed my fate of futility. We drifted further away from that spot as the day wore on, and by days end, we were too far to motor back. Just being a passenger in my partner's boat, I didn't have much say in the matter. I'd later find out that Steve went back to that spot with his other boat partners the rest of week, but never saw that fish again.

My other mistake was not knowing where I was on the lake to revisit the giant. We were fishing a new area at the time, and I was too focused on fishing. I never glanced at the GPS. It wasn't until we returned to Wisconsin when I was shown on a map exactly where that fish lived. To this day, I'm not confident Steve wanted me to catch that fish. When I was straining to entice her to bite, Steve made another cast himself instead of prepping the net. In hindsight, I don't think it would have mattered if he had the net sooner, but I'll never know. There are only so many giant fish out there. I could only hope to get another chance in my lifetime, and pray that I haven't used up my one chance.

"Let's make a run over to a spot that will make one of us happy, Split Rock," said Steve. I tried to brush off the monumental catastrophe of losing the giant, and agreed. On the boat ride over, the sky grew dark with mountainous clouds that spread faster than we motored. The once small chop erupted into a sea of white rollers. "We'll have to get rain gear on the second we stop. We're gonna get dumped on," pronounced Steve. Once the boat stopped within sixty yards from the Split Rock, we scrambled to whip our rain suits on. As we did, a piercing clap of thunder echoed across the bay. On the distant shore, we observed a blinding wall of rain screaming our way. We knew we were gonna get drenched, but we had the perfect drift heading into our spot, and the water was pumping through the crack, making it the opportune time for a hungry musky to feed. It was now or never.

My first cast with my green Reef Hawg plopped right in the sweet spot, tight to shore. As my luck continued, no takers trailed it back to the boat. I quickly switched rods to a double 10. I whipped it back to the exact same spot. This time, a nice musky ravaged the bait on the third turn of my figure eight. To my surprise, Steve was quick on net. I boated my first of the day, a decent forty-two inch musky.

As I placed the brute back to her home, the storm grew close and fierce. The wind intensified with gusts over forty miles per hour. I hastily scurried off the back deck to grab a seat. In sheer awe, Steve and I viewed the storm rage no more than fifty yards from us while we received mere sprinkles. Treetops swayed with branches snapped from their limbs. Lush green leaves ripped prematurely from there summer homes. It felt like we watched it from the comfort of our couch, while in reality, we were on the edge of mayhem. Mother Nature's show of power lasted barely as long as a commercial break during the evening news. Thankfully, her path of destruction was limited, and excluded us.

The quick-hitting storm behind us, King Island was our next milk run. The whole bay was littered with twig and leaf debris. One tiny island, with a single white pine, had its top twenty feet broken off and now lying in the water. Fishing would prove to be tough. The next two hours got us less than nothing, if that's possible. As Steve and I finished working a rubble rock shoreline, a familiar boat pulled up next to us. Come to find out, our friend Tom and his son Tim were staying at King Island Resort.

Timmy was grinning ear to ear. He couldn't get out his digital camera fast enough to show us, as Tim had just entered the Fifty-Inch Club with a new, personal best, a fifty-one and three-quarter inch behemoth. It crushed a Cowgirl just as the storm hit off a windblown point. While we chewed the fat with Tom and Tim, Steve's Cowgirl sat alone in the water. Steve had left it there after his last cast when Tom and Tim pulled up, and completely forgot about it. All of a sudden, all hell broke loose behind us.

Steve gazed down and witnessed a large musky inches from his bait. He snatched his rod and ripped into a large circle. Like a clash of lighting, he managed to hook a musky. Being only a foot away from the boat, the water spurted a million drops of shirt-soaking spew into my face.

The whole ordeal may have set a world record for fastest hook, set, and net combination. It took no more than five seconds from strike to net. Tom and Tim looked on in utter disbelief. Neither could say a word. They just shook their head as Steve withdrew her from the net for a quick pic and her length check. Forty-eight inches later, it was time for high fives and musky-slime handshakes once Steve slid her back into the lake. "I can't even believe you. No wonder they say you have a horseshoe up your ass," laughed Tom. Steve bowed, and with that, he started up his motor, and Tom and Tim took off. "I think he's pissed off. Tim mentioned Tom hadn't even seen a fish today, and we're not more than a few hundred yards from their lodge!" Steve chortled, "shit."

"I thought you had a big head BEFORE," I uttered. "Once again, looks like I'm the new leader for the Big Fish Contest. I like my odds for back-to-back championships," boasted Steve. I learned a lot from Steve, mostly musky fishing. But humility was never his strong suit.

"Let's stop by that reef in front of Musky Alley on the way back," I declared, attempting to change the subject. Motive was, Steve's brother, Stewart, had seen a fifty-inch albino a few times over the last few years in that hangout.

So we pulled over on our homeward bound journey, and I tossed in a Cowgirl, while Steve opted to fish a black and green Top Raider. On our first cast, I see a six-inch wake blaze behind Steve's bait. He conjured up his figure eight, but found no takers. As Steve recast, I peered down and noticed something in the drink. I dropped my Cowgirl in and spun a figure eight. All of a sudden, my rod loaded up. I quick set the hook and shriek to get the net.

Within minutes, I boat a forty-one incher. "You stole my fish, you lucky bastard!" said Steve. "Au contraire. You gave up on her because you lacked the skills to figure eight her," I joked. I couldn't even finish that sentence without bursting into laughter. Chalk one up for old Brad!

BY BRAD MATHEWSON

CHAPTER XXVI

ADVENTURES WITH JAN

The sweet aroma of bacon sizzling in a cast iron skillet awoke my aching stomach with somersaults. There is nothing quite like bacon. Its uses are too many to list. It's so good, it even claps for itself while it sizzles in the pan. The scent alone can make the most religious man question their beliefs. Bacon is so encompassing, I think it literally speaks to you. "It's OK. Take me. Eat a strip, religious boy. I won't tell anyone." Bacon arouses all your senses and will force you eat until it's completely gone. Damn I love bacon.

As I strolled into the kitchen, Rod cooked the bacon and whisked two dozen eggs that would sooner be poured into a turkey pan and slipped into the oven. I decided to forgo my usual healthy ways of daily protein shakes for some sinful bacon and scramble eggs with toast. When in the great north woods of Canada, one must do as if in Rome. "Hey Jerry, we're having bacon and eggs this morning. No need for that crappy Sugar O's cereal you eat every damn day," I exclaimed. "There's nothing wrong with my cereal. Got all the vitamins and minerals a growing boy needs to start the day off right," said Jerry. I rolled my eyes with a simple head-shake. "Jerry, hate to tell you this, but sugar, cocoa powder drenched with high fructose corn syrup might not contain the correct vitamins a sixty-two year old man should start his day out with," I thought. Apparently, Jerry thought he was still a ten year old at musky camp. He heaped two bowls of Cocoa Puffs every morning. I ain't his wife, but that just doesn't seem like good 'old man energy food'. I try not to bust his chops too much, but you gotta pick on him for goofy shit like that. It's just what buddies do.

To say the breakfast was deliciously filling would be an understatement. Having thrown caution to the wind, I alone consumed nearly a dozen sauced baby chickens in a single sitting, not to mention a pound of greased swine. But during my personal gluttony, I did manage to wash it down with a bottle of crisp, spring-fed Canadian water. So, I was at least a little heath conscious, right? Later that morning in Jan's boat, I revealed the secret to Rodney's special scrambled eggs. Rod pours the left over bacon grease over the eggs right before he served them to us. Tasted fantastic, but two hours later, the grease started to do its dirty work on our guts. They rolled something awful, enough so we occasionally sprinted to shore to use mother nature's toilet (aka, a fallen log).

BY **BRAD MATHEWSON**

Overnight, while I got another lousy sleep on my fifties era couch with complementary rusty spring in my spine, a large storm had blown in. It down poured with lightening and forty-five mph winds, and according to my cell phone, it all started around 3 am. A not-so-welcome cold front greeted us that morning and the boys decided to not roll out of bed till 8 am. There were rain squall warnings until 8:30 am, so I wandered to the main lodge after Rodney's famous breakfast. The shitty router for wireless internet was submitting a piss-pour signal, restraining my laptop from obtaining the weather information we required for the day.

"What can I do you for," asked Jenny as I emerged into the lodge. "I can't get a decent signal on my laptop. We have no idea what the weather is going to do today," I said. Okay, I need to explain a few things before pressing on. To protect the identity (and to not slander), there is no 'White Birch Lodge' on Lake of the Woods that I'm aware of. That being said, every bad thing I have written about this lodge has been absolutely true. In fact, I've left many things out because some of it is just ridiculous and I'm not writing about the lodge, I'm discussing fishing. (That could be an entirely separate book about that shithole). Anyway, it's imperative that your guests have the weather forecast every single morning before they venture out. L.O.T.W. is a beautiful, peaceful place. If you happen to be out fishing in the main basin and a severe thunderstorm kicks up, your smaller boat could easily capsize and drown you, or in extreme cases, you get zapped by a lightning strike. It's the job of the lodge to make sure you are forewarned of any impending weather. A full forecast should be posted at the main lodge every morning. At the 'White Birch Lodge', safety has always been a back shelf item. They only care about your almighty American dollar.

"I guess I can check that out for you," complained Jenny. She flipped on the French speaking weather band radio. Jenny nodded her noodle in acknowledgment. My eyes crossed. Sounded like pure gibberish to me. Knowing the English version spat out after the French, I twiddled my thumbs in an attempt to be patient. (Not my strong suit). Finally, the voice behind the radio mic suddenly changed from French to English. Problem was, the guy spouted the temperature in Celsius and the wind speed in kilometers. Agitated, I still had no clue what the hell he was yakking on about. Just as I'm about to blast off into a full blown whine, an American forecast emitted that I could actually understand: Winds down to twenty mph with light drizzle most of the day and temps in the low sixties. It was far cry from the eighties and sunshine we were blessed with thus far. I requested a couple of bags of ice for drinks that night, as our crew of ten consumed gallons worth of Whiskey Old Fashions a few hour before bed. Oh and they do charge you a handsome $10 for every 3 pound bag of ice, even though they have a very large ice maker. Nickel and dime is the name of their game.

"Can't believe these guys don't know french," I heard Jenny say as I walked away. I belted out, "Awe, we Wisconsinites are all Norwegians."

By the time we all hit the water, it was 9:30 am. This day would require rain gear on all day long. To add to that wet mess, it was one of those days where everything that could go wrong, did. Even with my PMA (Positive Musky Attitude), it was tough. Northern winds topping out at twenty-five mph, and the damp drizzle that seemed to hover in the air, made it feel more like an autumn chill, than summer. My only saving grace was a new Gore-tex Guide suit my wife had found for me at a local sports shop. It kept me nice and toasty all day long. It sure beat my old, cheap, big-box store $10 rubber suit I used to slap on. That piece of shit felt more like sauna than rain gear. I'd get wetter wearing that than if I went bare-ass naked. Rubber doesn't breathe at all, and your body sweats something awful because of that. There are some items that you just can't skimp on quality, regardless of the price: Toilet paper, condoms, and rain gear. You go cheap on any of those things, you'll pay ten-fold for it in other ways.

This was the first time I'd fished with Jan, and I was excited to learn some new spots that the other brothers hadn't fished before. They would share information amongst each other, but you never just give up your best spot to anyone unless you're fishing it with them. Jan took me to all his favorites that morning, and by noon, we were both completely dumbfounded by the lack of nibbles. Apparently, the fish knew I was there. With Jan's hot spot's ice cold, I suggested we hit Split Rock. Jan agrees and we mosey on over.

When we arrive, the wind bellowed straight onto the outside point of the massive boulder. Jan insisted that I made it my first spot to cast, but my tube bait produced squat. When Jan's tube bait slapped down in the exact same spot, a thirty-inch musky smashed it. Fish one on the board. We spent the next twenty-five minutes laboring the area around Split Rock with no further luck. Jan decided that we should check out the shear rock wall adjacent to our current location. Before we knew it, fifteen minutes whizzed by. Once again, not being known for my patience, I quickly determined the spot was featureless and a total waste of valuable time. As I was about to declare we should jet, a mid-forty inch beast hammered Jan's Tiger Tube. Just as it got boat-side, it unbuttoned and bid us farewell. The wonderful tube bait: definitely a fish shower, but hard to actually hook the fish and keep it on long enough get a net on it. I remembered a previous trip where Steve and I went 0 – 15 in one day on tube baits.

Jan and I ended up spending forty-five minutes more working that shear wall. When I say shear wall, I'm talking a forty foot cliff with thirty-six feet deep water. We battered the cliff pool for nearly an hour, and Jan managed two follows while I dabbled with a low forty twice, but couldn't manage to keep him hooked. I decided to keep my mouth shut for the rest of the day (which may be the greatest accomplishment of all time), for when you fish with someone more seasoned than you, it's best to heed there advice on spots you deem useless.

"Where to next Jan?" I inquired. "Let's run over to Maggie Island and get your fish," Jan suggested as he maneuvered the troll in the lake. My blood instantly began to bubble. Not two days earlier, I had raised a fifty-incher twice in the same spot without her eating. It was time for redemption. "So how did you and Jerry fish this spot before?" It was rare to be asked how to fish musky by these seasoned veterans, so I was a bit taken back with pride. "Well, we started fishing the saddle between the two boulders, then work our way onto the reef. That fat brute has been on the edge of the reef," I explained. "You're on point and in control. Let's hit it the same way," Jan asserted.

The saddle was strewn with hundreds of desk-sized boulders almost on top of one another. Deep crevasses gave the perfect ambush location for a hungry musky. Every sense I possessed was on high alert. My eyes were that of a hawk, searching for the torpedo shape or unnatural shadow lurking underneath the surface. My heart thumped at two hundred beats per minute. The hunt was on. As we approached, my gut warned me to switch bait. I ripped off my green Reef Hawg, and snapped on a black Cowgirl with silver blades. Jan angled his lime green Tiger Tube.

"I'll cast outside and let you have the inside so you can catch her this time," expressed Jan. I made three deliberate casts to very specific hiding places, each cast more intense than the previous. My eyes trained three feet behind my lure begging for that fifty-inch musky to appear. Every stroke of the figure eight was textbook perfect. Even Joe Bucher would approve. Finally, once Jan couldn't watch anymore, he took his first cast: a long bomb ten yards out from the point. The second his tube nipped the water, a submarine with teeth and bad intentions the size of a killer whale destroyed his bait. Instinctively, Jan slammed steel into her. There is an almost rod-breaking bend in his eight foot Fenwick. The tip danced to the rhythm of her head-shakes After ten seconds of dancing with the devil, the rod snapped back and line flopped limp. I'll say it again if I have to: tube baits are hard to get a good hook set on.

"How big do you think that was?" I questioned. Jan simply smiled and laughed to himself in his usual carefree demeanor. "I just don't know, but it felt massive. Just the way it goes, sometimes," pronounced Jan. He may have come across carefree, but deep down, you could feel his gut-wrenching turmoil boiling within. Jan, not one to make overreacting decisions, was now the one having second thoughts about his bait selection.

"OK Jan, no more playing around let's work the inside and see if the lady of the reef is home," I said.

Jan quickly changed over to a Double Cowgirl and made a back cast to the very water I had just dissected with 'Fresh Water Hall of Fame' like skill. When his bait was about halfway back to the boat, his rod loaded up. Jan and I locked eyes, and by the look on his face, I knew it was something hefty. In pure awe, I observed his line scream from his reel like it was attached to a stolen Trans-Am in the seventies. At that point, Jan was just along for the ride. He dipped his rod low to the water attempting to prevent her from jumping. Somehow, his rod was outside the trolling motor and tight against the shaft as he struggled to lift it up and over. Beyond reasonable comprehension, the musky torqued with unbridled power. "Bitch is gonna break my rod!" Jan screeched. The shaft warped like it was toting a bowling ball. "I had no idea a rod could bend that much and not break," I gawked. Finally, with a quick upward jerk, Jan freed the rod from underneath the trolling motor head and he was back in the game. Or so he thought. The extra pressure placed on the fish caused the hooks to heave out. "I never even saw it. There was absolutely no way I could stop it. I've never felt power like that before. Unreal. Where is the toilet paper, cause I need to shit," said Jan. Yup, that was Jan in a nutshell. Give her hell, and then brush it off.

We beached the boat as Jan tore his boat apart, searching every compartment twice, until he found the ass-wipe. I'm not exactly sure if his feet ever actually touched dirt, because I've never seen an old man fly into the woods quite like Jan did. The next five minutes were nothing but bear grunts and sighs while Jan did his business. Once freshly dumped, the apparently lighter Jan skipped back to the boat with a walking stick in hand. "That was the first time I have ever had to drop one on an Island before. Last damn time I eat one of Rodney's special breakfasts," snarled Jan. "Unless I'm due for a colonoscopy." Jan nearly shit his pants again with his own quick humor.

It was now going on 4 pm, and with four and a half hours of light remaining, we still hadn't developed a pattern of any sort. We decided to scurry on over to the next island, hoping for different results. "Brad, I want you to cast to that point. I'm just going to sit back and watch you catch a musky," said Jan. Sure enough, I cast my double 8 bucktail just beyond the point, and as I'm bringing it past, it got nailed. The fight was strong with this one, and the fish felt large. For some reason, I just knew it was too good to be true. Jan netted the whopper, a forty-inch Northern Pike, and my heart sank a little. I mean no disrespect to such a large, beautiful pike, but it's no musky. That said, my PMA was still intact despite the long fish-less day.

Something I try to keep cognizant of is to never give up. Every next cast could bring that fish of a lifetime. This is an attitude I've noticed most successful musky hunters I have fished with seem to share. Without a good PMA, there would be no way a person could put up with getting kicked in the face twelve hours straight, day in and day out. Every spot on the spot cast you make, every textbook figure eight you do, could be the one that resurrects your musky soul and fetches your CPR (Catch Picture Release).

"Where to?" Jan asked for the hundredth time, even though the man knew the waters as well as anyone. Hell, the guy practically shoved fish on the hook for me. On this day, I knew my friend worked his ass off. He was putting me in the right places and situations to be successful, but some days, the muskies just don't cooperate. And that's fishing.

Jan must have sensed my disappointment. We were near the lodge, but he veered off our track line. "Where we heading?" I wondered. This was a bit out of character for good old Jan. "You want to catch a musky today, don't you? I know of a small reef, but you gotta be careful. It tops out at only a foot deep," explained Jan. Willing to give anything a shot, I quickly agreed and we zoomed out again.

On my first cast on this shiny new reef, my body surged with an unknown energy. It flowed through every nerve ending like a virgin touching home base. The Force must have been strong with me, because I just sensed something big was about to happen. My heart thumped rapidly in my chest. Then it happened. A slight tap was all I felt. Someone once told me, "hook sets are free," and instinctively, I went for it with the all-or-nothing hook set that would cross a Great White Shark's eyes. It was only then that I realized what I had done. The air extinguished from my lungs with the jolt of a sucker punch. I accomplished the extremely difficult task of hooking the top of the reef. Across the boat in the fading Canadian sunset, Jan observed the whole incident. "Do you have one?" requested Jan, as if he didn't know.

"Nope," I replied, hoping the whole scene would just pass by. "But I watched your rod and it loaded up on the hook set. Don't tell me you hooked the top of the reef on your first cast!" barked Jan. I'll give him credit, the bastard played his cards well. "Shut up." I knew this would not be the end of this. I just hoped it wouldn't stick with me for years to come. Jan just snickered to himself and tossed out his line.

I gave my rod two quick snaps and my double 10's pop free. On this trip, I came prepared by jumping up from an eight foot rod to an eight foot, six inch pole. What a difference it was. My forearms didn't need to Popeye from having to pop baits free of rocks. In Canada, they say if you're not bumping rocks once in a while, you ain't catching fish. I can tell you from personal experience, I pretty much hit or hooked every rock in that damn lake, and all I have to show for it are dull hooks and severely chipped baits.

While on the subject and to remind you again, it is very important to sharpen your hooks after any encounter with rocks. It doesn't hurt to check them when gunning to your next spot. One fish CAN make or break a trip, especially if it's the 'once in a lifetime' fish. A short list of must haves includes: two files - coarse and fine, with backs for both, two pairs split ring pliers, a box of split rings, and lastly, a good assortment of new hooks. LOTS OF HOOKS.

On my retrieve back to the boat I attempted a quick figure eight in the darkened water. Unfortunately, it was only to have my rod tip scrape the bottom again. "I guess we are really shallow," I observed. Jan gave me a 'no shit' gesture. He made his first cast while I wrote my name in the stone. I watched in disbelief as a large wake pushed behind Jan's spinner bait and then abruptly stopped halfway to the boat. "Did you see that?" Jan yelped out with unusual excitement. I acknowledged with a hand raise.

I'd seen better wake in my day to cause more commotion than that. "I don't think you understand what's happening. Just watch real close," Jan requested. He whipped another cast up onto the reef. Sure enough, another big wake followed and then stopped halfway. "Why won't he follow the bait back to the boat?" I questioned.

"Because, he's on the other side of the reef. He can't come over the top because it's so shallow. I can literally feel my blades hitting the top of the reef!" giggled Jan.

"Let's go around to the other side and try to catch her," I said.

"It's getting too dark and dangerous to poke around on the other side. Plus, we have to navigate through a shallow boulder field just to get there. No fish is worth breaking equipment over," proclaimed Jan. Hard to argue that one, unless it was a bona fide sixty-incher. And of course, it wasn't my equipment.

BY **BRAD MATHEWSON**

On this day, it wasn't meant to be. Once again, the rocks kicked us in the stones and we retreated to a hard-earned steak dinner with a few Canadian Whiskeys.

CHAPTER XXVII

ULTIMATE DEJECTION

Today would be my last day on the water, and I was scheduled to be with Stew. It would be abbreviated as we had to trailer up and stow our gear before dark, meaning we would fish no later than 6:30 pm, and that was pushing it. I quietly pleaded with every non-boat driver that had come on the trip to see if they wanted to leave early so I could stay. Just like my fishing – no bites. Steve was nice enough to offer up a spot to fish three in his boat, with his son Allen. I debated that, but three in a sixteen and a half foot boat meant you're one bad cast away from a trip to the emergency room. Against my gut feeling, I graciously declined.

I was back to where it all started, fishing the day out with my near seven foot tall fishing partner. By the way, I'm not even 5' 9" anymore, apparently mother nature has cast her shrinking spell on me early in life. It had to look like the white equivalent of Shaq O'Neal fishing with Spud Web. It wasn't until the last day on the water that I noticed his toes were nearly as long as my fingers. Kinda gross, I believe he could hang upsidedown like a bat if he tried. The weather douche was calling for upper-eighties, bluebird skies and no wind. Terrible musky hunting weather, but what are you gonna do? "So what's the game play for today?" asked Stew. "If we start drinking now, we can be drunk by noon. Then, take a long nap, and wake up just in time to make supper for the boys," I half-heartedly jested. "That's not a bad plan. Problem is, we don't have enough whiskey to pull that off. We'll have to go fishing instead," said Stew, playing along.

It had been a stupid-hard week of fishing. The fish weren't biting for nothing, and the ones that did were crammed into very small feeding windows which were surrounded by long periods of nose picking. Every damn fish we had landed was in the late afternoon, making the mornings dull and challenged our PMA on a daily basis. "I think it best to hit the areas where we saw big fish and forget the numbers game. Time to swing for the fences," I boasted.

"I'm up for that," said Stew.

By noon, it pushed near ninety degrees, with no wind and hazy skies. It felt more like a Florida skunk's crotch than the great north woods. I was basting in my own armpit juices and reiterating PMA over and over in my head, desperately laboring to trick myself into thinking there was a damn musky behind my bait on every cast. We musky fishermen are gluttons for punishment. It was to the point where I needed to take my shirt off and soak it in the lake. As I was dunking my shirt, I eyeballed a musky eyeballing me. Probably wondering what an albino human was doing on the surface. The musky apparently followed in on my last cast and found benefit from the shadow of the boat. I quickly snatched up my rod and whipped a figure eight, but never saw that fish again. Upon further analysis, the pure blinding of my whiteness and the sun's reflection off my bald scalp most likely terrified him into permanent retreat.

While pondering deep in thought on my next move, I'm suddenly awoken by Stew. "Hey Einstein, we need to find some shade before we spontaneously combust, it's lunch time." Now you're speaking my language, I'm one who never needs to be told twice to eat if you know what I mean.

"Brad, this has been a tough week. It's been hotter than hell and the fishing has been so hit or miss. Maybe we should try to convince the guys into going two weeks later next year. By then it's September, the summer heat should be gone and the fish should be more concentrated on shallow reefs sunning themselves trying to put the feed bags on," said Stew. I didn't entirely disagree, but with a later date brought more volatile weather conditions in Canada. You'd be subject to the potential strong North and Northwest winds that fall brought, not to mention the significant temperature swings. You never know what you'll get in Canada on a daily basis.

After a quick lunch, it was back to running and gunning only big fish spots, but with very few fish sightings. With no discernible pattern, the fish gave no interest in our offering that day. By early evening, we were dog-tired and the long boatride back to camp came easier than any other day on the water. When the rest of the boys came in that night, we were shocked to hear eleven muskies were achieved by the group that day. Stew and I nearly peed our pants with stunned disbelief. If you let incidents like that dwell in your head, no amount of PMA will overcome the rational of feeling like a piss poor fisherman.

Friday morning Stew and I were up at 5 am. And were out the door and on the road by 6, before any of our crew had crawled out of bed. Strong thunder storms were in our path all the way home. When we arrived back into Northeastern Wisconsin we were shocked to see all the property damage, trees had been uprooted, broken branches covered the streets, standing water sat in peoples back yards, the power seemed to be out as the stop-and-go lights weren't working. Come to find out 60 plus mile an hour straight line winds had ripped through the area, I was lucky the only damage I had were a few missing shingles and a yard full of small broken branches and leaves to pick up.

Reviewing the tale of the tape didn't makes the trip a harder pill to swallow, you can't hammer them every year. But once would be nice.

MUSKY TALE OF THE TAPE - AUGUST 2011

BRAD - 23" 41" 42"

RODNEY - 33" 25" 42" 20" 40.5" 39" 38.75"

BUCKY - 40" 31.5"

STEW - 35.5" 41.5" 37" 38.5"

JERRY - 40" 43.25" 31.25" 37.25" 39.25" 43" 34.5" 38.5" 40" 29" 45.25"

BRIAN - 42" 42"

ALLEN - 31.5" 34.5" 41.5" 42" 43.25" 40.75" 40", 47" 38.5" 40.5"

JAN - 37" 36" 38" 31" 44.5" 34"

JOE - 44" 39" 42.5" 37.5" 41"

STEVE - 31" 41" 35.5" 32" 41" 28" 48" 32" 37" 41" 36.5" 37.5" 38" 39.5" 41.5" 43"

Personally, I felt like the trip wasn't a complete failure. I knew deep-diving analysis of my techniques and gear was required if I was going to make any improvement before our next journey. How deep, and more importantly, how truthful, could I be with myself? That would be the difference between three fish and sixteen fish.

BY **BRAD MATHEWSON**

MUSKY HUNT - AUGUST 2012

Somebody once said "all good things must come to an end." In 2012, we didn't stay at the White Birch Lodge. Frankly, the reasons were too numerous to list, even in a book. To say it was long overdue was an understatement. All that said, I couldn't help but feel a little sad about the move. That dump was my first introduction to Canadian Shield fishing, and the flea ridden place we spent our honeymoon at. I'll admit, it was not a happy honeymoon, but thankfully my wife is a forgiving woman. Our new digs was a forty-five minute drive away, in Nestor Falls, at a place I'm going to call Musky Lodge for the sake of the book. A guy in my local musky club told me all about this lodge. Where loads of walleye fishermen flocked in spring, but come the end of summer, the business was sluggish. They were on a recruiting initiative for musky hunters to fish these slower months at a reduced rate. Tim the owner of the resort also a name change for there book and I exchanged a few emails, and after a discussion with Jerry, we were booked for our annual August trip and uncharted waters.

I tossed out a quick call to my old musky partner, Stew, and we were set, at least so I thought. A problem arose, for this year, it was my turn to bring the boat. That meant a couple, not so pleasant things. Number one: I wouldn't be able to jump from boat to boat and fish with whomever I wanted every day. It was time to captain my own vessel. I won't lie, it made my tummy rumble. The last time I captained a boat on L.O.T.W., my wife and I nearly drowned. Pushing the anxiety aside, it was vital to get my rig in tip-top shape for the trip. This would include new batteries, a spare prop (I know, I should have already had an extra prop, but I'm cheap and like to live on the wild side!) and a standard tune-up. The annual 'wallet cleansing' preceded the annual hunt.

BY **BRAD MATHEWSON**

CHAPTER XXVIII

OFF TO A GREAT START

Stew arrived at my house shortly after 6 am, and within ten minutes, we hit the road to meet the crew at the typical gas station to start the haul to the lake of muskies. We noticed an abundance of construction work clogging the highways in our perfectly planned route to Canada. Because that's just annoying, we formulated another variation in our itinerary by switching the town in which we border crossed. Instead of the usual Baudette, Minnesota, where they give you a nod of the head out of shear boredom, due to the fact tht only ten people cross the border each day, we would be crossing in International Falls, Minnesota. This place was so heavily guarded, no terrorist could even sneak through cheap whiskey without paying the liquor duty tax. I've heard horror stories of hour-long bumper-to-bumper waiting just to get into

Canada. The thought of prolonging our road-trip to the lake of giants curled my lip.

We arrived in International Falls around quarter-after two. We maneuvered across the bridge, right up to the guard house. I was stunned. No traffic jams, long lines, or honking horns awaited us. Just a pretty, young Canadian guard working her post, who took our passports. I smiled and made small talk, hoping she would lust for my Wisconsin blue-collar charm and let us pass, even though we were over our limit of alcohol (3.5 Liters of whiskey and a thirty-pack of Bud Ice). When she asked about our booze, against my better judgment, I spouted the truth. She smiled, probably believing we were a couple of drunks, and sent us on our way with no duty paid. I know what you are probably thinking while reading this: why the hell do you need so much alcohol for just one week stay in Canada? Yes, it may seem excessive, but there is a good reason. It all started on our last trip up to L.O.T.W.

Last year, after Stew and I had crossed the border, we decided to stop at the duty free liquor store and buy a case of Labatt Blue. We needed to ensure we had a few cold brews for the two nights we'd have fish fries. Unto our surprise, the price we paid for that one case of beer could have easily paid for two cases of the same beer back home. We ponied it up since we were on vacation, knowing sometimes you just have to blow some coin on stupid things. Our third night in Canada, we finally had enough fish to fry, so I went to grab us a couple of beers. Upon my arrival at the cooler, I found someone had helped themselves to a few of our beers. I was irritated, but was fine as there was enough for the fish. Two nights later, I went to grab a couple of beers and noticed that's all that was left and now I was pissed off.

I had overpaid for beer and someone else drank over half the case. After some investigative work, a few guys had seen my friend Jerry had enjoyed some fine Canadian suds on my dime. So I did what any mature adult would do in this situation: I found his case of Bud Light and shared it with other thirsty members of our group without Jerry knowing it. Yeah, we managed to consume the whole case in one night. The next evening, when Jerry went for a cold one after a long day on the water, all he found was a case of empties. Not very nice, I know, but effective. The scowl on Jerry's face when he realized someone had drank his beer with two nights left was priceless. He was madder than a wet hen, cussing up a storm to anyone who would listen. And the best part was, nobody told him who drank his beer. I offered up some of my cheap whiskey to him, which he begrudgingly accepted. Long story short, hauling extra refreshments for this trip would prepare us for any would-be suds stealers.

We arrived at the lodge in Nestor Falls just before five. It was a beautiful, two-story, rustic, split log lodge with a massive one thousand square foot deck wrapping around its second story. The view from the deck was directly at Nestor Falls, so you could enjoy a sunset while watching water cascade down flat, rugged granite and pool into a perfect, beer-like, froth. To my surprise, the owner Tim and his dog "Sam" also a name change, don't want to be sued by a dog for slander, greeted us as we stepped out of our trucks. It was already a nice change of pace from our past lodge owner. Tim was very friendly and personable, and showed us around the lodge. He then brought us up to our cabins at the top of a steep hill. When I say steep, you almost required rock-climbing gear just to reach the peak. Thankfully, we were able to drive it. Once up top, there were three cabins, each with two bedrooms consisting of three single beds and a bunk bed in each room, meaning you could sleep up to six cats per cabin.

Being that there were ten of us, sleeping arrangements would be comfortable. Steve came up with a great idea, benefiting me, Stew, Steve, and Allen. The plan was to announce that everyone should stay in the same cabin as their boating partner, so you would get up together in the morning and pack lunches, while planning your day without having to run between the cabins. Steve's next brilliant plan seemed a little selfish. He stated that all the cooking and a majority of the food storage would be in one cabin. Being that the other clowns didn't analyze the situation, it was agreed upon without discern. Because of this, our cabin consisted of just the four of us (two per room) and they would be sleeping three to a room plus all the cooking, eating, and partying was done away from our quiet and clean cabin. It was great, because we could live it up over there and stumble back to our place for a nice shower and quiet sleep while the rest of the boozers partied. I almost felt bad about the whole setup, but after numerous twelve-hour days on the water, you really needed to rest, it's a long week.

BY **BRAD MATHEWSON**

Once our arrangements were dictated, it was time to get all five boats into the water. Normally, this would be somewhat comical when we stayed at White Birch Lodge due to the tight backing situation around a tree, between the lodge and down a granite shelf without wrecking anything. At Tim's place, everything was situated next to the well-maintained blacktopped public boat landing which offered overnight parking for your rig if you so choose. Tim insisted we park our trailers on his lawn and our trucks next to our cabins so the general public, whom wanted to use the boat landing, would have ample room. I had a little trouble getting my boat started, but once I realized I hadn't pumped up my bulb on my fuel line, it roared to life. As I attempted to dock my boat in our assigned slip, I reached for the dock rail, to tie off, and was greeted by a rusty nail that tore a nice triangle into my left hand. This sucked on toast for many reasons. Number one: it really hurt. Number two: It's the hand I palmed my reel with. By itself the pain would subside in quick time, but knowing the reel would wreak havoc on it all week was a concern. Upon my palm skin tearing open, the red river flowed. Words of wisdom: make sure you keep your first aid kit in your boat and not on your workbench at home. I rushed into the lodge to see Tim, who promptly asked, "what the hell did you do to your hand?" I told him to take a hammer to his dock to prevent such happening in the future. Tim rummaged around and handed me some paper toweling and black electrical tape for my paw. Not exactly top-notch medical care, but what do you expect in the middle of nowhere. Once the dizziness and blood transfusion were complete, I found my super glue. Super glue is probably the most important tool in my boat. After long days of hot sun, your hands will chap and split open. I applied just a little dab of glue over the searing cut, and it felt as good as new. From my understanding, doctors use the same quick fix on patients, along with duct tape. It's all part of the Obama Health Care Program, so I'm told.

With two hours of fishing time left, we decided to give it the old college try. We didn't know the water around Nestor Falls for nothing, so we didn't plan on traveling far. Just as Stew and I climbed into my boat, I heard the all-too-familiar plead for help. "Hey Brad. Do you know how to pull up the Lake Of The Woods map on my GPS?" whined Jerry once again. There it was. That was my horn signifying a new fishing adventure in Canada was about to begin. It was clockwork. It was an endearing annoyance. As always, I told him I'd take a look at it, but the whole while thought of ways to drop kick the damn thing to the bottom of the lake and make it look like an accident. After twenty minutes of searching Jerry's mildew-stained instructions, I unfortunately had his GPS up and running. One of these years, I thought, that damn thing will finally break down and he'll have to get a new one. One could say that about Jerry, ha ha.

Stew and I sailed a quarter mile from the dock to a pair of promising Islands that hosted a nice saddle between them. The air temperature was ninety degrees and dreadfully humid, with the sky dull gray with menacing black clouds rolling in rapidly. Just as we arrived, a deep rumble of thunder rattled the boat, followed shortly after by a second roar. I shut my motor down and peaked at Stew. "Well Brad, we should try to get in a few casts before the storm hits. Let's stay around these two islands so we can run back quick if the lighting starts up." It was our first minutes into the trip. Didn't have to ask me twice.

My rod sported a Top Raider in baby loon, my favorite bait in this type of weather. On my second cast, a small musky torpedoed into the sky, my Raider snug in it's mouth. I set the hook without first feeling the fish, which is a big no-no when it came to top water baits, and one rule I break quite often. On my next cast, another small musky struck. Now, they were small, but anytime you get back-to-back hits, your heart rate rises with excitement.

Thirty minutes in, the sky churned into crackled glass. The electric charge in the air raised our hair. We fished on even though a light rain began. The anticipation from a year's wait had us taking risks we normally would avoid. As the rain and lightning intensified, we begrudgingly admitted it was time to chug back to the safety of the Lodge. We still had all week, and no fish was worth a life, especially mine. As we neared the dock, someone turned the shower and light show off. Stew and I looked at each other, wondering if we were being tested to see if we were dumb enough to fight Mother Nature. I have seen her fury in the past, and respect everything she has given me enough to know not to mess with her.

With the storm having passed, new life sprung our will to push on. "I think we should fish by the falls Tim told me about. Somebody catches a fish there on a daily basis," I mentioned to Stew. "Lead the way, Brad!" We scooted the short way to the small, foaming falls and baited up. I grabbed a black and silver Showgirl bucktail and made a cast tight to the white rapids. I let the bait free fall for a few seconds before engaging my reel. With a quick rapid burst of my reel, I felt the blades tickling the rock bottom. Sure enough, a dark, mid-forty inch silhouette gave chase to my bait as it neared, but darted away at the sight of the boat. I've seen this behavior many times before on some of the crystal-clear lakes in Wisconsin. This would happen many times before the light of day succumbed to the evening.

The sun set and treated us to Mother Nature's canvas sky, a wisp of vibrant orange, red, white, and pink all pouring out of the western sky. Every evening, I'd be in awe of the Canadian sky. It is just breathetaking and you forget all your problems back home. We all could use a break from life now and again, and that's what L.O.T.W. does for me.

At the cabin, we awaited the crew before starting supper. Unfortunately, our meal planner and grocery buyer hadn't planned for a Friday meal. If you ever want to see nine guys go from happy-go-lucky to pissed off, withhold a meal from them. Just make sure to keep your room door locked while you sleep. Thankfully, we had enough junk food and cheap whiskey to keep the lynch mob at bay. We warned him that an oversight like that would be forgiven only once. By the time I crawled into bed, a nice cool breeze swept off the lake. The intoxicating air sped me into a musky dream sequence where every hook set would stick a fifty-inch pig.

BY **BRAD MATHEWSON**

CHAPTER XXIX

ASS-HANDING

When we awoke, the chewy-thick humidity was long gone and now replaced with cold wind and cloudy skies. The barometric pressure had done a one-eighty, and we were staring at a cold front with a thirty-degree temperature swing. Nineties were replaced by low sixties. For musky fishing, with the added bonus of rain and twenty mile per hour winds, we knew it would be a tough day of hunting. To say we took our dear, sweet time getting ready in the morning would be an understatement. I've never seen a bunch of guys so dejected in all my life. It was like being around kids who received tighty-whities and tube socks Christmas morning.

Once we got our sorry butts out the door, our first stop of the day happened to be our last stop from the previous afternoon. We spent a good thirty minutes working the area in and around the falls across from camp. Tim had informed us bait fish would stack up near the falls as autumn neared, attracted by the oxygen-rich warmer water. That told us our favorite toothy predator wouldn't be too far behind. He mentioned a client in November had caught a fifty-one and forty-nine incher on back-to-back casts using a Suzy Sucker. It was the last week of August, and fall in Canada wasn't more than a big northern blow away. Stew and I made a pact to fish the falls everyday on our way out in the morning and when we returned at dusk too, in hopes of catching fish on a spot the rest of the group ignored.

The light mist that had greeted us upon our first stop soon became a full blown fireman's bucket brigade. I couldn't help but snicker out loud. "What's so damn funny?" asked Stew. "The guys made fun of us for putting on our rain gear in the light drizzle. Some of them never brought rain gear, and the others will be digging through their boat searching while getting totally drenched. That's Karma for you," I joked. Stew's gut bust open. "You know what, Brad? That is funny! Those poor dumb bastards!"

I gazed toward the western sky, and dark gray puffy clouds appeared, along with the first crack of lightning. It was miles away, though, and we were hoping it would steer clear of us. Which seemed probable as the rain came and went for nearly an hour before it slugged us with massive thirty plus mph wind gusts, rain, and lightning. We were fishing about a mile and a half from the lodge at the time, hammering wind-blown points, attempting to not fall out of the boat. The real problem was holding our position long. I determined that I needed a kicker motor (add it to my bill next year). In my experience, it seems when the winds are too strong, the muskies will move on the downwind side of islands where an eddy will sometimes form. Knowing this dictated our next move, until a lightning bolt struck an island nearby and made me think better about standing three feet above the water line with a 8'6" graphite lightning rod in my mitts. We took cover in a nearby bay and made short, side-arm casts while keeping our rods pointed toward the water. It's not the smartest thing I've done, but Canada came one week a year and I had to make the most of my opportunities while trying to be safe and knowing my 6'9" partner was my sacrificial lamb, made me feel safer. The lightning lasted an hour and we had a few gully washer rain squalls mixed in. By noon, it was down to a light mist, and we hadn't moved a single fish.

"What's your new plan of attack?" Stew spouted. "Eat lunch under a dry shelter and recharge our mental batteries," I decided. After a few minutes of searching for a dry place to eat, we broke open our gourmet meal of sandwiches, chips, and zucchini bread. We rushed through our meal to get back to the musky grind. Unknowingly to us, the next few hours were uneventful, with no muskies and no pattern.

Across the bay, a familiar boat bounced in the waves. "Let's see if Steve and Allen have seen any fish or have a pattern figured out yet," I griped. We cruised through the chop and slid next to Steve's yacht. "You guys catch anything?" requested Stew. "Nope. Moved a few fish and lost one next to the boat in the last hour during the moon rise," announced Steve. "I bet you were using one of those old Lindy Tiger Tubes, weren't you!" I joshed. "Those damn tubes. The fish we've seen were in the weeds and slowly popping. Damn Tiger Tube has gotten a few lazy follows and one reaction strike, but she wasn't hooked very well and escaped, just like most tube fish do," clamored Steve. "Sounds like it's time to go weed whacking and find one or two chamber fish that want to get their picture taken for Musky Hunter Magazine," I pronounced with stoic demeanor.

My bait of choice for hunting big fish in the weeds was none other than the Slop Master (no, that is not my porn name). You can fish this spinner bait were no other spinner would dare go, and not be fouled up with tons of weeds. I found that during cold fronts, with a big swing in barometric pressure, the muskies have a tendency to burrow into the weeds. It's hard to get a good presentation in front of them down there because you are dealing with many a none aggressive fish with a very small strike zone, so you have to be spot-on-the-spot casting or you'll see nothing. Downsizing your bait does seem to help, too, but nothing is foolproof. Sometimes a musky will just lie on the bottom while baits are only inches from its mouth and still no bite will occur.

I stuck to casting out the Slop Master to every fish hiding weedy forest, I could find. Time after time, I whittled through the mess without as much as a nibble to show for it. You would think with all the weed whacking that at the very least I would have a lazy follow or two. Nope. Not even a northern pike dabbled with my Slop Master. Discouraging.

BY **BRAD MATHEWSON**

So with my arms feeling like rubber after so many empty casts. The only thing better than being on the water all day chasing those elusive giant muskies was being back at the cabin with a cold drink in my hand and warm food in my belly. We all got our asses handed to us that day. Cold, windy and wet conditions made for a miserable day. It was more suited for bow hunting whitetails than hunting muskies. Out of ten guys, we saw four fish and apprehended jack squat. Musky fishing has a way of humbling even the most die hard nuts. Everyone has days like this eventually. It's unfortunate we had to experience one of these during our week long trip. A valiant effort was made, but sometimes Mother Nature and muskies win, even with our $10,000 dollar arsenal of black magic baits.

CHAPTER XXX

MORE OF LESS

"Today is our day!" I proclaimed as I scrambled from bed. "The sun's shining and Mr. and Mrs. Musky will surely hit every bait I throw at them!" A quick look of the forecast told me things were looking on the up and up, but it was still gonna be a tough day. Our one-day cold front was gone and highs were to be in the mid-seventies with south winds up to twenty-five mph. A nice, welcomed change, but another huge swing in the barometric pressure meant tough fishing ahead.

A windy day to me means swift current, so our first plan of attack was to fish windblown points with double 10s. On our way to Cyclone Point, I identified something black in the water. As we approached, I could see it was a two-year old bear, probably 120 lbs soaking wet. Being typical tourists, we withdrew our digital cameras and got some nice action shots with young Yogi alongside my boat. He was a long way from land and paddling at a decent clip. Note to self: Don't attempt to outswim a bear. They obviously don't tire easily, Michael Phelps better watch out.

We spent the first three hours angling windy points with nothing to show for except some much needed morning exercise. When fishing high winds in an aluminum boat, you get the full brunt of whatever Mother Nature throws at you. Better hold on for dear life or you'll be in the drink. The constant bobbing up and down wears down your legs. Your knees act as shock absorbers and your gut is a washing machine on spin cycle. But who's complaining, we're on vacation! Being that we were doing "Sweating to the Oldies" tapes the entire morning with nothing to show for it, I decided the point bite wasn't happening. And a new plan of attack would be for us to fish a few garages in neck down areas.

Our next spot was a small group of islands in front of the entrance to Big Camp Bay. The current chugged south to north through a forty-yard gap between two islands. The west island had four garages that beckoned to be probed. The first two garages held nothing, of course. But the third garage was the cat's meow. A low forty-inch fish swam hot on the heels of my green Reef Hawg, but broke off the chase not ten feet from the boat. I knelt down and gathered my rod equipped, with the most frustrating bait ever invented, the Tiger Tube. I casted it in the same spot and Mrs. Musky was back nipping at my tube. I ripped the bait back at a faster cadence, but once again, she sank away a mere ten feet from the boat. "You had your chance.

Now it's my turn!" barked Stew. With that, he cast a Bobbie Bait her direction and slowly brought her back in tow. Again, she pulled the same Houdini trick and disappeared.

"I think we should give her some time and come back in a few hours," said Stew.

Having had enough of her teasing us, we made a run up to Big Camp. We motored on into the bay and seemed somewhat sheltered from the wind. There were two fingers that fork to the left and one that heads straight ahead. We took the first one to the left and unearthed nothing but dead weeds. The second finger was much like the first, only I did manage to see a twelve-inch baby musky that tried to eat my Slop Master. Why we even went up the third finger was beyond me. Strange to think we were at the end of August and some weedy bays were already dying out. That's Canada for you. A very short summer period and then it's back to a long hard winter. Let that be a lesson to some of you looking to fish L.O.T.W. There is a lot of water to fish and explore, but time is limited. You have to share information with your buddies and other guys at your resort. I can't stress this enough. Your one week on the lake is a very short period of time to learn such a vast lake. I have friends who have been fishing the lake for over twenty years and still learning new water. Add to that, this lake seems to change from year to year. A bay that had beautiful cabbage one year can be devoid of life the next. If there's a lake that you need to find a pattern on, this is it. The weather is ever-changing, and you'll have to work hard every damn day to develop a pattern just for that day. If you're really lucky, a stable front moves in and a pattern can hold up all week long. You can form your own milk run and still discover new areas that have the same type of fish-holding structure or maybe even that fish of a lifetime.

From Big Camp Bay, we made our way down to GoHere Bay. (Duh, why didn't I think about 'going here' sooner?) Stew and I spent a couple of hours drudging the sandy, reed-filled bay with spinner baits. We did see four nice muskies in the forty-inch range, but the fellows acted like they were being paid by the government on an hourly wage, because they lollygagged around and wouldn't figure eight no matter how much we begged them. We methodically fished our way out of GoHere Bay by late that afternoon, with nothing to show for it but this short paragraph of faded memories.

Once the front of the boat came around a bend near an island, I noticed a large bald eagle perched on the top of a sixty-foot white pine. The aged pine appeared twisted from high winds, as all its branches were spun off. It was common to see twenty or more eagles in a day, but we hadn't seen one with its chest puffed out and wings stretched wide, sopping up the last of the day's rays. Mr. Eagle resembled a peed off football coach about to lose a foot in one of his star player's back side. I watched him shake his head at us with disapproval, over the last two days with no fish. "You losers should take up perch fishing," I thought I heard him say.

On our way back to the lodge that night feeling defeated once again, we attempted one last stop at a small Island sporting a very large log cabin. As we got closer, the cabin seemed to overshadow the entire island it laid on. I voiced to Stew to cast around the boat docks and see if we could make something happen. If you have ever been to Lake of the Woods, you will notice people tend to put ropes across open waters between the docks to detour fishermen from casting. One angry Canadian once bawled that I was "Casting on his property!" and explained what he'd do to "You's tourists dat ruin his lake!" My partner and I just smirked and wished him a good day. There's different types of folks that use this lake. Some are fishermen, but some are nature lovers who actually hate fishermen and think we're exploiting the fishery. Some in our group have experienced the latter, so my best advice is to smile and be on your way. Keeps all fishermen in a good light, regardless of what deplorable things spouted from their pie holes.

I casted my Baby Loon Top Raider through a series of ropes and docks, and see a three-inch wake push behind my bait. I speed up my retrieval and a thirty-inch musky crushed it boatside. The fish immediately makes a beeline for the back of the boat and before I even know whats happening it dives under the motor. I quickly race to the back of the boat and try to free my now tangled line from under the lower unit. I yell for Stew to trim the motor up and in doing so I can see my line is very frayed from rubbing on the skeg. In a quick attempt to free him I dipped my rod underwater and the musky goes berserk and now wraps the line around the prop. So I throw down the rod and try to hand line her in with Stew standing over my shoulder shaking his head and snickering. Meanwhile I'm in the battle of my life with a thirty incher as she wears grooves in my hands with an eighty pound Cortland Master braid. It took some testicular fortitude, but I manage to get her back to the boat and it was the hardest earned fish I've caught in years. After her release and ten yards of now frayed line Stew looks at me and says, "Maybe that bald eagle was right. We should take up perch fishing." And I couldn't disagree with him, we were a sorry pair of musky hunters.

We fished until dark only capturing an important lesson: Always be ready. You never know when a fish will strike a cast. Could be the first toss of the day or when you're dead tired, dreaming about supper and cold brewskies. I wasn't concentrating on fishing when my musky hit my Top Raider. I was only going through the motions. That relatively small musky made his run and tangled us up. I should have easily overpowered him with my 8'6" St. Croix and eighty lbs. braid line. If that were a fifty-inch fish, or even a personal best, I could never forgive myself. Make every cast count, and make a good figure eight every time, or if you're lazy at the very least a figure J. You never know when your life will change, or end.

Our dreams of becoming a musky pro and fishing the PMTT tournament full time were squashed for yet another day. It was time to snap back to reality. Our next big adventure was cooking frozen ribs on a stick, a real treat for supper for ten hungry dudes. (Apparently, our chef for the evening had forgotten to DE-thaw the ribs.) Our brilliant chef had a quick fix idea for the unforeseen problem. He placed the frozen pork treats on the grill grate to cook. Being frozen, the juices were sealed in, leaving it extra moist. Unfortunately, he soon found the grill had no top rack, nor temperature control setting other than 'bonfire char'. Ten-inch flames lapped our frozen sticks of barbecue delight. I'll give him credit for trying, because James did the best he could, but burnt outside and Popsicle inside would only lead to sore tummies and violent bouts of Old Faithful diarrhea in the morning. After twenty minutes, the science experiment had gone badly and needed to be stopped. I took the reins and finished baking them in the oven. I'm happy to report all was well, though we required an extra bottle of BBQ sauce just to mask the blackened exterior. And no one squirted up the bathroom the next morning.

BY **BRAD MATHEWSON**

CHAPTER XXXI

PRACTICE MAKES PERFECT

A Positive Mental Attitude (PMA) is arduous to retain when you're punted in the baby-maker day after day after day. Even with that, Stew and I managed to get our sorry carcasses out of bed the next morning. I was at the point where I literally prayed to the Musky Gods before my first cast at every stop. As always, my pleas went unanswered. Catching muskies must not be on the top of the big guy's list. Something I still don't understand.

The local weather-honk stated low eighties and south winds blowing up to twenty. With a thirty percent chance of rain by early afternoon, and another low-pressure system moving in afterward, our time was fleeting.

Learning new water presented challenges, especially when we had an established milk run year after year previously. Our confidence soared when we drilled our best spots. That said, in order to become a better musky angler, you must focus on your weaknesses. Be it working a certain type of bait properly, knowing your electronics inside and out, or learning a new body of water, you must develop a sound strategy and solution. By noon, I threw that damn book out the window. PMA could kiss my ass! The high-pressure system held strong as the low-pressure system never developed. We were stuck with bluebird skies and a few light, wispy clouds mixed in. Even that didn't go well for us.

"Stew. Stew! There's Steve and Allen. Let's see if they found a pattern yet," I woofed across the boat to the melancholy man. We scooted across the water and trolled up to the familiar yacht. "You catch any yet?" asked Steve as he chucked out his line. "Steve, we couldn't catch crabs from a ten buck hooker," boasted Stew. Steve smiled and began reeling in his line. He wore a stupid shit-eating grin, so something was up. "You guys caught fish. You got that stupid smirk again," I mocked at the boys. Allen couldn't contain himself. "Dad took a forty-seven and thirty-seven incher, and I nabbed a forty-four and a half inch beast! All within the last hour!" Stew gnawed his bottom lip. He glanced over to me and gestured to his belt. We both did an about-face and dropped our drawers to offer our 'full moon' to them. Lucky bastards.

"There are supposedly two really big fish not too far from here according to Jerry and Brian," muttered Steve as he deflected his eyes from our moons. I quickly raised my shorts and whirled around. "Jerry is camping on one of the spots. Go to the floating LP tanks at the entrance to GoHere Bay. There should be a shallow rock reef with large boulders on top of it. It's about four feet deep and drops off to twenty feet on both sides of it. There was a nice upper-forty inch tubby hanging around. Rod and Buck saw her, too. The other spot was just southwest of that. Two islands adjacent to a large weedy bay, that's where you'll find Jerry heaving bulldogs for a phantom fifty-incher." I dug deeper in search of more Steve wisdom, with little to no help. "I landed my forty-seven incher in a reedy cove out of the wind and my thirty-seven on a shallow rock reef. Allen lifted his on a saddle between two small islands containing a nice, chugging current. All on double 10 Cowgirls, but no real pattern," explained Steve. "Now get your bony white asses out of here and catch some fish!" As we cruised away, I yelped over the motor "Hey Steve! Could you help me with this suntan lotion? I don't want my ass to burn!" Little Al chortled. Steve offered me the one-finger salute.

"Finally! Something to go on. Double 10s for me the rest of the day," I proclaimed. If there was anything I learned in my years of fishing with Steve, it was to listen to the man when it pertained to muskies. I was excited to have extracted some information from him. It felt like a new beginning full of potential. My PMA was back in my quiver.

We found LP reef right away. On my first cast to the rocky reef, I hooked into something solid my first turn of the reel. It wouldn't move. "Do you have a big one?" questioned Stew.

"OH YEAH! It's so big, I doubt I'll get my buck tail back. Only question is, does catching the reef count?" Stew practically dropped his rod into the lake. "WE JUST GOT HERE?!?!" I shrugged my shoulders. Stew ignited the trolling motor while I raised up the tip of my rod to give it a dozen or so quick snaps. Finally, my bait broke free. Meanwhile, the motor scraped the top of the reef, ruining any hope of catching fish. Yet another hot spot shot on the dot by yours truly.

Here's an example of me breaking my own rules. I wanted so badly to fish an area where a nice musky resided, I ignored a key point. One must remember that if you don't know a spot, then only a damn fool would rush right in and start casting. Always review the area with your locator on side-scan or down imaging to help understand the particulars in said spot. If nothing else, look at your darn map. Too many idiots rush in and cast without knowing if they drove over the prime real estate. Have a plan of attack before battle to tip the scales in your favor.

With his PMA fully intact, Stew blurted, "Let's fish the back side. Maybe the fish are hard of hearing over there." I hoped he was right. I had messed up enough fishing holes this trip. I started feeling awful for Stew having to deal with my ineptness. As luck would have it, our first cast both had fish chasing hard. Both came boat side and once around in a figure eight, went and disappeared. "One O'clock and those were the first muskies all day!" Stew sighed. We continued to ease our way back to where we started, but no further window shoppers. In agreement, we decided to return after sundown to see if we could convert a double.

BY **BRAD MATHEWSON**

As we made our way over by Jerry, Brian stood up waved his arms. "What the hell are you two doing over here? Didn't you see Brian waving his arms?" howled Jerry. "I'm working this whole area for a monster musky. She nipped at my Bull Dog a few times but wouldn't eat." "How big do you think she was?" inquired Stew. "Fifty-three. Maybe fifty-four!" "So, maybe a high forty-inch fish. You're old and your eyes are shot, Jerry," I quipped at the geezer. Jerry laughed and ordered us to get the hell out of his area so he could catch the big one. I explained to him that the great white whale was long gone, so Jerry snapped back with, "Have you boys even caught a musky yet today?" Bastard always went straight for the jugular. "We are trophy fishing. It's a new world record or nothing!" I yelled over as we pulled away. I parked my butt back on the seat and turned to Stew. "We really need to catch a musky, don't we. "Yep," uttered Stew as he rubbed his brow. This was starting to get embarrassing.

"That weed choked bay. Let's see if anyone is home," I stated. As we rounded the corner of the island, we see James and Danny catching walleyes one after another. The closer we neared, my locator lent reason to their success. The screen was stuffed with dark clouds, or better called, bait balls. We were located between a shallow bay and a sharp break that dropped from five feet to twenty-five feet in a dozen yards or so. No wonder Jerry had raised a big fish here. "Why aren't you guys musky fishing?" I wondered. "Just taking a break to catch some fish for our fish fry tomorrow," explained James. Stew and I slowed down just enough as to not disturb their fishing frenzy.

If they were gonna waste their musky fishing time on my behalf, by all means, I didn't want to stop them. Watching them made my gut rumble for fresh fried fish food.

Instead, we headed straight into the shallow bay. I was startled to find nice red cabbage with a tint of green algae bloom that percolated within the hour due to decreased wind. I swiftly excavated my tackle box for a white, tandem spinner bait while Stew snapped on his black and green Ace bait. We found a pleasant thirty-minute nonstop northern pike action spot. Frankly, I was happy to finally have a jerk on the other end of my rod. For a brief moment, it felt like we were real fishermen again. They weren't muskies, though. We kept two for the pot and traveled to a map spot back near Big Camp Bay.

Our intended spot was a protected cove off the mainland. It offered a sandy bottom, reeds, and was windless most days. It was the kind of place a fat, lazy musky should hang out. To our dismay, we weren't the only ones there. A family of beavers had taken up residency. We could see a large beaver lodge next to shore with downed trees providing ample cover for muskies to hide. As we made our casts toward the beaver's lodge trying not to get snagged in one of the feed piles. I knew we'd see something. Within minutes, I had a nice musky follow toward the boat, only to disappear with no interest in my figure eight whatsoever. Even the beavers got into the action. They'd follow our baits to the boat and stare at us, endeavoring to figure what we were up to. Normally, beavers are very nervous and don't want you near their lodge. They'll swim to the surface and slap their tail at you, warning the others of impending danger. I thought it best we move along. Like a chick I knew back in the day, that's a beaver that will bite back.

We fished a few more fishy spots on our way back to the LP tanks, and managed to see six fish. Could our luck be changing? "Feel that, Stew? It's our luck changing for the rest of this trip. It's momentum. Tonight, on our last spot before dark, we're gonna land a double," I pronounced without a glimmer of hesitancy. "That's some wishful thinking there. Your PMA must be back," laughed Stew. Laugh all he wanted, the Force was strong in this one. I could literally feel our luck shift from shit to shamrock.

The plan was to fish the outside points of the reef so it wouldn't leave any chance that a certain somebody could hook the top of the reef and mess things up again. The setting sun dripped below the horizon, with the sky a smattering of fire and salmon pink. I watched intently for any deep follow that resembled a dark shadow under the fading light and shimmer of the lake's rippled surface. On my final cast of the evening, my body tingled as if I was in-tune with Mother Nature herself. A slight tap of my double 10, I reared back and drove home a devastating hook set that could have turned a reef into an Island. "Get the net! I finally got one!!!!!" I screamed at Stew. Stew was a bit dumbfounded that our plan had actually worked out for once. I powered the fish straight to the waiting net, and once secured, it was time to get her unhooked. Time for a quick measurement and a picture. As I held up my fish in the last light of day, all I could think was PMA (Positive Mental Attitude). You can't quit if you want to be successful in this sport. It's the guys who fish longer and harder that are rewarded. Sometimes, it does mean getting your butt kicked all day. All for a few minutes of happiness in the remaining minutes of the day, makes it all worthwhile.

"How big is she?" Stew requested, as he stood over me. "Forty-one inches," I said proudly. As she swam away strong, I was reminded of 'Time on the Water', my favorite fishing book. These are moments like this at the end of the day, that only a fellow musky hunter can understand and appreciate.

BY **BRAD MATHEWSON**

CHAPTER XXXII

FISH TALES

The morning dawn broke with a whim to return to the sights and sounds of the most memorable experiences you've had on Lake of the Woods. That place for our group was known as the King Island area. A place where the many reefs, coves, and small islands have names that only our gang would recognize. Places like Whale Rock, Bucky's Bay, Musky Alley, Split Rock and many more. My comrades had been learning this area for over twenty years, and I had been privy enough to many of their honey hole which have produced muskies year after year. These milk runs were forged through years of trial and error. You could literally fish this milk run from dawn to dusk and not hit all the spots. It's not just generic area, either. There really is a spot-on-the-spot to each location, and if you aren't within inches of that spot, you aren't catching fish. I can't say this too many times about L.O.T.W.: If you don't know the sweet spots, you aren't catching numbers of fish. That's something I really worked on every trip to Canada. You must be extremely accurate with your casts and dead focused in. It is of the up-most importance when musky hunting.

Steve and Jerry consistently catch twelve or more muskies every trip because they've mastered the key essentials to musky hunting, particularly on L.O.T.W. It's not due to their 'secret spots,' because we all share information. When I fish with them, I noticed they don't waste casts. They hit the prime spots with deadly precision and swiftly move on. Even their time management is formulated to perfection. They tend to think about the next area while casting the first. There is no, "Hey, let's look at a map and decide where we're going to fish next," and at the same time they're trying to develop a pattern of what the fish want for baits and speeds that day. The people at the top of the musky fishing industry aren't that much better at locating muskies than you or I. Yet the Pro's conquer musky hunting at a whole other level, leaving us bait chuckers in their wake. Their secret is, "The Devil is in the Details". Do all the little things, the fundamentals, correctly every time. For example, they are able to read a musky's mood while going into a figure eight and give their bait more than one dimension and thought than just a halfhearted figure eight. Because they think of their bait as three dimensional, many more fish convert into eaters instead of 'almost' stories.

Other details they are relentless with are having needle sharp hooks at all times. Meaning they check their hooks and retouch them with a file every time they make contact with a foreign object. They are quasi-MacGyvers, too. They have a fix for every solution. Extra parts, assorted tools, reels, line, and two of every bait they own, just in case one is lost. I've witnessed these pro's go as far as keep a spare locator and trolling motor in their truck. (Must be nice to have unlimited piles of cash in their piggy banks). Lastly, but more importantly, they take a spot and dissect it with surgical casts and convey speed changes, direction changes, and force action into every cast, imparting their bait a different look than all the others. I could go on and on about what the pro's do and most don't do. When it comes down to the root causes of our failures, most of us are just plain lazy when it comes to many of the fundamentals. By adopting a few of the pro's bag of tricks, any of us could put another musky or two into a net each year. That alone is worth the extra effort.

Speaking of extra effort, it seemed that technology had finally made its way to Canada on this trip, in the form of the World Wide Web. The first few years, the WI-FI in the cabin was horrible. It would literally take twenty minutes just to pull up weather info. With everybody having smartphones now, you can check the weather throughout the day without needing to run back to the lodge to pull it up. If you spend a summer week on L.O.T.W., you'll be nailed with at least one good gully washer. Make sure you have a good app on your phone to know when to head for safety and seek cover. There were many times where we pulled into someone's open ended boathouse to get out of the rain. Unfortunately, I still rely on Mother Nature's flashes of lighting to motivate me to safety. My old fashioned flip-phone is only good for conversation. (Imagine that?!?!)

"Allen, what's the forecast today?" I asked, as my phone presented nonstop thinking circles. "Looks like clear skies and ninety degrees. No wind," declared Allen. "So what you're telling me is that we're about to be roasted like a chicken." It may sound like I was amused. Trust me, I wasn't.

On our way over to the King Island area, I'm reminded of staying at White Birch Lodge and fishing our way toward King Island on a daily basis. This time around, we approached from the opposite direction with a good twenty minute boat ride with the throttle at three-quarters open to save on gas. When gas prices at the lodges in Canada are as crazy as possible, we always made sure to bring up our own five-gallon plastic tanks, lots of them. Some resort owners complained we weren't buying from them and others don't care. Using my high school degree for something, I worked the complicated math formula, and found it does pay to bring your own gas along. At the very least, you know it's clean and the correct octane.

Our first stop of the day on our way to King Island was Split Rock Narrows, an epic area a mile long that narrows up to a only a football field wide. It's anywhere from twenty-five feet to as much as forty-five feet deep. With an east or west wind, the area created a strong current and drew in crappies and walleyes, and Mr. Musky is never far behind lunch. It was a big fish spot, with many big pigs seen in this area before. The garages along the shore act as current breaches or food shelf's for muskies, as the basins drops straight off tight to shore.

BY **BRAD MATHEWSON**

We parked near a Volkswagen Bug-sized garage, with a five-foot deep shelf bordering thirty feet of deep blue. I casted a black Cowgirl with silver blades, and the first crank of the handle divulged a light tap. As I set the hook, believing I had landed a small northern, I was surprised to find that I had probably just won the 'tiny musky contest'. At the end of my line, a chubby twenty-seven and one half inch slob musky awaited my grasp. "Looks like I stole one right out of the crib!" I laughed. "After all these years of musky fishing, I'm still surprised at how a small musky will eat something so large," said Stew.

Only twenty minutes passed after I released my Canadian giant back to it's home, when lightning struck again. We were only a few hundred yards from the first landing location, fishing a very similar garage with no other garage for at least a couple hundred yards. Sometimes if you find something irregular in an otherwise featureless shoreline, you may have found a musky hot spot. Our favorite spots are isolated shelves next to deep water, it's a good current break situation and the muskies feel safe. Stew's fish hit on a rainbow trout-colored Cowgirl, with only a crank or two of the reel. We were discovering if you landed your bait on their heads, you'd get a reaction strike from fish that might normally be neutral. A quick scoop of the net and I had Stew's first fish of the trip: a thirty-eight inch-er. We needed it. "Today is the day, Stew! Two fish in twenty minutes. I just hope I have enough memory on my SD card for all the musky pics we're gonna snap!" "It feels like a weight has been lifted off my shoulders. Now I can stop pressing and just enjoy the week!" sighed Stew. It was a struggle this year to land a musky. Having finally done so, we both felt the pressure of failure subside. But relaxing was the last thing we could do now that we were finally on fish.

The next couple of hours were spent in 'The Narrows' angling more garages with only two lazy follows to show for it. "I think it's time to head over to King Island. More importantly, over to the Split Rock," I said with a smile. Split Rock is, by far, the location that makes me recharge my PMA with pure excitement. When I lay in my bed in Wisconsin I dream of fishing this location. It's what personifies Lake of the Woods for me, it's my happy place.

It had been an entire year since I'd visited my favorite spot in the lake. A car-sized boulder broke offshore and left a four-foot exposed crack with a nice shelf next to deep water. This is a scorching hot spot for muskies, especially when the quick current is present. Split Rock accounted for more fish in our group than any other spot in the whole lake combined. In the few years I had been there, over twenty fish were apprehended, and close to a hundred follows. If it were a matter of life or death, and I could only fish one spot in the entire lake, I would bet my life on this spot. That's saying a lot for a fish as frustrating to catch as a musky.

We passed quite a few nice spots on our way to my favorite. Probably not the smartest idea to pass good spots just to get to another, but I'm a musky hunter. Nobody said we were bright. As we ease up to our spot, I shut off the big engine and advised Stew to drop the trolling motor down, but to not use it. Instead, we drifted in for a sneak attack. The wind was beyond perfect. I'm like a kid on Christmas morning and everyone is still asleep, I can't take it any longer I need to open at-least one gift. I finally long bombed a cast. Stew gawked with disapproval, sensing I should have waited until we got a little closer. Lucky for me, my new 8' 6" St. Croix rod loaded up nicely for those required Hail Mary casts. My bait plunked exactly in the slot next to shore. As my Cowgirl drew up to the boat, I beheld a mid-forty inch tubby in hot pursuit. Four times around in a figure eight and he vanished as fast as the money in my wallet when the wife finds it. I'm about to make another cast when I spot my fish lying in the shadow of the boat. I grab my throw back rod and try a larger circle with a small Suzy Sucker and pow, she nails it boat side, seconds later a very green forty inch musky is in the net.

"I can't believe you pulled that off, maybe our luck is changing," said Stew.

A quick pic a release and it was now Stew's turn, I won't lie I did feel a little guilty about getting the jump on him. Now on Stew's first attempt, he cast to the exact same spot as mine, and his magic rainbow trout Cowgirl brought in a mid-forty inch musky to the boat, only this one lagged further and further behind. When it got closer to the boat, it disappeared. Stew frantically whipped a few figure eights to no avail. "I told you we'd see a couple of fish here," I boasted at Stew. He hadn't had as much luck with Split Rock as I had, so he wasn't nearly as excited to go there as I. My promise of visiting muskies here was met with a halfhearted, "We'll see."

After three spot-on pounding passes and one musky, we left the hot spot a bubbly froth and elected to head out to an area deemed 'Musky Alley.' Its location was such a secret, only our group fished it. We never saw another soul in that area. In fact, ten years earlier this had become a Mecca, of sorts, for big fish. The area was fed by a creek, and possibly underground springs, as the water is crystal clear and feeds a unique ecosystem. It's the only area in the lake we found wild rice, giant Lily pads, coontail and red cabbage growing together at the perfect fish-able depth. This area was a half acre long and oxygen rich, with an average depth of six to seven feet and secluded from most of the lake. At any time you could be gifted a showing of deer, muskrats, beavers, otters, bears, and at one time years ago, a moose.

A quick check of my cell phone read eleven o'clock. The sky consisted of a hazy blue, and you could almost masticate the humid air. It felt like musky fishing on a lake of molten lava. Sweat seeped from every orifice and dribbled into every crevice. It was a day where clothes melt right into your skin. "What the heck are we doing out here, anyway? It's gotta be near ninety already," moaned Stew. I had to admit, on days like this the old saying "When the going gets tough, the tough get going," was never a truer statement, PMA would help us through.

"It's time for the good old redneck air conditioner!" With that, I dunked my shirt into the lake and slapped it back on. I may have looked like an idiot, but it worked for a good two to three hours. Give it a try next time your balls drip salt water. You'll thank me.

BY **BRAD MATHEWSON**

As we methodically fished our way through the weedy bay and into the "Ally," I found rusty crayfish skeletons resting on the bottom, along with some very much alive crayfish munching local greenery. Many muskies we've caught through the years had beat up red mouths and a few bad mannered ones even pooped out rusty crayfish into our boats. Muskies are very opportunistic feeders, capitalizing on any critter they can get between their jaws. I had no idea a musky would bottom feed until I noticed one take a dead shad off the bottom in a Wisconsin lake.

As usually was the case when musky fishing, out of nowhere, only ten feet of line separated Stew from two excited muskies giving chase to his rainbow trout double 10. As luck would have it, the muskies must have seen each other spooked in opposite directions, leaving poor Stew with an untouched bait. I'll give him credit, my constant disappointment showed on my sleeve. Stew had a unique ability to brush it off without dwelling in the least.

"It almost looks like a wall green of angle haired pasta just ahead," said Stew, without batting an eye. The green noodles were a plant named wild celery. Stew mentioned he tried some himself once, and it tasted just like celery. (Disgusting) Frankly, there's nothing wrong with weeds when they provide cover for fish, big and small. However, when celery grows ridiculously thick, fish can't even use it and it's more of a detriment than a help.

"I saw an albino musky," said Stew, seemingly out of nowhere. Apparently years earlier, Stew and one of his brothers where casting spinner baits when a white musky trailed his bait to the boat. They claimed it was a low-fifty inch torpedo, and found it two years in a row in the same location. And Stew thought this was a very similar spot. Of course, with me along, no great white hope would be found that day.

That signified how the rest of our day went down the old crapper. We fished Musky Alley until almost four o'clock without a peep from another musky. We did manage to put a northern pike into the live well toward the evening, so all wasn't completely lost. A nice pike to our ever growing stash back at the cabin meant we were in for a massive fish fry, that night. Stew kept the day lighthearted by telling me old "You should've been fishing Musky Alley ten years ago!" tall tales. Isn't it funny how everything that ever existed was always better in the past? Somehow, time and memory tend to lead to delusions of grandeur. With fishing tales, well, those become tall tales seconds after it happens. Hell, I've had a guy tell me a line of shit when I was literally right there with him when it happened.

With it getting dark, we needed to get back a little earlier than normal to set up shop for the fish fry. Come to find out, we'd be a few guys short. Rod and Bucky snuck out with our host to another lake. They made plans to trailer our host's boat to a lake named Dawg Paw. Later that night, drunken Rod and Buck stumbled into the cabin just as some of us were heading to the fart sack. My eyes were sandbagged, but I had to find out what the hell those two were up to, considering they were strolling in near midnight.

BY **BRAD MATHEWSON**

"Did you guys eat any supper yet?" I asked to start my prying discussion. "Nope. Didn't eat much all day. Mostly a liquid diet!" slurred Rod. "I'll heat up the leftover fish and fries while you tell me all about Dawg Paw Lake." "Well, there's only one boat landing on the entire lake, and the damn thing is privately owned by an old Native American woman. Our host had to go up to her house and pay fifteen bucks to access the boat landing, but apparently our host butters her up by always palming her twenty-five bucks cash. In return, she grants you permission to use the landing. She also hands you a small amount to tobacco to place on the lake surface as a gift to the Gods, who will then bless you with a good day of fishing," explained Rodney.

"This smells like a line of bullshit," barked Stew, as he meandered from the shitter. "That's how things work around here, I guess. The Native Americans have access to the lake through their land, so they charge you what they want." "Fine and dandy. Now, how many muskies did you guys catch?" I blurted out. I didn't give two shits about all the other garbage. I needed to know everything about this fresh new musky water world. Rod adjusted his junk while plopping down on the couch. "None. But we did raise ten fish, and every damn one was around the fifty-inch mark." "Seems like a giant waste of time, to me. You idiots traveled all the way up to the greatest musky factory in the continent, and lose a day sampling an unproven new lake," Stew blurted out. Rod puffed with lack of amusement. "The problem was, the water was so clear, you could see down fifteen feet." I scrambled over hauling the two lugs their grub. "My question is, why are you both three sheets to the wind. Your eyes seem glassy. Were you guys smoking wacky tobacky?" Most of the cabin exploded into laughter. "We're not gonna sit here and be grilled like a couple of kids," said Buck. "Bullshit if you ain't. Fess up, potheads if you want to get your grub on with this fried fish and fries, you'll tell me every damn thing.

"Here's the deal. We drank two bottles of booze and a case of beer for lunch. Before that, we almost got killed in a boating accident. Our host drove the boat, spinning stories while racing forty mph down the lake. Suddenly, he released the steering wheel and whipped around to mix up three more drinks. I glanced up just in time to see us speeding towards a huge iceberg of a bolder only ten feet from the boat. I shouted and cranked the wheel to the right as hard as I could. Somehow, we just missed the rock and screamed by. Man, I thought we were dead, for sure. Even braced myself against the boat thinking my quick wheel jerk was too late. Only thing died was my underwear." The room grew eerily quiet. None of us could tell if this was just another fishing story, or true life. Both guys, though bombed off their asses, never wavered from their adventure story.

I flopped down on the couch next to Rod. In the dead silence, I leaned over to Rod and sniffed. He peered over at me like I'd lost my damned mind. "Yes, Brad. We were offered pot, but only Buck and the guide smoked a few joints." "Bullshit! You are just as messed up as Buck That 'I didn't inhale' crap only works when you're running for president!" "Quiet idiots! Here comes our host!" The guide plowed through the door, totally blitzed. He weaved some hefty bullshit about how many fish they had seen that day. And how disappointed he was he couldn't get Rod or Buck hooked up with a couple of them. Bullshit or not, he meant well. Whether the boys got a pic with a whopper was irrelevant. They had their 'fish tale' for the trip.

CHAPTER XXXIII

OLD FARTS AND GREENS

Two guys with forty-seven inch muskies leading the 'Largest Fish' contest made me wake up at the ass crack of dawn with a new sense of urgency. I had delusions of grandeur, because my goal for this trip was to not only catch the largest musky, but also break the magical fifty-inch mark these ass-hats had rarely accomplished.

As I gathered up my equipment for the morning fish, Stew spouted a few obscenities in the background. "Cheech and Chong ate all our leftover fish and French fries!" I meandered into the kitchen, thinking bullshit the whole way. "No way. There was almost two full gallon bags of fish and probably two pounds of fries." I dug through the garbage, and sure enough, two empty bags lay waste. "Damn, that pisses me off! I was hoping for a nice fish sandwich or two. Dammit. Now I'm stuck with turkey sandwiches." Stew rummaged through more of the drawers in the refrigerator. The more doors he opened, the harder he slammed them shut. "WHERE DID ALL THE LUNCH MEAT GO!!!!!" Stew slammed the refrigerator door shut and stomped off. "It looks like we have a deli thief on our hands, this sounds like a case the Royal Mounted Police could handle," I said.

I slid over and checked it out myself. Sure enough, all of the Oscar Meyer family sub packs of meat were gone, except for a couple slices of bologna the scavengers must have missed in their munchies bonanza. We had all pitched in for groceries and James bought them. Two sub packs were allotted for each day. After a little investigative work, we managed to crack the case. Here, one of the 'large' gentleman from our group liked to make super meat lover sandwiches, two inches thick, along with inhaling multiple slabs of meat for breakfast, leaving the rest of us to be on a 'like-it-or-not' diet.

As Stew shuffled back into the kitchen, he shoved his wallet into his back pocket. "Let's run to town and get more lunch meat. We don't have much gasoline left for the boat, any ways." As a guy who's gone to Canada and always brought his own gasoline, here's a little piece of advice: I know it's nice to help out the local economy, and us fisherman do make an impact, but buying liters of dinosaur squeezens in Canada ain't cheap. I did the gallon/liter conversion, and they jack you for nearly six bucks per gallon. That's crazy expensive, and I was only running around in sixteen and one-half foot Aluma-Craft, with a 90 H.P. Evinrude. I can't image what guys zipping around in the 620 Rangers would spend. I'd have to take out a second mortgage just to cruise water in one of them. People who utilize high-end, overpriced luxuries make, what I like to call, 'F-You' money. The problem for me is, I made 'F-Me' money. I'm just lucky I wasn't using a dinghy with a make-shift paddle consisting of tree bark and duct tape.

By the time we ran to the grocery store for lunch meat, bread and some of the Queen's gasoline, it was almost ten in the morning. Stew tossed out the idea to check out the second long-fingered bay a little northwest of us. We hadn't seen a soul travel up that way all week, and we prayed it held a few hungry muskies longing for our tasty baits.

A small cold front had moved in overnight leaving the daytime high to be only seventy degrees, with winds out of the north at a shy twenty miles per hour. We were fishing near some boathouses when some wrinkly old fart waved us over to chat. Me not being one to turn down a chance at some information, or just shoot the bull, motored on over. "You gentlemen having any luck with the muskies?" the old-timer asked. "We try hard. Does that count for anything?" I blurt out. The old man snickered as he nodded his head. "This has been one of the worst damn years of musky fishing for me. I wasted my whole damn summer musky fishing every damn day. Nothing but the pits. I've seen about half as many muskies as I have in the past, and the ones I did see were little short nippers and won't hit a damn figure eight. I hit a way point on my locator and come back to fish them when there's a condition change, but they're nowhere to be found. Damn muskies been on the move all season. Don't even have a damn core home range like most years, damn slippery bastards," he said. Stew rubbed his forehead. "Well, damn. We've definitely experienced fish not wanting to follow a figure eight. If they do, their interest is lost quickly." The old fart nodded with complete understanding. "Well, at least I'm not the only sucker soul fishing this damn lake. Good luck going forward." With that, the old timer ventured off, having left us with an even worse outlook on the week.

By early afternoon, our little science experiment was over. It was time to hit our local community honey holes and find out what was going on. We slogged around Wolf Island. Stew hooked and lost two nice low forty inch fish on tube baits, indicating that oil slick seemed to be the hot color. But it wasn't until three o'clock when things really turned around for Stew. We were back in the Split Rock Narrows casting to isolated garages. I had a couple follows on my new black spinner bait with featured black chrome blades. I even managed to catch a thirty-five inch northern pike. Suddenly, out of nowhere, Stew roared that he had one on the line. I quickly shook off my snake and manned the net. "She's barely hooked, so be careful!" Stew worked the rod like a pro, weaving back and forth. Knowing he had it on a tube bait made us both nervous. I eased the net into the capture position. Netting was the one thing I had become a pro at on these trips. I wouldn't let Stew down. "Nab her as she makes the pass," Stew ordered. "If she's too green, I won't even try," I nudged at Stew. "Screw you! She's too green. You net that pig!" woofed Stew. As Stew managed her next to the boat, she journeyed toward the stern and right into my waiting net. Ka-ching.

To give some subtext to me blasting Stew about a fish being 'too green', a few years back, a couple of Steve's buddies came up to Canada and one of them hooked a very large fifty-plus inch musky. When it got near the boat, his net man apparently got worried about a very angry green musky going crazy once it was in the net. As the fish came to the boat, it went straight toward the waiting net. At the last moment, the guy whisked the net away just as the musky was about to swim in. He whirled around, only to declare the fish was "TOO GREEN". With the surface commotion, the brute went on a deep sea run, straight under the boat, where the line became frayed. As it sawed on the keel and promptly snapped the line, never to be seen again. That net man was all too lucky he wasn't never seen again. What should have been a great day with a fish of a lifetime, converted shattered dreams into homicidal nightmares. I, personally, don't believe in the notion of a fish being 'too green' to net. I own a Big Kahuna net. There isn't a musky that suspends in a deep Cisco-filled lake I couldn't net. Even from a conservation stand point, the quicker you can get that fish in the net and released back to the abyss, the less stress is endured and less lactic acid is built up. A brief handshake and quick picture is the name of the game anyway, right?

"How big is she, Stew?" Stew slapped his bubba on the measuring board and yelped out that it was a solid forty-five inches. After several high-fives and a slimy-paw handshake, it was back to fishing. I don't know about you, but I get just as jacked up about my partner catching a musky as I would my own. I love the renewed vigor you get after a successful CPR (catch, picture, release). It's like golfing. You hit terrible shots over and over again, but it only takes that one perfectly straight drive down the middle of the fairway that you remember, and it keeps you coming back for more punishment.

Six hours later, and none the wiser, another small cold front shut things down for good that day. We were fortunate to catch that one fish. We attempted to slow things down by me working a lime colored Reef Hawg and Stew hurling his slick oil Tiger Tube, but we saw no other fish. By day's end, we both were mentally drained and physically exhausted. Fishing for nearly thirteen hours straight is damn hard work. But I wouldn't trade that workload for anyone's on the planet, except maybe the baby oil guy on the Sports Illustrated Swim Suit shoots. That's a gig I'd like to wrap my hands around. (Pun intended).

CHAPTER XXXIV

DEER IN OUR HEADLIGHTS

It was here. The day most guys in Musky Camp look forward to the most. Steak Night! Twenty-four ounce slabs of pure porterhouse heart-attacks awaited our return from another long day on the water. As much as we drooled our way through this scheduled bliss, it was also a depressing day, as this always signified the last full day of fishing. The next day would be cut short by two hours to set up the fish fry and party at our host's lodge.

The daily forecast by the weather-goon called for eighty degrees, light winds out of the south at five to ten, and bluebird skies. Stew yanked up the waistband on his shorts and pursed his lips. "I'm confident that with today's conditions changing for the better, we're gonna have a great day." Usually it was I who would offer a vote of confidence for the day to come. I was more than stoked that it was Stew that was boasting of grandeur. I must have been rubbing off on him.

Eight long hours later, we had fished isolated garages, shallow reefs, rocky spines, saddles, and protected sandy coves. All that hard work offered us zero fish raised. It bore the resemblance of a local chamber fish going on strike without a head's up about the work stoppage. It was one of those days were you wanted to throw in the towel and say screw it. It's in these moments were the pros will push on and the amateurs will give up. I am not a pro, nor do I think I'm even close, but I model my 'on the water' work ethic after them, and occasionally it does pay off.

"That's it. Get the map out. We gotta regroup and brainstorm," I said. Stew nodded in agreement and yanked the map out. We perused the schematics of the area in an attempt to find something, anything, that would stick out as a potential hot spot. Next to the Split Rock Narrows read an area named 'Deer Bay' that ensnared my peepers. "Steve was telling me about Deer Bay last night. He said it had some nice looking coontail and lily pads, but they hadn't seen any fish," Stew pointed out. "We got nothing to lose at this point. Let's head there and check things out for ourselves," I utter in frustration.

As we entered the bay, I spotted an isolated patch of lily pads near shore, resting in five feet of water. Stew casted his Rainbow Trout Cowgirl and I my white bucktail spinner bait. On my very first cast in, I managed a thirty-inch musky to swipe at it, but failed to hook up. Not five minutes later, Stew made a cast to the inside corner of the weed bed. Out from under the heavy pads marched a fifty-inch fish nipping at his Magnum Flashabou all the way back to the boat. Stew vexed into a figure eight, but it was too difficult being clutched in coontail. He ended up with a rod tip covered in weeds and stirred up cloudy water. Without using our heads to think things through, our lack of a game plan led us to bash that weed bed over and over until it looked like it had been put through a food processor. The better plan of attack would have been to leave her alone and venture back at last light or a condition change. We worked the next two lily pad beds with no luck, when Stew made a long bomb cast toward the deeper water off the left side of the boat. With that cast, he managed to sucker another musky, this one in the upper-forties, damn near pushing fifty-inch class, follow up to the boat and sink away.

"I believe we're on to something, Brad," said a jovial Stew. I made a cast to a weed point when I finally hooked into something. It felt like a fighter, and my heart skipped a beat. After a few moments of wrestling, we discovered the boxer on the end of my line wasn't a musky, but a beautifully marked, rather plump, thirty-five inch Northern pike. We spent a total of four hours in Deer Bay casting all the potential hot spots. A few times we went back to where I had Way Pointed those two big muskies, just seeking to make something happen, but to no avail. I truly wanted to stay until nightfall in hopes of having another shot at a big fish, but it was time to start fishing our way back to camp. I had to have supper ready for ten famished carnivores.

By **BRAD MATHEWSON**

On the drive back to camp, we made plans for the next morning to head straight back to Deer Bay, bypassing all our routine stops along the way. It was time to swing for the fences. If we wanted to win the largest musky contest, it was gonna happen in Deer Bay.

CHAPTER XXXV

DELUSIONS OF GRANDEUR

Seven in the morning is not exactly 'early bird catches the worm,' but when we are home, we're all very early risers. On average, every guy at Musky Camp drags their ass out of bed before five. At Musky Camp, its encouraged to sleep until at least seven. Just make sure it isn't later than half past seven, or your fishing partner will botch the next net job to teach you a lesson. I remember my first morning at musky camp. I had my alarm set for five that morning, and when it went off, I sprung from my bunk to have a quick breakfast, packed my lunch, loaded my gear in the boat and applied the much needed sun screen to my pale body. I had all this completed by five-thirty.

I meandered back into the cabin after loading the gear in the boat and there was nobody even up in the cabin yet. So I sat on the couch for the next two hours until our crew stirred from their slumber. Only at that moment was I told by Steve, if I ever woke up that early again making so much damn noise, I'd be sleeping in the truck!

Down at the docks, I loaded our gear into the boat for the last day on the water. We took out all gear from the boat every night and stored in the main lodge's basement. This stems from the fear of our stuff being stolen because we were next to the public boat landing. Some thief had taken the lodge owner's tackle box earlier in the year, so we weren't making the same mistake. Luckily, I had just enough gas for the last day as I topped off the fuel tank with ten gallons of Canadian gold. Unfortunately, I'm not talking about maple syrup on my pancakes filling my gut. An actual fuel tank, and the gold being gasoline.

Stew and I decided the night before to make the twenty minute run straight to Deer Bay where we had our eyes on some very nice muskies. Whether we happened to completely forget about telling our group about a potential hot honey hole was a moot point. Part of going with our group is we make fishing fun and include everyone in on what the hot bait or technique that's working, or where Joe Blow had raised a large fish. We kept no secrets. But we're men. We don't share our feelings, so why should we give away ALL the best spots. Rule of note: Always have a card or four up your sleeve, just in case. I assumed every putz in camp kept something for themselves.

The chilly morning air sliced through my tee and had me shivering to the point I almost dug out my buried rain jacket in a feeble attempt to warm up, but who know's how long that search party would take in my now disaster of a boat. Old Stew was just as bright, sporting a tank top and shorts. Not the wisest decision one could make on a fifty degree morning, but we were the only morons on the water, and when we left our little protected bay, we found the rest of the lake still as a winter's night. I'd never seen L.O.T.W. so peaceful. It was like driving by a scenic billboard painted by Terry Redlin. As the morning sun scorched the clouds from existence, cold pockets of air that had slapped us mere minutes earlier, had gave way to warm puffs. Mother Nature opened her oven door and the aroma of her creation drifted out. It was quite tranquil. As we entered the bay, I noticed right away our musky-filled weed bed was washed in the sun's love. The musky gods were literally shining down on us. If that wasn't a sign that there is a God, then I don't know what is.

"Can you believe how perfect this morning is? One of those days where something special's gonna happen," I preach to Stew. "Ya, I can feel it, too. It's almost an eerie calm," Stew replied. "We're gonna catch a fifty inch fish in here today." I proclaimed. Sure, maybe I predicted that every single time we went out on L.O.T.W., but I'm an optimist. Don't get me wrong, there's more to musky fishing than just catching a fifty inch brute. But it was not only my lifelong dream to accomplish, every man in that group was gunning for that caliber trophy. Hell, reality was, most days I would shit my pants at

BY **BRAD MATHEWSON**

any musky, much less a fifty plus inch cow. But we all have our dreams, and every cast gave me a shot at mine.

Our first casts of the morning were to the right side of the bay, which held nice coontail and large lily pads. They covered an area of five acres, with a depth averaging six feet. We had seen four quality fish there the day prior, so maybe we could convert a follower into an eater. The game plan this day was to make precession casts to all openings within the lily pad field, and methodically pick the weed bed apart section by section. If you see four fish in one spot, there's probably twice as many lurking around in the weedy depths with them. I worked with a black chrome spinner bait which had a large number ten blade that you could feel thumping through the rod on every turn of the handle. Thirty minutes into working the first acre, I felt a strong tap. Quickly, I drive the hooks home and one second of excitement turned into that of disappointment. I had captured a twenty-six inch northern. Whining aside, we needed meat for our fish fry, so he was a tasty start and I shouldn't complain. Many musky guys get irritated by catching northern pike. I even hear about a few bad apples that kill every northern they catch because young northern fry will feed on musky fry because northern pike spawn first. Whether that is true or not I don't know, but I find the Northern Pike a worthy adversary and I am proud of everyone I catch. Besides, there's some true trophy pike in the forty to forty-five inch class swimming around LO.T.W and a few pushing that 50 mark. From my point of view, it's better to fight a pike than waste your day fending off shear boredom. Fighting any good fish will keep you sharp and on your toes and give you plenty of practice in hook removal. Fish twenty-six inches and under are mighty fine table fair if you master the removal of the Y – Bone. That isn't hard if you have an experienced fish cleaner show you a few times. Hell, even I can do it, so I know anyone that can hold a knife can handle it.

We hadn't moved far when I had another hit. This time, I reeled back empty handed. A quick check of my hooks told the tail. I had forgot to sharpen my hooks after my last fish, a mistake that has cost many musky fishermen countless fish each and every year. It's why I've mentioned it numerous times in this documentary. To me, it's a golden rule, and I somehow had broken it. When that crap happens, you spend the rest of the day assuming the one that got away was that fifty-inch hog and kick yourself for ignoring the fundamentals.

Towards the end of the massive weed bed, the lily pads spread apart by twenty feet or so. We took the same approach as we drifted through them. Stew would fish everything on the left side of the boat, and I would fish everything on the right side of the boat. I noticed a huge lily pad and decided to heave the long bomb cast. With one crank of the reel as the blades on the spinner bait start spinning, something just crushes it. When I set the hook , I knew it was a great fish, as a significant head popped out of the water. It was a new personal best at the end of my line. "Stew, get the net! Get the net! I got a big one!" I screamed like a little girl. "Calm down! Carefully play the fish to the boat," Stew instructed. I fight it out with that powerful fish. The damn thing kept burying itself deeper into the weed bed. So I'm not just fighting the weight of the fish, I'm also pulling on twenty pounds of weeds with it. And not the good kind of weed, that's a joke meant for potheads, for which I'm not. Finally, I extract her from the jungle and give a little prayer in my head for everything to go right. Up until now, it had been "Shit-luck City" for Stew and I. Even my extraordinary high level of PMA was not so great earlier that morning. I tried to convince myself that if I ain't dead, I ain't quitting. For a brief moment, my persistence felt like it was gonna pay off. My eighty lb Cortland Master braid held strong. I powered that fat heifer with a acre of weeds from the back of the boat toward the front, into Stew's waiting net. It was a textbook net job, once Stew untangled the net in the front cleat. This was another golden rule in my boat. You don't want your hard-earned fish to swim off, or worse, get tangled in your net and perish. When I looked into the net, all I saw was a salad bowl full of weeds and my line in the very center. "WHERE IS SHE!?" I screamed. I quickly rip the weeds out of the net like a crazed madman thinking old Stew had botched the net job and when the garden was weeded, there lie a massive beast for which I will ever be grateful. A warming of my soul not much different than when one meets his newborn child for the first time. It's a special feeling that only a fellow musky nut can appreciate.

"Remember what I said on the way up to Canada?" I quizzed Stew. "Hell, Brad. You say a lot of useless stuff I don't listen to. How am I supposed to pick out one of the many bullshit things you spout out?" I was in such a good mood at that very moment, I let him slide on it. "My one goal was to break my personal best. I held a forty-three and a half inch fish with Steve once before. Today, I have surpassed it!" Stew dug out the camera, glove, and release tools and laid them on the deck and walked over to the net. "Let's just get her unhooked and on the bump board and find out," blurted Stew. He was trying to speed me up as I was soaking in the moment over this absolute lake hog, but he, too, was anxious to find out what we had. "She's double hooked right in the old snot box." As I tried to withdrew the hooks from her I noticed the second trailer hook was crossed over the front and under and through both jams. Meaning they were pinned shut and she couldn't breath. "I yelled to stew grab my Knipex wire cutters quick." With a couple fast snipes the hooks were served and I removed the pieces and laid her back down in the bottom of the water bag. Almost immediately her gills started to flair slowly and she began to breath once more. I sat there with emotions running wild, here in the net was the biggest musky I had ever caught and in my own selfishness I had failed to noticed that this musky couldn't breath, my heart began to break and the air from my once puffed up chest disappeared. Stew and I sat there on the gunwale of my boat in complete silence as if we were in a loved ones hospital room praying for our beloved one on life support, to make it through.

"How could I be so blind to the situation," I said. "Don't beat yourself up too much, it happens to all of us," said Stew. But Stew's attempt at making me feel better was to no avail and the lump in my throat returned. Now all we could do was sit and wait.

BY **BRAD MATHEWSON**

Twenty minutes went by and the haze in her eyes disappeared and she began to spark back to life, soon she was ramming the side of the bag to get free. When she sprayed water onto the boat with a flick of her tail I knew she had been brought back from the verge of a almost certain death. If we had immediately done a Catch, Picture, Release, (CPR) and returned her to the lake the lactic acid that was built up in her system would have surely killed her. "Glad to see the purple and green disappear from your flush face and the burnt lobster one side, pasty white on the other, of your skin has returned as well," said Stew.

"It's time, I said to Stew." As if he had read my mind Stew wet the bump board. Yet another tip that helps to keep the fish's protective slime mucous intact to help prevent infection. Learn it, live it, love it. I gently cradled the brute onto the board and stretched it out. "Looks like she's forty eight inches. Nice fish, Brad."

There it was. My personal best Canadian Shield musky. It took much longer than I'd have liked, but when you accomplish a goal, a dream, some would say a miracle, you must soak in that moment to ensure you never forget it. After some very quick pictures to help me remember that moment forever, and to prove to the other snobs at camp this wasn't no fish story. I whisked her back up off the board and placed her back in the water. After about thirty seconds of revival, she swam away strong and hopefully breaking many a fisherman's personal best as she matured. I gave Stew the traditional slimy hand shake and even slipped in an unwanted hug accompanied with a few musky hunter war cries. That adrenaline high was incredible. I had netted my personal best and had taken over 1st place in our Biggest Musky Contest. I needed to sit down for a minute and reflect upon what had transpired. I'm man enough to admit it; a single tear dripped from my face. In looking back at it, though, I believed it was probably just irritated from the pesky gnats. We'll go with that.

By eleven o'clock, Stew was in desperate need of an Island bathroom break, so I took him to shore. He scurried up a rock wall with his toilet paper in hand. He looked like a damn mountain goat climbing up that wall. Back in the boat, Stew and I hatched a new plan for the afternoon. We had worked over the bay thoroughly that morning, and we had a 'hot tip' from Stew's brother, James, and his son Danny. They had apparently missed two very large muskies while bulldogging the shear walls in the Split Rock Narrows. When they said something about their encounters to Tim, our host, he informed them that the crappies would stack up along the ledges of steep drop-offs.

The Narrows had a max depth of forty-four feet. There was some nice current flowing through because it was a neck down area, and Tim had seen some very large fish using the ledges as an all-you-can-eat buffet. If you've ever been to an all-you-can-eat buffet, you know that the clienteles' average weight per person is well over three bills. And that's the average. So you can imagine how excited we were to perhaps find a musky food trough. Wouldn't have been shocked to find a sixty inch, seventy five pound record-breaker.

BY **BRAD MATHEWSON**

The plan was to throw crappie colored double 10s and let them sink for a five second count, and then slowly crank them back with our low geared Revo Toro Winches 4.6:1 until we could see them. Once we got eyeballs on them, burn them the rest of the way, mimicking fleeing crappies. It was different to fish casting up against a shear wall and letting your bucktail free fall in hopes it wouldn't get wedged in a crack. On my second cast right, when I turned on the afterburners, I noticed what appeared to be a dead musky floating belly up. Only it wasn't floating. It was screaming fifty mph on its back after my Cowgirl! I was in complete shock. This insane fish went into a figure eight, mouth wide open, nipping at my bait like a thirsty bar hag. I watched that unhinged musky whirl around at least ten times, never once chomping on my bait. "I can't say I've ever seen that before! That fish must have been lying under a ledge, and when your bait went by, he swam vertical up the wall until your bait moved out away. Then the crazy thing inverted itself because he had nowhere else to go!" said Stew. "Thanks for the play by play, Stew. Dammit. I really thought that was a dead musky floating by. Got lucky with muscle memory that I went in to a figure eight without realizing it. Too many times a guy gets into a LOTW trance of cast retrieve cast, but one must be on the ready and always do your figure eights. Guess that's why we fish muskies, cause you can never predict what the hell they'll do next," I announced, as I tossed out another cast to try again. "She looked to be a good forty-four inches or so. Very wide across the back," Stew declared, as he wound in his own line.

As always, Mother Nature seemed to have it in for us that afternoon. Temperatures soared in to the low nineties, with virtually no wind, bluebird skies and high, wispy clouds. Our energy boost from earlier in the morning was all but sucked out of us, along with our ability to stay hydrated. The high pressure system was winning this fight. A check of my phone revealed it was almost six o'clock in the early evening, and there ain't no snooze button to hit to extend our musky dream. We had exactly one hour was left to make something happen. It had been six long hours sense our last follow, and Stew's magical rainbow Cowgirl had raised three times as many muskies as I had. But even his Houdini like voodoo seemed to lose its musky drawing power, and I had tried everything in my box with the same empty handed results.

That hour slipped by quickly, as all hours fishing in Canada tend to go. On our way back toward camp, we stopped at a small island at the entrance to Big Camp Bay. The island was maybe thirty feet across both ways, but had some grass and one lone white pine growing on it and some small wooden sign that at some time in history had said something, but weather had beaten it unreadable. We both joked that whoever clutched a fish here would have the island named after them. Earlier in the week, we had both raised a couple nice mid-forty inch fish here. Now was the time to cash in on those encounters. A few casts to the wind-blown garage was all it took for Stew's magic to reappear. A nice low forty-inch fish emerged, did the standard figure eight dance, and promptly swam back home. "For whatever reason, the fish haven't really responded to the figure eight like they normally do," Stew complained. "Yeah. I've tried different styles of the figure eights, and nothing seems to help this week," I confirmed for him.

Around to the back side we go to get the hell out of the wind. We find another garage and Stew's rainbow warrior lands perfectly. This time, a mid-forty inch fish peeks out and presents a little square dance with Stew, and was suddenly called home. I react by grabbing my throw back rod equipped with my favorite baby loon Top Raider and firing a Bucher missile into her lair. With the full power of the Canadian Shield, she exploded from the water in a fit of rage. I slammed the hooks to her and felt a tug, but the next thing I know, she was gone. She was either not hooked very well or she was just mouthing the bait and decided to let go and break my heart. Muskies can be real teases at times. Stew's next cast is only fifteen feet down the shore from the garage. Guess who followed back to the boat for a look see...the same infatuated mid-forty inch looky loo. After a once around in the figure eight, she goes back again. You had to be there to believe what I'm going to say next. That same musky played bucktail fetch SIX times and never once bit his bait. On the last trip back to the boat, I told him to dead stick his bait right next to the boat and see if we could get a reaction strike. So Stew stopped his Cowgirl next to the boat and the musky just froze inches from his Magnum Flashabou, which fluttered in the light current. The inquisitive musky just stared intently at the taunting, tempting meal while I did my best impression of Mel Gibson in the movie Braveheart. "Hold, hold, hold, hold, hold, NOW!!!" Stew held close

to five minutes and I could tell he didn't like my Mel Gibson impersonation. With her nose on the bait and her nipping at the Flashbou, Stew finally ripped the bait away. I thought for sure she would blast his bucktail, but instead she swam off toward deeper water without a care in the world. She apparently had grown tired of the games and wanted a real meal. Stew simply turned to me, shrugged his shoulders, and grabbed a can of soda. Wasn't much else a guy could do.

"Well Stew, my phone says its quarter to seven, and we have to be back in fifteen minutes to prepare the last fish fry and pound down the remaining Whiskey," I lament. On the boat ride back to the lodge, I thanked the musky gods for the week of fishing. As tough of a week as it was, we managed to raise many mid to upper forty inch fish, and even spotted a few fifty-inchers. The prior year, the same group of ten schmucks grasped sixty-nine muskies. This year, the total was down to thirty-seven. Most of that was due to being on new water and learning its secrets instead of being on well-scouted blue and attacking the hot spots on a daily basis. Both tactics have their benefits, as it's pretty damn exciting to find a brand new honey hole and nabbing a giant

When we got back to the dock, Brian and Jerry were waiting with shit-eating grins on their faces. "Alright. What's with the stupid faces? What did you catch?" I quizzed. "A couple nice fish. The last one was just ten minutes ago. On a whim, I stopped on a fishy looking spot as we made our way back to the lodge, and Brian struck a forty-eight and a half incher!" Jerry bellowed. My heart sank into my gut. I had spent the day knowing I was about to put the big fish contest cash in my wallet, and just like that, it was ripped from my fist. "Let's see the pictures," demanded Stew. We glanced over the pictures of Brian's fish, and instead of seeing a fish, we were smelling a rat. "That's the smallest forty-eight and half incher I have ever seen Brian. Strange how the picture of my forty eight inch beast looks so much bigger," I jabbed at the two idiots. "I think you two are full of crap! That musky is probably only forty-two inches." Jerry started chuckling in his stupid way. "Alright, you got us. Its only forty-four inches. But there is a cool story behind it," Brian admitted. "I made a cast to some reeds in a sandy cove, and worked my Manta when a nice musky appeared as it was nearing the boat. If you ever tried to figure eight a glide bait, you know it ain't gonna happen. I figured I had no hope of catching this fish." Jerry, never one to let a good story go without his two cents, chimed in. "I saw Brian struggling, so I grabbed another rod that had a Double Cowgirl bucktail on, and we did the old bait and switch on her," said Jerry. Taking his story back, Brian spoke up over Jerry. "I started into a new figure eight the second the Cowgirl entered the water, and the musky seemed to get more aggressive instantly. She crushed it on the second turn. I'll admit, without Jerry's help, I would have never held that fish. Hell, I should have never even thought about trying such a bone-headed idea, but it worked," giggled Brian. It was a great story that they spun, not so much for its content, but the adrenaline each man still had from the hunt. But to me, the most important part was that it was only a forty-four inch minnow. Meaning, I was about to be crowned

BY **BRAD MATHEWSON**

big fish on campus champ! And frankly, it was all I cared about.

Back at the cabin, word of my fish had gotten out. I must have retold that story a half dozen times. It was a nice feeling to have some bragging rights over such an experienced group of musky hunters. The handshakes and slaps on the back were nice, but the two hundred dollars pot for largest fish that was presented to me by Rodney was the best catch of the week. It paid for the gas in my boat that was burned by a week's worth of Canadian Musky fishing.

Tim, our host and lodge owner, came over during spirits and fish, and listened to our annual end of the week bullshit sessions. He perused the pictures and seemed genuinely interested in everyone's stories. Whether he genuinely was interested or not was a moot point. Either way, this was a huge upgrade from the place we used to stay at, where we got more of a boot out the door than a pat on the back. Tim even invited us all down to the main lodge for some Polish beer and a little surprise. Once the crew arrived at the main lodge, I was awarded the trophy for largest musky. Something that I had been pursuing for years. But it wasn't the only item on the agenda for handing out. Steve was awarded a nice Melines fishing vest for "Most Muskies Caught" at six, and Brian was awarded a trophy for "Best Musky Tale". To have our annual team pictures taken, we all lined up as best as half-drunk fishermen can do, and Tim snapped the photos. Somehow, apparently, the flash must have temporarily blinded poor old Brian. He flopped clumsily around with his trophy and lobbed it through the air to the cold, hard lodge floor. The trophy, with the nice gold musky, snapped into pieces and skid across the floor. Brian managed to enjoy his best catch for all of ten seconds. Typical.

By midnight, I had had enough of the Polish beer and whiskey, and decided to jaunt back up the steep hill towards our cabin. As I neared, I noticed Buck was holding the staggering drunken Steven up from falling on his face. Buck whipped the door open and released Steve, whom immediately collapsed to the floor like he himself was a flopping fish. Pure poetry.

"Hey Brad, could you give me a hand?" giggled a slightly inebriated Buck. As we lifted the slobbering drunk to his feet, Steve slurred out the normal drunken rhetoric of loving us and being glad we were there to share the experience together. Laughing myself, I kicked him in the ass to his bed and ordered him to sleep it off. When guys get drunk, there are three different ways they'll act. The old "strongest man in the room" routine, which generally leads to wanting to fight everyone. Secondly, they think they're Jeff Foxworthy; the funniest guy in history and the life of the party. Thirdly, they cry and tell you how much they love you, and that you're the best person in the world. The first two are acceptable and quite common musky-bum behavior. The third should be reserved, and only used on your wife when she says you should probably miss one year of your annual musky trip to go on a family vacation. When that 'request' is stowed upon you, you'll need to pound down a few choice beverages to ease the pain.

Saturday morning I awoke and looked at the alarm clock it read 5:39 am and I realized we had overslept our pre-agreed wake-up time of 5 am. I could hear the boys sawing logs, sleeping off there drunken binge. "Stew are you awake, I asked?" "Yeah, I think I'm in a bad dream and we overslept," said Stew. "We did."

We quickly get dressed and started packing, Stew went in Steve and Allen's room and shook there butts out of bed. Somehow we had the cabin cleaned out and trucks loaded in 20 minutes, there wasn't even a soul stirring in the other cabins. We drove down off of Mount St. Helens and down to the boat landing and loaded up both boats. Just under 40 minutes not too bad for four guys who stayed out till 12 or 1 and one guy still legally drunk.

MUSKY TALE OF THE TAPE - AUGUST 2012

BRAD - 48" 41" 40" 30" 27 ½"
STEW - 45" 38"
JERRY - 42" 42 ½" 41" 40"
BRIAN - 46" 40" 38" 23"
BUCKY - 47"
JAMES - 43" 38" 33" 28" 22"
DANNY - 39" 42" 24"
STEVE - 47" 37" 30" 39" 42" 44 ½"
ALLEN - 44 ½" 39" 43"
RODNEY - 34" 39" 39" 34"

MUSKY HUNT – AUGUST 2013

August 2013 had me spending every waking minute of free time pounding the local waters for my favorite toothy predator. As fun as that sounds, something was missing. After self-reflecting while kickin' it on my boat one morning, it kind of hit me. Once you've been spoiled by the greatest musky fishery, nothing else compares. The beauty and opportunity that Lake of the Woods presents to the avid musky hunter is unparalleled. Sure, you can go to a Minnesota lake and get in line to fish all the community spots. Maybe you'd even catch one and have some fun doing it. But a better investment of your time is to head to Canada and find your own spots. Nowhere else on the planet can you see so many muskies. If you're any good, it's not unusual to catch ten fish in a week, or even more. I don't know this from personal experience, of course, but my compadres do. I give them a hard time, but they are some of the best fishermen I know.

Heading into the 2013 Canadian musky hunt, things were gonna be a little different. My fishing partner for the last two trips had been Stewart, but this year he and his family 'decided' to take a family trip to California instead, leaving Canada out. Sucker. The man replacing my 6' 9" inch buddy was his brother James, a former college defense of lineman who missed being drafted in the NFL due to a bad knee injury late in his collegiate career. He stood only a mere 6'7", and tips the scale over 350 pounds. Don't be fooled, he's surprisingly light on his feet for such a big man. A one-time school teacher, James was well spoken and very intelligent. He never swore, which might not seem like a big deal, but I knew it would be interesting to have this choirboy in the same boat with my 'sailor' mouth. Especially when f*cking sh!t hit the god-damn fan.

CHAPTER XXXVI

TIMES A CHANGIN?

BP gas station at 6:45 am. Same as it ever was, and that, to a creature of habit, is comforting. I motored into the parking spot and noticed we're the last one to arrive. As I hop from the truck, I observe Jan purposely dumping gas on to the black top. Now remember, this is during the peak of the great 'Big Oil Profit Scheme', when they accumulated record profits at all consumers' expense. So the fuel he was dumping out was like lighting a match to a wad of bills.

"Hey Jan! Why are you dumping gas all over the ground?" I blurt out as James and I made our way over. "Just had some dirt inside this old gas can. Figured I'd get rid of it out here rather than the boat tank," Jan explained. The stinky puddle that spread around his feet expanded beyond a normal 'can cleaning' volume. "Sure looks like a hell of a lot of gas just to clean out some dirt," I noticed. "Yeah, it's probably a gallon or so. It will just evaporate in the sun," Jan said, with a laugh and a shrug of his shoulders. Like I've said before, I run with a different group of guys, haha.

After the normal bullshit session, the caravan takes off to the Canadian border. As we get closer, I can literally smell the fresh open country that is awaiting us. The ride there is always exhilarating, as the anticipation almost gives a guy the meat sweats. It's 4:24 pm by the time we pull into the public boat landing. James and I are the last ones to unload our boat, as we head over to the general store and gas station to buy our fishing licenses. Once inside, the friendly lady at the front counter asked me for my Ontario Outdoors Card. I explain to her that it had expired and I had not yet received a new card.

She informs me that they already issued a card, and I either lost it or it disappeared at the post office. Not exactly the way I wanted to start out the 2013 hunt, but it was pretty typical that some bullcrap would occur. If nothing else, these adventurous trips to L.O.T.W. taught me to expect the unexpected. So much so, the unexpected was expected. Thankfully, the lady was nice enough to sell me a $19.00 temporary Outdoors Card. Grateful I could continue on my merry way, I accepted begrudgingly. Thanks, Canada.

Marching a little straighter, having gotten rid of the extra wallet weight again, we were off to cram in a few hours of fishing before dark. A quick check of the time read five o'clock. "Where do you want to go?" asked James. I had spent the better part of the last year dreaming of hitting a very specific location on the water. Once we were at our destination, and James uttered those words, I spewed out terms quicker than I could think them. "Headin' out from Nestor Falls, there's a point on the left side. If we keep going straight about a half mile, there's a lone island slightly to the right. It looks like the waves are crashing into the north side," I spouted in quick rhythm. James merely blinked, and nodded his head pretending he knew what I was talking about. Whether he did or not, who cared. WE WERE FISHING IN CANADA!!!!!

The temperature was a balmy eighty-five degrees, with winds blowing fifteen-to-twenty mph Both of us were fan-casting spinner baits to the point. Analyzing the situation, it seemed the waves were coming in a little too hard at the moment, so I took us around to the right where a white pine had fallen, creating a nice current break. Being the guy running the trolling motor, I naturally took the first cast tight to the downed tree on the non-current side. Low and behold, if a darn musky didn't grab my spinner bait the second it touched aqua. As is on par for the first day on the water, it was a short-lived thrill.

The hook wasn't set deep and came unbuttoned almost as fast as it grabbed hold. But it gave me enough time to ascertain that the beast was a good forty-inches. "Forty or not, you got to get them closer to the boat in order to count it," said James. Whatever.

Ten yards further up the shoreline was a rocky finger jutting off the coast. It was made up of bowling ball-sized rocks and had me feeling extra greedy. I took the first cast five feet from the tip. This time, the musky went skyward with the spinner bait in its mouth. I fought her tooth-and-nail all the way to the boat. Just as James lowered the net into the water, she touched the net against her body and it spooked her enough that she surged away and came off the line and disappeared. "This is bullshit!"

Two fish back-to-back and nothing but dual kicks in the nuts is all I get to show for it!" I bellowed out. It was early in the trip, but I could tell my luck wasn't gonna be any different. James chortled deeply, seemingly pleased with my distress. "You're funny. This is going to be an interesting trip."

After my mini meltdown, we went around the backside of the point. James spotted a single garage just begging for bait. He fired a quick cast, and before I could even react, a nice mid-forty inch musky, with its nose on the skirt, followed back to the dinghy and goes around twice in figure eights before returning to its home. Tempted myself, I decided to give the spot a try. The same inquisitive fish came back out again, but this time sunk away before I could get a dance with her. Tease.

"Not a bad forty-five minutes of fishing, that fish was pushing 45 inches, we'll have to remember her for tomorrow morning. Already got two fish hits and one fish follow," I boasted. "That fish you had to the boat and lost was all my fault. I should have been quicker on net," James admitted.

It was refreshing for a fellow angler to admit guilt, whether accurate or not. "It's not your fault. Things just happen sometimes. If she was meant to be in the net, she would have gone into the net. Probably wasn't hooked all that well," I retorted.

Only an hour in, and it felt like karma might finally be on my side. We close out the evening throwing our favorite top water baits, but have no suitors.

BY **BRAD MATHEWSON**

CHAPTER XXXVII

NOT THE ONLY ONE

When I awoke the next morning, the humidity weighed heavy on my lungs, you could almost chew the air, for today was going to be a long one. The weather jerk on the radio, declared it was finally time for Canadians to shed their long underwear and wool stocking caps, it was now summer for at least a couple of weeks before the eleven months of winter set back in. A stable warm front seemed to be upon us, too, which meant a lot of muskies would be seen. How many would be caught was always the ultimate question. Even at the butt-crack of dawn, it was already in the mid-seventies, with highs for the day calling for upper eighties, with winds slapping out of the south in the mid-twenties, partly cloudy skies. It was just the kind of weather to get the big girls stirring.

You can probably guess what the plan of attack was for the day, if you said wind blown points and sand flats, then you're right. Wind and wave action tend to invigorate rock dwelling muskies, so the weather forecast dictated our plan of attack. The current wave action disorients musky prey, making it easier pickings. Once the wind disappears, that pattern falls apart. Then, generally speaking, the muskies that rise during calm moments from the rock ledges are usually neutral fish, using the sun-rays to help metabolize their last meal. All that said, the old standby of rocking and rolling doesn't always work, and the sand bite can really turn on when the wind is really cranking. So pick your poison. We decided to progress down our musky checklist of baits, speed of retrieve and cover types until the puzzle came together. That, or exhaust ourselves undertaking every darn thing on the list. Whichever came first.

James and I hopped into the boat for our sunrise ride. Just a couple of fools in search of some trick-able muskies that would eat our shiny baits made of plastic, metal, tinsel, deer hair, in every color imaginable. Baits equipped with sharp hooks that resemble absolutely nothing in nature. But hey, they seem to work, so I quit asking the question "what is this bait supposed to resemble?" years ago. After purchasing several hundred, and mostly only using a few, what was the point in asking anymore?

As we motored along the water, something grasped my attention up ahead. "What the heck is swimming by the Island?" James turned his face and squinted. "I think it's a black bear," suggested James. Sure enough, splashing through the current up ahead was a solitary black bear making his way through the lake with only one thing in mind, acorns. Through the years of coming up to Canada, we routinely would see deer and bears swimming island-to-island in search of the nut. I'm truly amazed at the distances I've seen deer and bear swim. We've seen them go up to a mile through rough waters just to eat a few ripe nuts. I'm amazed and impressed at their abilities and sheer determination. When you think about it, though, it's not like they can meander to the local grocery store to pick up a frozen pizza. That would just be weird.

Spotting the bear paddle across the bay reminded me an encounter I had with James' brother, Jan, while musky fishing in Northern Wisconsin one June. After a plentiful supper that night, we only had a few hours of fading sunlight remaining, so we put the boat in at Big Lake, on the Cisco chain of lakes, as it was just down the road. With the sun setting and prime time before us, I spotted a doe swimming across the widest portion of the lake with her fawn in tow. We kept on fishing, but we both would periodically glance over to witness their progress. They weren't easy to find, being nearly a quarter of a mile away. Some thirty minutes had passed since our first sighting. We both felt something was wrong. The mother was a good hundred yards ahead of the fawn who seemed to be slowing in pace. As we surveyed the situation, the mother spun around and swam back to the struggling fawn in attempts to coax him along. That didn't last long. The mother started swimming toward her intended destination once again, leaving the fawn to navigate the deep on its own. From where we watched, we could hear the fawn bleating frantically. The mother doe had

no choice but to keep trucking on for her own survival. After a few minutes, mother was nearly 3/4 finished with her swim, while the small fawn was barely halfway and swimming in circles. We observed its little head disappear underwater at moments, and then briefly reappear to gasp a breath. You couldn't help but have heartache watching this little life struggle.

I understand that one isn't supposed to interfere with nature, no matter how cruel it can seem to be. At the same time, I couldn't help but think that maybe we were right here fishing on this night for a higher reason. I peered over at Jan, whom was thinking the same thing I was. That little fawn was gonna be turtle food if we didn't do something. "Yeah we better go give the little guy a hand," Jan replied. Then he yanked up the trolling motor and jumped back on the tiller. We speed toward the fawn as she started swimming slowly again. By this time, she had whirled around inadvertently and was on her way to the opposite side of the lake than her mother had gone. As we pulled up, her head once again went underwater. I thought we were too late, but a couple seconds later she reappeared, panicked and bleating. There wasn't much fight left in her by the time we arrived. Not thinking, I barked out to the fawn to "come here." After a moment, I realized she wasn't a dog and wouldn't listen. But a funny thing occurred that backed my thinking that this was meant to be. The little fawn turned and swam straight toward the boat! Once within reach, Jan nabbed her by the nap of the neck and handed her to me. The fawn was shaking and bitter cold. She laid down in my lap like a small puppy cuddling to get some warmth. Jan and I were shocked at how tiny he was. He couldn't have been more than a few weeks old, definitely not old enough for long distance swimming. I quickly removed my sweatshirt and wrapped him like a newborn baby. I could feel his heart beating a hundred miles an hour and extreme shaking from the cold dip. But within minutes his breathing and heartbeat seemed to return back to normal and the shivering stopped, the young fawn began to relax and almost snuggle in. We pulled the boat up to the same spot where his mother had exited the water and placed him on solid ground. As we slowly pulled away, the fawn softly bleated a couple times and his mother reappeared and approached her little fawn. I knew it would take a while for the fawn to warm up, but he immediately started to nurse. Jan and I were immediately warmed at the sight of their reunion.

Now, I'm not normally some kind of bunny-hugging, tree-kissing, nostalgic sissy. I am an avid bow hunter whom loves a nice, juicy venison steak as often as possible. In spite (and because) of all that, I needed to help a creature that had given me so much joy over the years. Oh, in case you're wondering, yes I did try to smell him and its true fawns have no smell, it's natures way of protecting them when their young.

I spun this story to James as we continued our musky hunt. He retorted, "You guys are the freaking Batman and Robin of nature." Nice and sarcastic, as expected. "I just hope that doe repays the favor by bringing a large boyfriend past my stand this fall," I requested. She didn't.

Our first action of the day took place on a small island complex at the entrance to GoHere Bay. I was casting a double

BY **BRAD MATHEWSON**

eight bucktail with silver blades and a black Marabou skirt. I find that Marabou is heavier when wet and can be cast more effectively in strong winds, while the Flashabou gets pushed around in the wind which makes long bomb casts into the wind impossible. We cast feverishly to all the main, wind-swept points when a large boil appeared next to the spot I had just cast. Apparently, I peeked the interest of a dominant musky. Unsuccessful on that specific toss, my next cast was a throwback lure I had a lot of confidence in. It was a Shallow Raider in blue and chrome. I love to burn it back to the boat with short quick jerks, and then slow it halfway for a few feet before resuming the jerks. It seemed to really get them fired up mimicking an easy meal, trying to escape. On this cast, a fifty-inch tank charged hot on its heels. The brute of a fish followed hard, it's back a mere inch or so under the water surface pushing a six inch wake. On the entry to my figure eight, I dove the bait deep with the help of my eight and one-half foot St. Croix rod. The musky reacted by diving straight down. It's powerful tail jetted purposefully from the water, splashing me in the face with water. I considered her a 'hot fish', meaning she was gonna eat and not just screw around. I went around and around with this fish ten times, changing my figure eight up by moving my bait three-dimensionally, varying my depth and speed. I pull out every damn trick I had in the book, nothing would trigger her to bite. In these cases, two sayings come to mind: "There's a reason why she got so big," and "There she was... gone."

By early afternoon, it was time for a much needed change in scenery. The windy points and eddies on the backside of the points failed to show us any more fish. Plus, fighting the wind with a single twelve-volt battery would cut our day short in a hurry, considering the day was a thirteen hour marathon. Physically, your body takes a pounding when fishing high winds in an aluminum boat. Your legs and knees are basically shock absorbers. When it's not happening on the high seas, it's time to hit sheltered weedy bays or sandy bays. My vote was to hit my favorite Deer Bay. I love to fish the slop when the big girls hunker down. I'm like Jacques Cousteau, exploring each open pocket for that one active fish. For this type of fishing, nothing beats a Bucher Slop master. You can really pick the weed beds apart with a Slop master where others wouldn't dare.

Once we had maneuvered into Deer Bay, it didn't take long before we had some action. I caught three northerns, the largest being thirty-two inches. Not record breakers, but nice practice and pure enjoyment. James also managed to boat three northerns, and raised an upper-thirty inch musky. By mid-afternoon, though, we both decided that small muskies and pike just weren't for us anymore.

We needed to find active, larger fish. Sandy bays was next on the docket. For whatever reason, these seemingly featureless sandy bays can really turn on during a big blow. And if you happen to find some reeds and a rock or two, all the better. I have found many times that muskies will be very shallow, even some of real giants. We cast double 10's in these types of situations. The stirred up sand can be near zero visibility, and the thump of the big blades of a double 10 will get the job done.

BY **BRAD MATHEWSON**

On James first cast to a wind-blown reed point, he hooked up with a plump thirty-inch musky. "It's no record breaker, but maybe it's a sign of better things to come," James encouraged. During the next hour or so, we raised six more muskies in that same area. Some off reeds and others just hanging out on the sand flats. All of them were quality fish in the mid-forties to fifty inch range. Then, just as things were looking up for us two musky nuts, Mother Nature turned the fans off and all went dead. The skies turned an eerie gray. You could hear a mouse fart it was so calm. The surface became mirrored glass. Most rational people would take that as a sign that Mother Nature was about to bring about something big upon your ass, so you'd better tuck tail and run. If you're a walleye guy, then that would be exactly what you would do. But we musky guys have a crazy side to us. That little voice inside our heads orders us to get to the nearest big fish spot, because the first couple minutes before a big storm (and immediately after) is prime time for the biggest of the big muskies. If your lifelong goal was to catch a fifty-plus inch Canadian Shield, this was the best time to make that dream come true. Navigating between lightning bolts and high winds was all part of the adventure, and would just add to the story.

We scurried to a reef just past Wolf Island, which was only a few miles from the lodge. Here it topped out at six feet deep and was surround by thirty-seven feet of water area. This was a popular walleye spot for local fishermen, and also a haunt for big muskies in search of an easy meal. As we motored to the reef, James stared over my shoulder to the looming skies behind me. "Holy crap. Those are the blackest clouds I've ever laid my eyes on," admitted James. I whirled around to witness deep thunderheads forming just over the tree-topped skyline. There was no question it was a menacing, intimidating sight that struck even the hardiest of fishing souls to wonder one's sanity. I chose to ignore the pending doom, and press on. Behind me, the black curtain headed our way, with reminders every thirty seconds of bowling alley rumbles that made your hair stand up. James' fear began winning his struggle with courage. "Let's get our butts out of here!" "We haven't even made a cast yet. Let's stay for a couple minutes, toss a few baits in, nab a sixty-incher, and then we'll blow this taco stand," I said with supreme confidence. Reluctantly, James put on his big boy pants and tossed out a line. He casted a perch-colored Bobbie bait, while I used a black sucker colored Hellhound. Suddenly, the boat dipped heavy to one side. I peep up to see James diving into a massive figure eight. "Do you have a fish going?!" I bellow out.

"I did, until she sunk away. As I'm finishing my retrieve, I did a little J for a figure eight. I ended it, I peer down and lying not a foot under the water and tight to the boat is a fifty-inch monster staring at me, wondering where her meal just went." James flopped down into the boat seat, partially out of exhaustion, and partially out of dejection. To even see a fifty-inch water cow is an accomplishment, but to have one on your bait and you prematurely ejaculate your bait is devastating on so many levels. James rubbed his brain, vexing to extinguish the anguish. I knew full well that would haunt his dreams for weeks to come. In a way, it was reassuring to me that I wasn't the only one to have these types of fiasco's happen to them. I felt horrible for James, but felt a little better about myself at the same time.

Moments later, a flash of electricity shard the sky. Cracks of thunder echoed the air. At that moment, between James soul-crushing defeat, and Mother Nature's ever-approaching disaster, I knew it was time to drop the hammer on the tiller and get the hell out of Dodge. Desperately wanting to make a pit stop at Nestor Falls on the way home, our better judgment prevailed and we escaped the storm a couple minutes before water poured down. Lucky for us, we managed to make it up the dock before being blasted by buckets. Our musky brothers were not so lucky, as they were all trapped out in a monsoon. James and I made our way back to the dry cabin, showered and enjoyed a much earned cocktail by the time all our soaked comrades showed up. The only downside for me was we were to have hamburgers on the grill that night, and I was to be the head chef. I donned my rain suit and did what any good chef does when faced with less than ideal cooking conditions... drank heavily.

CHAPTER XXXVIII

DANCING WITH GREATNESS

Not all days are created equal. Some days are plain, normal 'same as it ever was' days that are extremely forgettable. Others have greater value and hold a strong memory for years to come. And then there's the days that change the very foundation of your soul the rest of your existence. Little did I know that when I woke up this morning, the day was gonna be one of those days I would never forget.

The forecast for the day called for partly cloudy skies, with the wind out of the south at a mere five-to-ten. With the high to hover around ninety four degrees, it would be like fishing in an oven. For our first stop of the day, we thought we'd try out the small island complex James and I had fished when we arrived on Friday night. I had lost two muskies in that area, while James had managed to raise one. The first location at the island complex we stopped to fish was the laid down tree where I had hooked a musky. As James brought his perch Bobbie bait back, I couldn't believe my eyes. The same musky was being hypnotized by his cadence, though never committed to eating and swam back to her tree. We both attempted multiple cast backs. I used three different baits hoping for happy result, but it was not to be. As we made our way to a sandy reed filled cove, I noticed that the foot pedal on James trolling motor wasn't working. I did the old unplug and replug, but just like my fishing capabilities, came up empty handed. Since that didn't work, I pressed the power indicator button, which will illuminate red on either low, good, full charge or recharge, and it shot straight up to full charge. We were perplexed. The damn motor would go through all the speeds, but the trolling motor was unable to move from side to side with the foot pedal.

"James, where do you keep your back up foot pedal," I quizzed, still concentrating on the piece of monkey crap not working. "I don't have a backup," James admitted. That broke my focus to stare puzzlingly at James. "I hope you're fu**ing kidding me right now." James shrugged his shoulders. "You're telling me you came all the way up to Canada on vacation, spent all this money on gas, lodging, food and licenses and you didn't bring and extra $80.00 foot pedal?! You do realize that two of your brothers have the same trolling motor and lucky to get a full year out of any one of them?" This seemed beyond comprehension to me. If you own a Minn Kota Power Drive, you get my drift. I have owned a couple of them through the years since they are a very affordable option. But I understood that with some savings on the front end came a potential cost for backups because of cheaply made foot pedals. Anybody else I knew that had these always had a backup foot pedal in the boat. It was common sense. So James not having common sense left me fuming.

With really no other option, I ended up ripping the pedal apart in hopes of fixing it myself. After a few minutes of deep inspection, I couldn't find any signs of a broken part. James admitted that the foot pedal was over two years old and "probably past its prime." That just fueled my anger more. We were basically stuck here wasting fishing time. The only option I saw was to head back to the lodge, speed down to the local marine dealer and hope he's open and in stock of the correct foot pedal replacement.

We screamed back to the dock and hopped into James truck to speed to the nearest boat dealer down in Nestor Falls. Just our luck, no one was around. We then took a drive over to the local bait and tackle shop, but still no foot pedal. Back at the lodge, a worker tossed us a phone book to call around. After several attempts to what seemed the entire country of Canada, we found that we were screwed until Monday when the marina would open.

"I guess we either straight line troll or manually turn the top of the trolling motor to go left or right," I complained. Neither option was good, but ultimately was our only choice.

We decided on the latter, because I was way to antsy to dink around going straight line.

Three hours into me hand operating the trolling motor, my blood pressure rose by the minute. The thought of tearing the trolling motor off the front and tossing the whole works into the lake had crossed my mind several times. Pure frustration and sweltering ninety degree heat caused me to stomp on the foot pedal and let out a few choice words. Just then, the damn trolling motor moved to the right. "Did you see it move?" I asked, wondering if it was real or just the high heat frying my brain. With my right foot, I gently pressed the spring loaded base to the right and the motor turned right. Then I did the same to the left and it went left. I was happy as a lark. Whoever used the phrase "it doesn't pay to get mad because you'll just make matters worse" never had a trolling motor break down at the beginning of a week-long musky hunt on L.O.T.W. "I can't argue with logic like that, now let's go fishing," said James.

Once our mechanical issues were finally put aside, we pounded the waters tough again. By one in the afternoon, James hooked a northern pike we intended to have for sup-per that evening, but he measured at twenty-eight inches, which was within the protected slot and needed to be tossed back. One minute later, I managed to haul in a pike as well, but at thirty-one inches, she was too big as well. It seemed like most of the northern we seized were in that slot. The rules for northern pike here were only one greater than 35.4", and none between 27.5" and 35.4". I don't know about you, but I have a hard time killing a northern greater than thirty-five inches.

I'd much rather eat a twenty odd incher. I just feel that those majestic-sized fish should be able to be enjoyed by all, not just plugged on a wall. But that's just me, I guess.

For that afternoon, James and I managed to raise five musky, all of which came from isolated shallow reefs surrounded by twenty-plus feet of water. The problem was they were all neutral fish that were just working on their tans and were not fooled by our fake prey offerings. One musky in particular, a nice mid-forty incher, would just follow. We couldn't even entice her into a figure eight. Six times we raised her in a thirty minute period without as much as a nibble.

By early evening, we were fishing a not-quite 'C' shaped sandy cove. There was a ten foot wide channel stuffed with weeds that led to nearly forty acres of weed-choked bay. When the wind blew from the south, a nice current would developed right into the bay. This cove was also unusual in that it sported depth of four feet in the very back, and six-to-eight feet out front, and contained a nice mix of open sand flats and really impressive coontail growth. We were across from Wolf Island near Cyclone Point when the wind picked up to near fifteen miles per hour out of the south. We both could feel something big was going to happen. I casted in a black Slop Master spinner bait while James casted out with his perch colored Bobbie bait. Before I knew it, James hollers out that he's got a big slob on his line. The musky stayed low all the way to the boat. I jostled next to James with the net in the ready position. James struggled as he wrenched her closer. "Here she comes! Get ready!" gasped James. I could see her five feet under, heading towards the boat. Out of nowhere, she veered off at literally the last second, leaving my only shot being to take her from behind, going away. I stretched out as far as I could with the net, but thought it better to wait for a more realistic nab. The musky taunted us like a drunken floozy. She rose to the surface like a submarine, showing her girth and tremendous chest. We both gawked in awe. She was easily a fifty-two to fifty-four inch monster and only a mere ten feet away. She simply lied on the surface in an uneasy peace. We couldn't see the Bobbie, so we knew we all but had her.

"James, slowly apply pressure to her and lead her toward the waiting net," I whisper. My heart was racing. I couldn't even imagine what James was going through at that moment. He simply nodded his head. Just then, like almost every other musky hunt I'd ever been on in my entire life, it was over in an instant. The king musky spun violently into an alligator death roll and disappeared under the surface. Then it happened. James' line went completely slack. "SON OF A BITCH!" cried James. We were both dumbstruck by the rapid change of events. Suddenly, James shot out his arm, pointing into the waters. "There she is! To your left!" She splashed to the surface after breaking the line, violently thrashing her head side to side to throw the bait. I hopped on the trolling motor with the net at the ready. Just as we got close enough, she sunk under. I buried the net deep into the water in a last ditch effort to snag the beast, but missed clean. James sunk in his seat for a brief moment. Defeat was crushing his soul. But the fight wasn't over just yet. "She's on the other side of the boat!" I yammered, kicking the trolling motor up to ten to whip around. As I adjusted to take another swipe at the majestic musky, she disappeared before into the blue for the last time.

A few minutes passed by before either James or myself said a word. It was a lot to comprehend and understand what just happened, and to figure out what we could have done differently. The 'could have, should have, would have' started racing through our minds. "How did she break the line? You have 80 lb. braid," I wondered aloud. "You don't realize those gill rakes are so sharp, 80 lb is like dental floss to a giant beast like that," said James. Another few minutes passed by. "I just can't believe she was there one second, and gone the next." I ran the scenario through my brain endlessly, struggling to find an answer. Only one came to me. "It's my fault. I should have tried harder for her on her first pass by the boat, but I pulled up short," I admitted. "No, you made the right call. She was out too far and she would have tail-walked out, or worse," explained James. I appreciated him not adding onto my dismay, but it didn't help me feel any different about the situation.

We stayed in the cove for another hour playing the waiting game, but she never resurfaced. It felt like someone had punched me in the gut. I felt physically ill, even if she wasn't my fish. I could only imagine how James felt. When musky hunting, we work as a team. I probably get jacked up more than the guy catching the musky does because I know the kind of commitment it takes to be successful. "Let's go fish the weed bay behind the cove. When we're done, maybe we can take another look around for your fish. Hopefully she'll relax and surface again or at least wallow in the shallow where I can get a net on her," I wished aloud. It was already eating at me to get one last crack at her. Giving up, at this point, was simply not an option. Not to my musky-heart.

The second we finished working the weedy bay, James started his tiller. In fact, I hadn't even sat down yet and he was on the throttle. Maybe forty-five minutes had eclipsed, and we had embarked on a different kind of hunt. The kind, we hoped, would end in a life saved. For all we knew, the musky could be tangled up in line and unable to swim properly, or her mouth could be pinned shut from the Bobbie bait lodged in her throat. "Terrible way to go if she couldn't eat and would slowly starve to death," said James. "She might throw the bait and be OK. Let's check the shoreline for your bait or a white belly floating," I requested. After another long, extensive search with the same empty results, it was time to drive back to the cabin and tell the tale of what could have been. We weren't giving up the search, only putting it on hiatus. We would begin the next day the way we had ended this day. It was the least we could do for such a majestic fish. It deserved nothing less than all our efforts. And just maybe, it could be a happy ending for both the fish, and us musky hunters.

CHAPTER XXXIX

LEARNING THE HARD WAY

A full night of quivering over the details of the previous days fiasco brought some ease to my weary heart. All attendees on our musky hunt shared their own personal horrific experiences that were very similar to our ordeal. Many of their stories also happened with large musky and razor gill rakers. The shared adventures forced me to rethink my query. Was I underestimating the shear strength that Mother Nature had given to her creation? Even with all the respect I gave to the mammoth fish, had I taken them too lightly? Looking at the bigger picture, it's easy to understand how a lack of respect could develop. Technology is ever-evolving at a pace not seen in history. The nine- foot rods vs. the old five-foot pool cue, with the up to one hundred lbs braided lines and the low-profile reels with massive cranking power and the ability to bring in a double 10 with ease... leaves a fisherman with little-to-no fatigue. You lose perspective on just how daunting a task it is to collar the musky monsters. But even with all our bells and whistles, you can't beat nature every time. Our over-confidence in our tools tends to leave us scratching our collective heads in bewilderment.

As we silently readied ourselves for the day ahead, we knew in short order we'd soon be back at the scene of the crime. James had a fifty-plus incher stolen from him by Mother Nature, and a little bad luck. We barely said a word as we made our way on our nightmarish return. We felt it best if we stop the boat a distance away and slowly drift in like bumps on floating logs. If the big musky was wallowing in the shallows, we'd be sure not the disturb her this way. The boat drifted in from right to left at a fairly medium pace. I scanned the shoreline for James' Bobbie bait and/or a floating musky. Thankfully, and not surprisingly, neither were found. As we approached the far left side, I set the trolling motor to five and worked back to the right again only being a few feet from shore. Still nothing.

"I'm starting to think she threw the bait and is resting comfortably back in the weedy bay," I pronounced. That damn feeling of the unknown is the worst. Not knowing if she was dead or alive is a gut punch to the nuts. But analyzing the events from the night before, one wondered how any musky could survive with a bait that far down it's throat.

"It's a tough pill to swallow, but that's part of fishing. We do our best to catch these magnificent fish, try to handle them with the kid-gloves and respect, but sometimes... well, stuff happens. I'll tell you what, let's make it a point every time we drive past this cove we stop and fish it. Just maybe a positive can come out of this potential tragedy," I proclaimed.

The day's forecast was for more of the same - hot and humid with a light breeze out of the southwest pushing a whopping five mph. Clear skies and a high near ninety again. As a side note to the forecast, if any of you out there are fishing during these type of long hot days, you need to purchase a bottle of Gold Bond Medicated Body Powder. Just sprinkle it on the 'big Jim and the Twins' before you leave camp in the morning so it will absorb moisture, stop any itching and cool your tater tots all day long. If you trust nothing else from this book, trust this. I say it's a little piece of heaven tucked into every bottle.

Once we moved on from the nightmare cove, we headed to the infamous Musky Alley. We arrived shortly after nine-thirty in the morning, and upon our arrival, neither one of us could believe our eyeballs. The ever-changing L.O.T.W. had finally answered our prayers. The once, almost un-fishable, Musky Alley had been mostly rid of the wild celery that had plagued it for the past couple of years. The growth that was so tightly woven together that I'd seriously doubted any sizable perch could swim through it, much less a full grown musky. What remained was beautiful coontail, red cabbage and large lily pads scattered about its surface. It felt almost too good to be true. The ultimate question was left staring us in the grill: were the muskies back? "I haven't seen Musky Alley look this fishy in years!" James spoke with an out-of-character giddy tone.

The game plan was to keep the trolling motor on low and slowly fish our way against the current until we couldn't go any further. Then we'd turn around, drifting and fishing our way out. On my first cast down the middle of the channel, I obtain a nice low-forty inch musky follow for a short ways before getting spooked by the boat. On the very next cast, the same scenario repeated itself. James made a long bomb cast of his own down the middle with his Fire Tiger Bobbie bait and ends up with two muskies chasing it at the same time.

Both fish appeared in the mid-forty inch range. I viewed in amazement as these two muskies seemed to be jockeying for position as they approached the boat, but neither fish would bite. Attempting to do a convincing figure eight with a Bobbie bait was near impossible, so enticing them further would seem equally impossible. I watched as the bigger one of the two, a chunky forty incher, swam under a nearby lily pad and settled on the bottom. I grabbed my throw back rod, fully equipped with the most frustrating bait known to man, the Lindy Tiger Tube in motor oil color. I tossed it ten yards past the musky. With a quick snap of the wrist, the bait looped toward the surface. Then on the pause, its tentacles would flare and dance seductively towards the waiting fish. Just as it neared the musky, a twenty-four inch northern came out of nowhere and grabbed my bait. I'm instantly hooked up with a little runt. Apparently in me hooking the small northern pike, the musky thought that the pike was injured and took full advantage. It darted like a perfectly aimed torpedo and T-boned my northern tight in its jaws. It proceeded to swim away with its new meal, leaving me to fight both a musky and a northern all the way to the boat. As what seems to be very typical for me, just as James went down to scoop up my two-for-one special, the musky released and swam off, leaving a mauled pike for me to deal with.

A brief discussion between hunters convinced us that giving these two brutes some time would ultimately convince them to become eaters instead of followers. Upon leaving the channel, the waters fork to the left and right, separated by a sixty yard weed flat that's way too thick to fish. With a flip of the coin, we fish the left side all the way out, then would come back up the right channel as we would then fish against the current. It took us about forty minutes to work our way around, managing to raise five muskies in that low-thirty inch range.

Thankfully, we didn't have any hook ups with any of those little twerps. After the forty-minute fish around, we were back in the same location ready to attempt to nab those two musky. Glancing around, I spot my fish under the same lily pads as before. This time I decided to try a Bucher shallow Raider in a perch pattern in hopes that it would draw out the fish. Just like before, I fish it erratically past her, she followed to the boat, and swam back to her lily pads. I snapped on a Slop Master that produced the same result. Double 8, same result. Hell hound, same result. Lastly, a Suzy Sucker, but she wasn't interested in any of them.

"Must be a Lake of the Woods chamber of commerce fish," joked James. "Maybe it's time for a change in location. We're not too far from the famous Split Rock," I suggested, being sick and tired of these two teasing, government muskies. "I have never caught a musky there before. Though, I have fished it many times and I have witnessed plenty of muskies being taken there," admitted James as he wound in his final cast in this area.

I have talked at great length about this spot for a good reason. It's an incredible ambush shelf that holds muskies every time. Whenever a fish or two leaves, another one slides up to take its place. Secondly, the size structure of these fish tends to be in the mid-forty inch range, which is a quality fish. Of the hundred or so muskies caught there, I know of none being under forty inches, but none, that I've witnessed, being over forty-five inches. That taught me that when muskies pack up to hunt for food, like-sized muskies tend to stay together, just like perch. If you catch a six-inch perch, the whole school will be that size.

It's about one o'clock by the time we made our way to Split Rock, and the oppressing heat of the day is at full tilt. As sweat dripped down my brow, I instruct James to kill the motor within a hundred yards of the rocks to give the region an old fashion sneak attack. "I want you to make the first cast and place it deep into the narrow channel between the rock and shore," I ordered James. This was my bread and butter area, having fished it religiously over the years. Nobody knew this area any more than I did by this point. When I wasn't fishing it, I was dreaming about fishing it. James was using orange and black spinner bait that he refers to lovingly as his Ace bait. I never even had a chance to cast before I perceived a nice musky following deep behind his bait.

One thing I was taught by my friend Steve on my first Canadian trip was to watch three feet behind your bait, and out of the corner of your eye, watch your partners bait. There have been a good many fish seen that neither I nor my partner ever initially saw, but were able to warn one another. Now I'm not saying that every musky we spotted for each other were then nabbed, but if you have a head's up on an unseen fish, obviously your odds will be slightly better. Plus in my boat, we work as a team and share knowledge, baits and techniques. Just don't ask to share MY LUNCH...

"James, do you see that musky?" I whispered across the boat. "Yeah, I see him." The musky swam around nine times in the figure eight before James managed to drop a hook into him. We got it in the net, snapped a quick picture, and then slapped it onto the bump board. Forty and one-half inches. Not a Goliath, just a nice healthy fish.

As I placed the fish back into the water, I peered up at James. "Holy shit! You look a boiled lobster! Maybe we should get out of this heat and head on over to Tom B's cabin for some much needed shade and snacks," I suggested. James held up his bottle to try and see his reflection. He pressed on this cheeks and winced slightly. "That's the best idea you've had all day. Do you know what cabin he's in?" Of course I knew.

Our friend Tom B. and his family came up to Canada that same week, but they stayed at a place called King Island. It's a little bit more money there, but the trade off is you're right in the middle of a prime fishing area. We land-lovers like to bring our own gasoline, and enjoy the ability to meander over to the local general store if we happened to forget to bring something. The nearby general store is great for being able to purchase anything you may need, but that reliance always comes with a steep price. The down side to where we were staying compared to King Island was it required a long boat ride to our favorite part of the lake. That sucked up fishing time, so it wasn't perfect by any stretch of the imagination. But being cheap Wisconsinites will force you to pay a price in one way, shape or form.

We pull up to the island and see Tom's beautiful Crestliner Musky Edition, every aluminum boat lover's dream ride, tied up to the dock. Once on the island, I stroll over to the cabin that I believe to be Tom's and nobody is home. "You don't have a clue which cabin he's in, do you?" James inquires. I scratch my bald head in bewilderment. "Well, he was in this one four years ago when Steve and I paid him a visit. It's a small island. He's in one of these cabins. We'll just go door to door until we find him."

On a good note, it only took four tries to find Tom's cabin. It was nice to get out of the sun for an hour, have some nice cold ice water and eat some snacks. Tom and his boy, Tim, shared with us what had been working for them out on the water. To hear they weren't doing any better than us made me feel relieved. How they chose to spend their day on the water was much different than ours. First of all, they were on the water by seven in the morning or even earlier, and that included chowing down on a nice big breakfast with all the fixings. We didn't start until eight in the morning, and gobbled a quick bowl of cereal or a protein shake on our way out the door. Next, they came in for lunch and even took a short nap before fishing the rest of the afternoon until supper, when they'd come in again to chow down and then finish the day on the water until dark. When we fished, we are gone all day long, eat our lunch while driving to the next fishing spot, and don't arrive back to the dock until nine at night. Not until then do I go up to the cabin and start fixing supper with whomever I can guilt into helping me. We usually don't eat until nearly ten, have a couple cocktails with supper, and hit the fart sack around midnight. I'll let you decide what you think is more relaxing. Remember, we don't have any other option but the one we utilized. We fished too far from camp to come back early for lunch or supper. That would be a lot of wasted gas and time. Like I said, cheap guys pay for it one way or another. I think this is where the phrase "Time is Money" comes from.

After the brief visit and munchies with Tom, we head back to the water by three in the afternoon. The temperature is still similar to Death Valley, but managed to drop down to about ninety three degrees. The lake's surface barely has a ripple. The one thing that did change was an algae bloom was in the midst of happening. You wouldn't think that the water could change a different color in one hour, but we now were looking at pea soup. "We need to find some current areas where visibility will be greater," I suggested. Off we went to the only place I could think of that always seemed to have current: Split Rock Narrows.

BY **BRAD MATHEWSON**

When we arrived in the Narrows, the water was clear with no sign of green algae. We bulldogged our way back through the Narrows for a couple of hours, raising five fish in the first hour before things shut right off dead. There was an isolated sandy bay just off of the Narrows, so I thought we'd give it a try. This water had a heavy green tinge to it, but nowhere near the color of the water around the King Island area. I worked the front of the boat around a large boulder that I couldn't see until the trolling motor had collided with it. Luckily, I only had the power set to five, and no visible damage had been done. The location I was heading for, before I was so rudely interrupted by one of Mother Nature's wallet-draining gems, was a long finger of reeds that stuck out nearly twenty feet further than all the reeds around it. We casted around the point in every open pocket we found along the way, but the water grew worse by the minute. Anytime I would make a cast, I couldn't even see my bait coming back to the boat. It was so bad, I planned on initiating our departure after one last cast. Suddenly, I look down, and before I could go into a figure eight, I watch a low-forty inch musky grab my green and black Slop Master. In my excitement, I start fighting the fish without ever setting the hook. Within five seconds, I'm standing there holding my limp rod in my hands. Reminder - when a fish hits, you should always set the hook. I have, more times than I'd care to admit, gotten seized by the moment, had a total brain fart, and cost myself a quality fish.

After licking my wounds, again, we stow the trolling motor and made a run to the little weedy cove where the day before, the unforeseen tragedy took place. We were there to right a wrong. This place had weighed heavily on my mind. I could only imagine the terror that James was going through with the loss of such a monster fish. They say the only way to begin the healing process is to get back up on the horse that bucked you. I'd love to tell you that James made a bomb cast back into the beast layer and with a couple cranks of the handle, the battle was on with massive head shakes and aerial acrobatics that would make the Wallenda family proud. But that would be a fishing story, and a lie. We did work that cove and the subsequent weedy bay behind it. In fact, we purposely picked apart every fish-holding nook and cranny in hopes of a miracle. In my heart, I wanted James to find her and remove the Bobbie bait that we were both sure was lodged deep inside her mouth and possibly preventing her from feeding, or worse, impeding her breathing. No matter how sick I felt, I realized it's sometimes part of the game. Unexpected things happen. All we can do is learn from our mistakes in order to not repeat them. As night fell upon us, James realized what I was doing. "Thank you, Brad." Nothing further was said by either of us. With those simple words, I knew my friend had made peace with what had happened, and we could now move on.

BY BRAD MATHEWSON

CHAPTER XL

BYE-BYE BAITS

It's hard to articulate how much I looked forward to another day of bluebird skies, no wind and temperatures hovering around ninety degrees with oppressive humidity. That little voice in my head has thoroughly convinced me that I am punished by Venus, the God of Love, with Florida-like weather every damn year as Her way of reminding me that I forced my wife to go to Canada for our honeymoon rather than take her to the Sunshine State as she wished back in 2009. I'm praying that isn't a life-sentence. Maybe I can get parole for good behavior. Of course, for that, I'd probably have to start behaving sometime soon.

By ten-thirty the next morning, we were fishing the Lily pads and coontail in the back of GoHere Bay, right where the bay splits off into three fingers. We were working the right finger first in our attempts to land a fatty. Our collective thought had us believing that the fish would be seeking shade from the Canadian bake that was lighting up the skies. This is also something we should have been attempting ourselves, but apparently muskies are much smarter than we are. James used his Fire Tiger Bobbie bait and I, a yellow Slop Master spinner bait, tipped with a white grub. We were casting to the open pockets when a musky exploded from the surface, clearly a good two feet above the water, with James' Bobbie bait T-boned tight in its open mouth. It was the perfect ice-breaker, for we hadn't seen a damn guppy until that moment. There was no need for a net job on this one, as James snatched the thirty-two inch musky out of the water like it was a small perch and quickly sent him back home.

On my very next cast, I aimed my shot only twenty feet from where James had just hooked his fish from. As it splashed down, I notice a familiar flash. In an instant, my spinner bait vanished from sight and was screaming towards the thick coontail. I set the hook and knew it was a much larger fish than James had just played with. This fish got a step ahead of me, and managed to get itself buried deep in the slop. I knew my only chance to not lose this fish would be to kick the trolling motor into high gear and get right over the top of the fish as fast as possible.

"I can't see anything down there but a thunderstorm of weeds and muck," said James, as he peered over the side of the boat. We got directly over the fish, which put us in four feet of water. Problem was, I could no longer feel the fish tugging at the end of my line. It had either managed to spit the hook, or the line was so tangled up in the weeds that the fish couldn't move. I worried it couldn't breathe properly, if that were the case. "Take the net, push it all the way down to the bottom and try to scope up that entire mass of weeds. We'll find out if she's in there," I requested of James. I'm not gonna lie, it helps when your fishing partner was a former NFL-bound, three hundred fifty pound defense lineman with the ability to move large objects with relative ease. The ball of waterlogged weeds inside his net had to weigh a good hundred pounds and could have easily filled the bottom of most boats. When James brought the net boat-side, I spotted a tail fin, and nothing else. "Nice job, James! You got our fish!" I shouted with a mixture of surprise and excitement. "Would you call this a musky salad?" bellowed James.

After quickly untangling my line and removing most of the vegetation from Lake Of The Woods, I finally had my prize: a forty inch musky. Not my biggest, but certainly one that I would always remember. After a quick photo, I sent her back to the jungle.

For a brief moment, we thought that just maybe we had finally discovered a musky pattern. But of course, whenever you start to gain an ounce of confidence in your fishing abilities, the muskies must sense that. It was just like someone had turned the light switch off, because we couldn't even raise a fish the rest of the morning and into the afternoon. Our next bite didn't occur until quarter after three in the afternoon, when James switched over to an oil-colored tube bait when we targeted weed edges adjacent to deep water. Shortly after James had his nibble, I netted a nice thirty-six and a half inch musky with giant teeth marks on its side that seemed rather fresh. The fish itself was in good shape and swam off strong when I placed it back into the water.

Our skies had turned baby blue with only a frogs breath of wind, we were just a couple of roast ducks basting in our SPF juices. My pop-up meat thermometer read 96, I argue its still better to be cooked alive chasing musky than to lose your soul stuck in an air conditioned office or factory all day.

"We should spend a little more time working this edge. Maybe we'll run into our cannibal friend," I hoped aloud. Since the plan was to stay, work the deep weed edge while our boat floated in the sixteen feet of water range, and cast back to the four foot weed edge, I had to try a different bait. I was thinking something that looked like a real fish, since there was a cannibal in our midst. I went into my rubber tackle box and yanked out a sucker-colored Suzy Sucker. I'd had good experiences with this bait in the past, so I briefly allowed my PMA to bubble up.

Halfway back to the boat, my third cast retrieval received the attention of a large surface submarine. I quickly reeled in my bait and made a long bomb cast past the fish. The second it hit the water, I reeled as fast as I could for three seconds, then ceased. I mimicked this all the way back to the boat. Only then did I truly find her.

Ten feet from the boat hid a low fifty-inch fish with one thing on her mind. With a quick pause, she darted at the bait from the side and hammered it on her way through. I attempted a hook set, but she had bit down too far back into my Suzy Sucker and blasted it in half. My heart sunk. I knew I couldn't delve back into my rubber box and whip out another Suzy Sucker. That fifty incher just severed the only one I had. Unfortunately, not all of us musky guys have unlimited funds to stockpile lures. Hell, I'm usually pretty happy if I have enough leftover cash to stockpile fresh underwear for a week-long trip. If I couldn't do that, I'd have to go commando, where my earlier tip about the Gold Bond certainly comes in handy. As I lifted my destroyed bait out of the water, I felt like a kid whose single-scoop ice cream flopped off the cone and splattered on the pavement. "It's OK, Brad. At least you know that musky will get an upset stomach attempting to digest that big chunk of rubber," James snickered. Strangely, not one word of that comment made me feel any better. Smart-ass. At that James burst into Paul Bunyan laughter.

We worked that edge for another hour, where I apprehended a thirty-seven inch northern whom also managed to destroy my favorite yellow Slop Master. Somehow it discovered how to unhook the split ring and stole my blade. In an attempt to straighten out the bent pin arm, I snapped it off, leaving only a jig head and skirt. James thought that was funny, too. It wasn't a good day for my ever-shrinking tackle box.

One last stop before dark had us at the reef in front of Cyclone Point. Considering my options were much more limited than when the day started, I found myself throwing a blue with silver blade double 10. James utilized a black with orange bladed Ace bait. We maneuvered in a 360 degree circle, casting up on top of the reef but achieved no lookers. I contemplated trying off the rock spine that would be out in thirty-six feet of water, but felt something tackle my bait. I accomplished setting the hook, but something just didn't feel right. As I brought it up to the boat, we found that it wasn't a musky on the other end. Here, a hefty twenty-inch smallmouth bass with a monster appetite greeted us. "Can you believe such a little guy would try and eat a double 10?" In all my fishing adventures, I never envisioned a small mouth bass with such delusions of grandeur. Part of me wanted this guy to be brought home to my local lake to breed more super smallies. He was fun!

BY **BRAD MATHEWSON**

CHAPTER XLI

SOME GUYS HAVE ALL THE LUCK

The next morning finally brought about a condition change. The weatherman told us to expect winds around ten-to-fifteen all day, with overcast skies and a fifty-fifty shot of scattered showers and highs down in the mid-eighties. After nineties and ball-sweating humidity for the past few days, a little breeze and slightly lower temps had us enjoying any break we could get. Honestly, I was praying for those showers to cool us down a little more.

I woke up that morning with the instincts that the fish would be hiding out in windward side of any reed covered area we could find. There's two small islands at the entrance of

GoHere Bay, and were connected by a rocky spine with a nice reed bed. Truth be told, there were some nice reeds all the way around the two islands. But the wind had produced a nice current in the neck-down area, between the two islands, and it felt rather fishy. Reeds usually begged for a spinner bait because it tends to slide right between the reeds without getting hung up. If it does get snared, you can just flick your wrist and make the bait dance across the water like a fleeing bait fish. That has led to many muskies in the net. Just five minutes into our experiment, I had raised a nice mid-forty inch fish and hooked and lost a low-thirty inch musky at the boat.

"Let's go around to the backside where I can see an eddie forming, maybe someone is home," queried James. "I like the way you think." On the first cast into the eddie by James, I find a large wake chasing the rhythmic cadence of his Fire Tiger Bobbie bait all the way back to the boat. "I think you gotta forty inch fish on your tail, James." Like an angry drunk, the musky violently swipes at the bait but misses. It then tries again, and misses again. Third time was not a charm, either. This left James in a pickle. The fish was all but boat-side now, and you can't really figure eight a Bobbie with little to no room to maneuver. "Brad, come back here quick and figure eight this fish with your spinner bait." I head for the back of the boat and ensue a figure eight. The fish whirls around twice, but real deep and lazy-like. It gave the perception of being only half-interested, but suddenly struck and my rod loaded up tight. I deposit the hooks while James, in disbelief, dug for the tangled up net. Not until he scooped up my fish did we both realize it wasn't the upper-forty incher we thought, but a puny twenty-seven inch baby musky. James must have brought them both back to the boat, and when the big one wouldn't go for my presentation, the little guy shot in and stole the bait.

"Is that where the phrase "bait and switch" came from? Dirty buggers," James proclaimed. "I can't believe that little fish would even try to steal a meal from such a large musky," I said. Before James could say another word, he found himself back in the mix with another fight on his hands. This time, a tiny pike, probably no more than twenty inches long, had half the Bobbie bait down its throat and hooked so horribly it had to be part of our fish fry that evening. We would need it and a bunch more if we wanted to eat that night, anyway. This little guy was doing us a favor by volunteering. I don't usually eat many pike back home in Wisconsin, but the pike we do eat for our fish fries are some of the best tasting fish I have ever eaten. I believe pike are not normally kept for the grease bath because guys had a bad experience while filleting them. I will admit, until someone showed me how to deal with the Y – bone, I didn't like to clean them, either. But once the technique is sound, the chore is mitigated and taste buds are treated.

This brought about a change in tactics, as we had twelve hungry musky hunters' bellies to fill that evening. It was time to go on a pike parade. We spent the next thirty minutes throwing spinner baits into the reeds and apprehending pike to plate. We ended up keeping two more, one at twenty-six inches, and the other just a half inch larger. You're not allowed to keep anything between 27.6" – 35.4" and only one can be over 35.4". The rest must be under 27.6". Thankfully, we find the fish under twenty-seven inches are excellent table fare, and are quite robust for their length due to the lake's bio mass. I tend to have a hard time putting the fillet knife to any fish over the thirty-five inch mark. I'd rather put it back to enjoy another day. Besides, when a cold front comes in, sometimes the random pike we catch will help me alleviate the musky blues.

By half past noon, it was time for lunch and a much needed break. We anchored the boat in the calm water on the backside of an island, within a hundred yards of a weedy bay. During our lunch break, we watched Jerry and Wolfy working a nearby island complex. All of a sudden, Jerry started yelling for Wolfy to get the net. Moments later, the sixty-three year old Jerry whooped it up like a teenage school girl who just scored the game wining bucket. Jerry held up an extremely large musky in the front of the boat while Wolfy snapped a hero picture.

My curiosity was getting the best of me. "Should we go over and see what he got?" "Knowing Jerry, I'd bet he'll bee-line it over here once he releases it to rub it in our noses," James stated with a roll of his eyes. Sure as shit, a few minutes later Jerry's tiller fired up and he was in our grills as fast as you can say "suck it". "You guys catch anything yet today?" chortled Jerry with a shit-eating grin slapped across his puss. I puffed out my chest, and in the best impersonation of an overly confident musky superstar, I boasted with the story of how we duped a massive twenty-seven inch musky from the nursery and impaled him on my Slop Master. "Well, if you guys want, I could give you guys a few free lessons on how to catch full grow mature musky," laughed the glowing Jerry. My ax being ground pretty well by this point, I shoot back, "I was taught never to take advantage of the elderly, especially when they are clearly suffering from a case of dementia!" With his patience thoroughly drained, James finally spouted out," Alright Jerry, how big was the musky you just snagged?"

"I'll tell you this. We'll have a new leader on the Largest Musky board. She was a portly forty-six inch beast of a fish. While you boys were taking a siesta, us musky hunters were putting inches on the board, and slime on our hands!" Jerry voiced a diaphragm laugh. "Now you two enjoy your little picnic. We don't want to keep our muskies waiting any further," bragged Wolfy.

As Jerry and Wolfy sped away, I surveyed an eagle, perched on top of a large decaying white pine not fifty yards from us, swoop down and grab a small pike. It landed on the nearby pebble-strewn beach and mowed its lunch. I scanned to the west and viewed another eagle deep-dive down from his lookout tower and conjure up a fish sandwich of its own. With a suddenly renewed sense of purpose, I asked if James just saw what I did. "Mother Nature never fails to put on a beautiful show on Lake Of The Woods," said James. "Sure, it's all amazing, but something is happening here that we need to be a part of before it's over!" James cocked his head like a quizzical puppy. "Have you ever heard that when the eagles are fishing, so should you. If they just hang out in the trees, then you should be enjoying a cocktail instead of wasting time washing baits."

Some of you may scoff at that notion. You could say "Brad, you ignorant fool, you can catch a musky any damn time, whether the eagles are feeding or not. Or, whatever the lunar chart states don't mean jack, you Pagan-loving ogre!" Sure, that might be true, I'll admit. But there are many tools in any decent musky hunter's tackle box. One of those is observance of Mother Nature, be it by watching the weather or her living creatures. Many times a bite can take place when something as simple as a lake fly hatch occurs. This unpredictable occurrence can set in motion a chain reaction in the food chain that may only last a half hour. If you aren't cognizant that this natural occurrence happens, you could be missing out on what we hunters see as a window of opportunity to capitalize on the muskies kryptonite, food. A hatch seems to raise up all the biomass in the water column. Example – flies raise up out of the soft lake bed toward the surface to begin their life-cycle. Hungry perch and crappies are there to greet them at the all-you-can-eat buffet. When a large school of perch and crappie are feeding, Mr. Musky dreams of perch nuggets and coleslaw to fill his own growling tummy. It's the circle of life, and if you miss out knowing that fact, you'll have better luck fishing in the local grocery store. Though, that would probably be frowned upon.

Witnessing eagles feeding, and being aware of the feeding frenzy that was occurring at that very moment, James blurted out, "IT'S MUSKY TIME!!!!" We could see a nice weedy bay from our lunchroom, so I believed it to be a great place to start our search. While sputtering over to the water garden, something lurking captured my eye. "James, stop the boat. A large musky is sunning itself on the shallow rock bar. Wow, that might be in about a foot of water!" As the boat wound to a halt, I jumped up on the front casting deck with a rod sporting a pink Show Girl on the line. I casted out in the general direction of where I had last seen the musky, but as we pulled up, she streaked for deeper water. I was left hoping her charge wouldn't take her to another area code. Not really anticipating for the musky to show itself, I was elated to see a solid fifty incher appear from nowhere to within a couple of feet from where I was going to go into my figure eight.

I went into a large looping eight with my 8'6" St. Croix, but it never really committed to it. Instead, it kept on motoring right under the boat. We then made a short drift, fanning the water. I happened to glance over to the Locator and noticed perhaps why she was in the area to begin with. A large bait ball school of small walleyes appeared on the screen. I figured they were walleyes because James and his son had fished walleyes in the same twelve-foot hole, adjacent to the shallow weedy bay, three times the prior year and netted one little walleye after another, with a ¼ ounce jig tipped with a tiny mister twister tail.

"I'm going to lift up the trolling motor and scurry past the beginning of this hole in order to drift across. Maybe we can make contact with that musky, again," I voiced over to the ever-reeling James. "Brilliant plan." Upon reaching the end of the hole, we embark on our silent drift. James changed over to toss an eight-inch Fire Tiger Bobbie bait while I pitched out a walleye colored, regular-sized Bulldog. About halfway into our drift, I see James rear back and drive the hooks home like a champ. It was difficult to tell if this particular musky James had hooked into was either really smart, or really stupid. It swam back towards the boat at warp speed, forcing James to struggle picking up enough line to not allow slack. "Reel as fast as you can, James! Too much slack and she'll be long gone!" I barked out, getting the net at the ready. Before James could utter a word, she captured in my waiting net, and none-to-happy that her plan had been foiled. The old Bobbie bait had hooked her solid, obligating us to pare the hooks with my Knipex hook cutters.

While on that subject, we spend a ton of cash on our rods, reels, lures, and even electronics. All that said, I'm astounded at what some guys have in their boats for release tools. Now, this is just my opinion, but you should have a quality pair of hook cutters, (Knipex is the best on the market, hands down). You should also make sure you have two or even three pairs of needle nose pliers. It's almost guaranteed that you will lose a pair or two to the lake bottom. As I've said numerous times in this, sh** happens. Also keep a set of mouth spreaders, split ring pliers, and a set of release gloves in your boat at all times. Keep all this in one small, easy to access tackle box, labeled in bold lettering "RELEASE KIT". At minimum, we owe it to these grand fish, and to our musky brothers and sisters, to CPR (catch, picture, release) these beautiful fish as quickly and safely as possible, so they can be enjoyed for years to come by all. (Or, at least by me again.)

Peering into the net, I was expecting to find the grand fifty-incher we'd been chasing the entire trip. Instead, James had himself a respectable forty and one-half inch musky. After completing the C.P.R, I eyeballed the locator screen and found us to be right on top of that school of fish. This meant there had to be a few hungry muskies hanging around the area. Knowing that, the blood began to pump hard through our veins, and you couldn't cast out fast enough. But as with many best laid plans, it was not to be. We drifted the area three more times with not so much as a follow. Our once abundant bait ball had all but evaporated. The winds completely died, the soaring eagles returned to their branches, and Mother Nature flipped us the bird. (Pun intended).

Sunset was upon us as we hit our typical last spots of the day. We fished a reef near Wolf Island, where I had a low-forty incher miss my Top Raider twice, just off the north side of the reef. My last cast by Wolf Island hooked me up with a stud forty two inch Northern Pike. With our last stop being the reef in front of Cyclone Point, which always grants us a musky, provided a forty-inch raise for yours truly, while James raised a hefty forty-five inch musky on his Bobbie bait. But just like the waning sunlight, both were lazy and only left us thirsting for more.

CHAPTER XLII

TROUBLE FOR NOTHING

Just when you think you have Mother Nature all figured out, she spits in your eye and torques your junk. The next morning brought us a whole new weather pattern. Gone was the near ninety degree oppressive humidity. This morning slapped us with cool and crisp Canadian air, almost like an mid-spring day. The temperature was barely sixty degrees, with a northwest wind at ten mph. The local weather-jerk said there was to be a seventy-five percent chance of rain that afternoon, and highs would only tickle sixty-six. With that forecast staring us in the face, I crawled into my lightweight rain bibs and raincoat so they covered my shorts and T-shirt. Surprisingly, I felt quite comfortable.

I was a bit excited on this morning, which admittedly is every morning, but this one had our plan of attack consisting of a five-gallon can of gas. That could only mean one thing – a run over to King Island to fish the old milk run! James had a small sixteen-foot deep V with a forty HP tiller, and with five hundred pounds of bullshit and fish fries between James and I, it was a lot for that little motor to push around. Hence, the need for extra fuel.

The first stop on our twenty-five minute journey was a spot we called 'Whale Rock'. This locale had produced dozens of fish for our group over the years. The backside of the large rock consisted of a very small, shallow, reedy cove that was protected from the wind. And it always held fish from the mid-forties on up to over fifty inches. I never saw a puny fish in this area, so to me, it was a 'Hefties Hangout'.

A single boulder in the middle of the reeds received my first cast of the day. The moment my bait touched liquid, an enormous musky jettisoned through my black chrome spinner bait as if it were in an action movie. I struggled to engage my reel. The handle spun freely and the thumb bar stuck down and I couldn't get it to engage so I could set the hook. After moments lost, which was probably only thirty seconds, the thumb bar popped up and I was able to crank the handle to pick up line. By that time, it was too late. Mr. Musky was gone.

"What the heck was that!? Why didn't you set the hook?" yelped James. "This piece of crap wouldn't engage!" I barked back as I finished reeling in the slack. "I got a real good look at the fish. It had to be pushing at least fifty inches, maybe more. Good news is I saw her swim back further into the reeds. Think if we go around to the other side of Whale Rock, you might get another chance at her." The reel I was using was brand new Abu Garcia Toro 6.4:1 -HS, specifically for this trip. I had taken a few practice casts, and everything worked like a charm during the dry runs. Worked perfectly well all week until when I needed it the most.

With the trolling motor at half speed, we crawled into position for our ambush. Utilizing the same bait, James let me have a redemption cast. In an instant, it was living a déjà vu. The musky steamrolled my spinner, while my reel pissed its pants. You could spin the damn handle around a hundred times and it wouldn't pick up any line. I'm not a violent person by any means, but if the person who assembled that specific reel would have been within a hundred yards of me, I would have used my rod as a javelin, flung it at his heart, which would have repelled his ass and the reel right into the lake. I'd have then waited until his lifeless corpse floated near the boat's motor, cranked it on full throttle, and left them for the eagles to pray on. Actually, that's a bit unfair. The rod had nothing to do with this epic failure. No sense wasting a great rod over a piece of crap reel.

After cussing the whole reel manufacturer's family name into oblivion, that damn thing suddenly engaged. Being that it was five minutes too late, I'm convinced it was out of pure spite. To ensure this didn't happen a third time, I gave the reel a couple practice casts, but it would malfunction every time. I tried to turn every knob and button, but it had become utterly useless. I knew the retailer who sold me this lemon would replace it, no questions asked. But he was back in Wisconsin, and I would be down to only my 5.4:1 Revo Toro for the rest of the day. I had left my other high-speed reel back at the cabin, not thinking this hot mess would kick me in the junk. Plus, we both had agreed to only bring two rods each day, as there was only so much room in James' small boat.

"Brad, you might be the most unlucky guy I've ever fished with. You could have hooked a fifty inch musky two different times, and managed to come up empty handed," giggled James. "You'd think a three-hundred buck reel would be a little more dependable! I waited an entire year to come to Canada, which is really my only vacation this year. A trip where one big fish can make an entire trip worth every penny, and then in a blink of an eye, a Chuck Norris kick to the marble bag!" I whined. James nearly busted his own bag laughing at my dismay. "Remember the old PMA! (Positive. Musky, Attitude). There are plenty of muskies out there, just waiting for you to not catch them!" I strongly contemplated throwing my friend and that reel into the lake. After a brief moment, I realized that I needed someone to split the gas bill with, so I decided against it. The question that remained was, for how long before I thought better of it.

Two hours passed before we ventured back to Whale Rock to give it the third-time's-the-charm trick. It didn't take long to realize that nobody was home on either side of the cove. We found a small garage, cut right in the middle of the thirty-foot Whale Rock, so perhaps Captain Fifty was hiding inside. I swapped my spinner bait out for a black & silver bladed double 10. With a flick of the wrist, I placed it snug against the back wall of the garage. Halfway back to the boat, the bait garnered the attention of a nice mid-forty inch musky. I vexed whisking it back to the boat, but found the need for my high-speed reel was dire. The fish darted into the first outside turn of my figure eight with its pants on fire, but when I went three-dimensional by going deep, she lost interest and puttered back to her home. To counter, I exchanged to a baby loon colored Top Raider and fired it right back into the garage. A small wake materialized about ten feet from the boat. James gawked as he witnessed a wide open mouth in the deep, but disappeared before I could venture a figure eight.

By this time, my PMA was barely intact, but still had a pulse. I dove deep into my tackle box for a very specific lime green Reef Hawg. With my confidence shaken, but not stirred, I fired it back into that musky's cozy little home with every intention of finally landing that water pig. Within seconds, my heart skipped ten beats! I had finally hooked into a nice....ten-foot long branch. For a moment, I swore it was a new world record musky. Upon my discovery, though, I decided to release it back to its home. A hundred and twenty inches would have been a record, I'm sure, but it wasn't something I'd take a picture with.

"This spot has whooped my ass, royally!" I snarled. "I know when I've been beat." James reeled in his latest cast, chortling the whole time. "We're only a half-mile from the 'Dinner Table'. Let's zip over and give it a try." The 'Dinner Table' is a reef can't be found on any map. Truly, it's a potentially dangerous spot if you don't have it marked on your GPS properly. I have talked about this spot earlier (the real shallow water where I 'caught' a prehistoric rock fish), so I'll spare you from rehashing the details.

Anyway, Tracy and his boy, Garret, had been fishing this reef all week, at least once a day, and saw three fifty-inch fish. They even had one on the line, but lost it near the boat. After the previous failures, I was pretty pumped to be fishing a hot location. With one look to the North, my juices got flowing more. The partly cloudy skies were being dry-erased by a black cloak of fire swords and devil's breathe. James, always thinking ahead, tensed up at the anger heading our way. "Maybe we should head for cover before this thing blows up on us." I, on the other hand, had a different perspective. "Are you insane? This is the prime time to catch a giant musky! Studies say big muskies turn on just as a storm is about to hit. They also come alive within a few short minutes afterwards. There is no better place to be than on a musky hole when Mother Nature gets crazy!"

In my excitement over the darkening sky, I dropped the trolling motor into the blue. The sky crackled like an unwanted Christmas globe from your ex-girlfriend. The boat vibrated, sending shivers down James' spine. "That seemed close to me. I think we should head for cover." "Quit being a baby and start fishing! That bolt was a least a mile away. Besides, it's just Mother Nature's way of keeping us from raiding her cookie jar," I jested, as I tossed out the line for another crack. Another, louder cloud explosion erupted. "I think your brain's been raided and replaced with cookie crumbs," contemplated

James. Upon James stating "crumbs", an enormous, earth-shaking detonation nearly created white caps on the bay. I'll admit, that one even made my soul nervous. "Getting louder. Ought to wake up that fifty-incher!" James had had enough of my shenanigans. "Pick up the trolling motor! We're getting the hell out of here!" I nearly had my line back in the boat. "I've only made two casts," I said. Then, another ear-splitting crash lit up the sky. "What are you waiting for? Let's beat it! That streak made the hair on my arm stand up!" I cried.

As we made for shore, we spotted an old boathouse that resembled a dilapidated chicken cope. The closer we got, though, showed that it was protecting a dock that appeared to be a dry place to wait out the storm. Once we escaped inside, the skies opened a Hoover Dam floodgate. You could barely see ten feet in any one direction. The heavens erupted in a game of cosmic bowling where electricity filled the blackened lanes. It was about ten in the morning when we had entered our boathouse, and it wasn't until quarter after eleven before we deemed it safe enough to resume fishing. Of course, just as we pulled out from the shelter, a lightning bolt struck the ground maybe a quarter-mile from our heads. With that, it was back into the boathouse. Twenty more minutes passed with no further electricity raining down from the sky, so with the rain dwindled down to a light mist, we went for broke.

"James, I think we should fish Musky Alley. We're only a short boat ride away," I claimed as I made my way back in to the boat. "I like that idea! Need a few more Northern Pike for the fish fry, and that area is loaded with eater-size

Pike," James agreed. My thought was that since it was named 'Musky Alley', you know, for all the muskies living there. James thought of it as a pike residence. Go figure. As a short refresher, Musky Alley is basically a back bay behind an island surrounded by a bog with constant current and a long, narrow appearance reminiscent of an alley. I'm convinced there are natural springs that feed the area, because the water clarity is unlike anywhere else on the lake. Plus, the diversity of weeds is beyond compare, making it every musky hunters dream come true.

The plan of attack was simple. We'd drive up the Alley as far as we could, which usually was just before the weeds cut you off. During years of high water, you could drive the whole damn thing and come out on the other side of the Island. This clearly was not one of those years. We made it about three-quarters of the way in before James shut the tiller down. Picture a clear-running, almost river-like strip in the middle of a large weedy bay. The Alley itself has current and runs six-to-eight feet deep. It measures about forty yards wide, with large lily pads growing tight together for a couple hundred yards on either side. Where James stopped put us in the clear current floating back the way we came. The Alley was stuffed full of beautiful red cabbage and coontail, and the rain fell ever so lightly, barely enough to break the mirrored water surface. The muskies and Northern Pike have only a second to decide to eat or not in these conditions. Our scheme was to slowly drift toward new hiding places within this alley, and discover more hungry fish.

"I got one, James! Get the net!" I screamed out and I yanked on the rod with all my might. My orange and black spinner bait had glanced the water and was smacked by, what felt like, a damn nice fish. Upon a quick victory, I gazed into the net at my prize: a thirty-four and one-half inch pip-squeak stared back at me. At least it was a good start. "They can't all be fifty inches, Brad," proclaimed James. He was right, but you could have said that with every single fish I detained. I felt that one of these fish SHOULD be a fifty-incher. You'd think by dumb luck I'd eventually get my mitts on one of them.

After a quick picture, James and I went right back to fishing. After a light downpour, within five minutes, James hooked a thirty-eight incher on a black and orange spinner bait. Our trend line was going in a positive direction, though his fish needed extra attention. It had the trailer hook lodged in its throat, and the front hook pinned both jaws together. In a situation like this, the fish becomes more important than the bait. I swiftly deployed my Knipex hook cutters and dismantled the bait. Thankfully, the musky didn't bleed like one would think, being that it was hooked in the throat. When we released him, the musky swam off strong.

We were in a zone, and we both knew it. To support that claim, my next cast had a mid-forty inch fish sway up to the boat, only it had very little interest in the bait itself. Damn thing seemed to be checking out the boat. I clicked up the speed on the trolling motor and cruised back upstream to make another cast to that same spot. That same fish swam past my perfect figure eight and instead, rested on the bottom of the lake. James cocked an eye as he searched deep in the water. "It looks like that fish is missing scales on one side of his body." I nod my head in agreement. "His fins looked like they were split on the same side, too." It was an interesting sight, as those types of injuries wouldn't be natural. We found out later that night that a couple guys, who were residing at the King Island Resort, had snared that fish earlier in the day and thought it was a good idea to net the musky and bring it into the boat. While these intellectual giants processed the snapping of hero pictures, the macho fishing morons decided not to wear gloves and dropped the musky into the bottom the boat. The boat carpeting caused damage to the fins and scales before these two numb-nuts grabbed the fish and got it back into the water. Two guys from our group observed the whole thing happening.

Guys and gals, study the situation BEFORE speeding to your prove-it-picture. Keep the musky in the net, and keep that net in the water, with the net tangled in the boat cleat as to not lose it. If you feel you could cause damage to the fish by normal extraction, unhook your musky by safely cutting any hooks and remove them carefully. Only then, get your camera ready. Make sure your buddy is pointing the right side of the camera in your relative direction, otherwise you'll end up with a picture of his ugly mug instead of your trophy. To keep from getting painful gill raker cuts, make sure to toss your gloves on. Not until this moment should you raise the musky out of the net. Treat it like a baby. Support its belly with your opposite hand like cradling the back of a baby's head. Never hold a musky while only holding its jaw. I have seen way too many pics of guys hanging a musky's full body weight by its jaw. This can cause skeletal damage to the fish and even kill it. An old-timer once told me, "you wouldn't pick up your dog by his jaw and dangle him around, would you?" Lastly, never have the musky out of the water for more than thirty seconds. You wouldn't want me to hold your head under water for more than ten seconds, so be equally considerate of your catch.

Anyway, we were in a tight window of hungry fish. On my very next cast out I clutched another musky this one was forty inches. Needing the hero picture, I dove into my waterproof bag and came up empty. "James? Have you seen my camera?" "Ummm, I set it on the cooler after your last musky," said James. I peered at my cooler and resting there, in the pouring rain, sat the brand new Fuji camera my wife had purchased for me on Christmas. We stood at about a half hour of steady rain since James had taken a picture of my last musky. My blood was boiling.

"Forgive me if I'm wrong, but wouldn't it have been a better idea to, I don't know, put my camera somewhere dry!" "It's your camera," explained James. I was mighty tempted to see if my fishing partner could hold his breath underwater for a full six minutes. But he was right. It was my camera and my responsibility. Not that it mattered by this point, I shoved the camera back in its waterproof bag. I pulled my cell phone from my inside rain jacket pocket to get a quick check of the time. Sure as shit, it was also wet, and the screen was fogged. I was fit to be tied. With every passing second, this day was getting more expensive. Plus, this meant that my extra expensive rain jacket was no better stopping the water than a drunk girls white t-shirt at spring break.

Shaking off the flattening of my wallet, James and I caught nearly forty Northern Pike and raised eight more muskies over the next hour and a half. We kept three pike for the fish fry that evening and release the rest. "I know we're supposed to be catching muskies, but it's a nice change of pace actually catching fish. Renews the spirit, so the speak," I admitted. It felt dirty to admit that, especially knowing how much time, effort, and cash I spend going to Canada to specifically chase the Canadian Shield. Sometimes some action to get the heart pumping can invigorate the soul and push you through those ten thousand casts until your next musky strike. "The whole 'catching X number of fish' thing is more of a kid thing. But it sure feels good crossing some eyes from time to time," laughed James.

By the time our drift completed, the weather turned for the worse, and by worse, normal humans would say better. The sun came out, turned blue the previously disgusting skies, and the wind crapped out to almost nothing. We made another run up Musky Ally and drifted back again in hopes of repeating history. This time, no Northern Pike or muskies were to be found. Mother Nature pulled the rug out from under us once more. No matter which bait or technique we exasperated, we couldn't get anything to bite. "Time to blow this taco stand!" I uttered, my patience having been completely spent. "Deer Bay?" James gestured as he toiled around with the motor. Before the word 'Bay' left his lips, I could feel the excitement building inside.

Deer Bay was the site of my largest musky, which won me the biggest musky contest the prior year. For whatever reason, we had been on the lake for seven days and hadn't even given the bay a single thought. As we arrived at the mouth of the bay, the large weed bed that had been present last year was now gone. In its place, a new weed bed on the far end of the bay, that wasn't there last year, had formed. The unknown giants that had to be hidden in that newly formed shelter made the mouth drool. As we neared the new bed, the bluebird skies I despised for the last couple hours had been replace by a menacing strip of heinous clouds.

Unlike earlier, the first lightning bolt and rumble of thunder from this bad-ass had me stowing the trolling motor and us heading back toward camp. About a mile from camp, we realized that the storm had moved off towards the east and was going to leave us high and dry. Instead of crying over split milk, we yanked out our rods (no, not those rods), and fished our way back toward camp. After getting tied up to the docks, we ventured to the general store to purchase some dry rice in an attempt at saving my cell phone and camera. Somewhere I had heard people yapping about shoving their dampened electronics into a bag of dry rice, (brown the preferred rice because it was less dusty) in order to salvage their usefulness. Fortunately, I was able to purchase rice, but all I found on the shelves was one lonely bag of white, instant rice. White or not, I needed its healing powers to breathe life back into my modern day vices, just as it had sustained people for hundreds of years.

By **BRAD MATHEWSON**

Just when I thought things couldn't get much worse, James and I were devastated when we discovered the boat fly swatter in the shape of a hand had been broken at it's wrist. To those who have never been to the great country of Canada, there symbol is not the eagle, like that of America. It is the black fly with its piranha-like teeth and an unquenchable thirst for musky hunter blood. On each of my previous hunts in Canada, I had been quite fortunate never to have encountered these tiny demons. But I was well studied in the horror stories from my grandfather on a trip he had taken back in the seventies. I heard they can be brutal in the spring, but by summer's end, they all but die off. Apparently, for whatever reason, they enjoy biting your ankles while you're in the middle of a cast. This would leave you with a choice: start turning your reel just as the bait hits the water, which in-turn spins your blades immediately and possible enticing a strike, or swat, miss the bastard, only to have him return once again when your bait is mid-air and about to land on a waiting musky's lair. The choice, though painful, is obvious.

Back at the resort dock while unloading gear that we stored in the lodge's basement for safe keeping, I find another item the rain potentially ruined. My musky journal, which carried many of this book's stories, was drenched. I scurried back to my room and spent the next hour carefully separating waterlogged pages apart and begging for clothes hangers off everyone. I sure hope my observations don't evaporate like my luck has. All I could do was wait until morning to see what a new day brought. It would be a sleepless night.

BY **BRAD MATHEWSON**

CHAPTER XLIII

ALL LESSONS LEARNED

The night was sleepless and dreary. Thoughts of my Musky Journal being forever lost rattled my subconscious, triggering dreams to be dank nightmares. I had spent years carefully articulating events of my Canadian adventures into a memoir. The thought of losing them over something so outlandish stabbed my soul. No longer being able to pretend I was sleeping, I rushed to my hanging journal only to find that the pages appeared to be drying rather sluggishly. In search of something, anything, that could assist its salvage, I rummaged through a closet and obtained a small box fan. I nabbed a folding chair and placed the fan at an angle to blow the pages. I peered around the room and realized this was basically lighting a match to heat a church. The room provided the picture of clothes hangers laden with ink-smudged notebook papers decorating every conceivable nook and cranny in the entire room. Some pages had stuck together unbeknownst to me, leaving me the chore of plucking wet confetti apart in hopes it would stay somewhat legible. That morning, this was all that mattered. Even more so than hunting muskies.

"I think everything is gonna dry quite nicely with that fan," said James. I'm not sure if he was being sarcastic or not, but I had to take every bit of positive reinforcement from my friend I could get. And with that, I realized there wasn't much else I could do at the moment to save my written memories. The only thing left to do was make new ones.

There was a slight nip in the air, meaning in a week or two, fall inevitably would take over. For Canada, these were the last weeks of summer, and worst of all, this was to be our last day fishing Lake of the Woods. We would all journey back by seven o'clock that evening to enjoy our last night of freedom from the daily grind of life. Some of us would go back to our kids, our wives, those jobs we hate. But for one last day, we were musky brothers there to out-duel one another. That evening at the main lodge, our host, Tim, would be awarding our annual Biggest Musky Award. Since I was the defending champion, the pressure was on to prove I could hang with these big dogs, and ultimately prove that last year was no fluke. With that, I had to stare down my rival, the one man who stood between me and this year's grand prize: a brand new Musky rod.

"Well, Brad. Today's the last day. Good luck out there. I hope you catch a big one," offered up Jerry. His comment made my eyes twitch and narrow in thought. "I'm not falling for any of your reverse psychology crap, Jerry," I shot back. Jerry shrugged his shoulders and smiled. "OK. Don't catch a big musky, then." As Jerry meandered towards his boat, I barked across the lot. "I know what you're doing, Jerry. You're going down! This is my year! I've just been biding my time to build up the drama!" I may well have known my bark was worse than my bite, but it sure sounded good. Don't get me wrong, Jerry is a great friend and an even better musky hunter. He has grasped more muskies than I'll probably ever see in my lifetime. With that experience comes his very competitive nature, coupled with my own competitive personality makes beating him only sweeter. Plus, there's a big fish pot where everyone throws in ten bucks. This year it was at $120, so it was a nice offset to the gas bill. "Just remember, you have to beat forty-six inches to win!" yodeled Jerry, as he and Wolfy sped away from the dock. James leapt into the boat, "We're up here to have fun. Don't listen to him." "Au contraire, we're here to kick Jerry's ass and win the Largest Musky title! The fun happens when I get to rub his nose in it at the party tonight!" I announced as I sprang in the boat myself. "There's no time to explore new spots or to even fish old spots that produced in the past. Our plan must be to only fish where we've recently seen big muskies." Being the last day, it was a sound plan, and the only one that could net me back-to-back titles.

The first stop on the 'Title or Nothing' tour had us in the weedy cove where James had lost his big musky. We didn't necessarily think we'd catch her again, but more hoping to get some sort of closure on the whole incident. As we tackled the area for the last time on this trip, I did manage to raise a forty-incher on a yellow Slop Master. The follow up cast produced another follow by the same musky, only this time she turned on my bait on the outside corner of my figure eight and stole my white trailer grub. Apparently, that grub must have really hit the spot. We worked that area for another twenty minutes without another sighting. As James reeled in another empty cast, he joked with me. "That fish is going to be bound up for a good week. She could probably use a shot of Metamucil!" Nobody can make James laugh quite the way James can make James laugh.

On our way to the next hole, GoHere Bay, I got a quick temperature gauge reading. It was nearly nine in the morning and was only sixty degrees. The weather-dick had predicted bluebird skies and eighty degrees, with NW wind ranging from ten to fifteen. We had to hit GoHere Bay on our last day because days earlier, Jerry managed to hook a giant there, only to lose it feet from the boat. That meant the big bastard should still be around, and if I was gonna rub it in old man Hoelzel's face, what better fish to do it than with than one he let get away. Our plan of attack was to fish the outside edge of a deep weed line, which normally held a pile of small walleyes. I was betting that was where Jerry blew his chance at the fifty-incher. I casted on the shallow cabbage with an Elvis double 10, while James went parallel with the fifteen-foot weed edge employing a Fire Tiger X-Rap. From what I could tell, a large school of, what I perceived to be, small walleyes and large arcs danced across James' fish locator. Just as we found our way over to that school, James' rod bowed to the water. "Get the net! I think I have a big one! It just stayed down!" yelled James.

My heart raced with excitement. I was about to net the big musky Jerry had lost. I'll admit, I was quickly jealous of James, because I wanted to be the man to beat Jerry with the musky he couldn't get into the net. As with most every single damn apprehension in this documentary, all was not to be. The fish that appeared at the surface was really a thirty-nine inch Northern Pike only pretending to be a fifty-four inch musky. How deflating for James. Deep down, I knew the day was to be my day, not James. The competitive spirit powered through my veins. I couldn't allow Jerry to beat me, again. It's a damn long year of ear chewing when he wins the title. If any ear was to be gnawed off, I'd be the one doing it.

While working the edge all the way down until we came back up to the 4 foot flat, I couldn't stop thinking about the large arcs that ran across the locator. In my open-water experience, I found when you find a school of bait fish, or what some refer to as a 'bait ball', whether that be whitefish or ciscoes, or walleyes, perch, crappies, or whatever. If you see large arcs near them, nine times out of ten, those arcs are muskies. Now, just because you have muskies doesn't mean you have hungry muskies. Arcs that are tight to the bottom of the school of fish are the only ones worth casting to, because they are feeding. When you see arcs above or well below the school, it usually means they're neutral fish. It's not impossible to turn neutral fish into biters, but in my personal experience, it's not worth the time to find out.

You're far better off working active fish than trying to turn them into active fish.

"We have to drift this area one last time. I just don't want to waste any more effort if we don't at least raise a musky," I proclaimed to James. As we motored back to our starting position, I noticed the same arcs tight to the bottom of the bait ball. "Do you think those are muskies?", asked James as he peered over my shoulder at the monitor. "Not sure. Could be a pack of Northern Pike," I ventured to guess. There was only one sure way to find out. After deploying the trolling motor, I purposely sped past unproductive water to get us to that arced school. It was killing me to not know what was the cause of that arc. The best plan of attack was to circle the school to pick it apart from all sides. With a toss of my Elvis (the king), I reeled it back.

As it worked its way through, what I perceived as, the edge of the bait ball, I felt a light 'tap'. A second later, another. I abruptly set the hook and the battle was on. Whatever was on mimicked James' fish from early and forced its way down. "I'll bet you a hundred bucks it's a Northern Pike. Probably the same size as yours," I wagered. Sure enough, the pike came up next to the boat and into James' waiting net. She was quite robust, and as I went to unhook her, I found the need for a jaw spreader. Once she opened up for a quick surgery, I found an eater-sized walleye deep in her throat. That would explain the chubby figure of this girl. She liked to eat at the all night Friday buffet, where one serving was never enough. When I placed her on the bump board, we found she was forty and one-half inches. This was the first time I knowingly held a pike that was hunting together in a pack. If muskies do it, why not pike. Plus, it's typical to have fish of the same size hunting together, so it made sense. With that information confirmed, there was no need to work the school any further. We were there to catch big muskies! (Though, pike are fun, too).

The next few hours drifted unproductively. Before we knew it, it was one o'clock. We must have tried at least a dozen spots in a 'run and gun' style, with no luck. My thought process convinced me that if we could narrow down to one big fish spot, we could raise a big one and either camp out or wait for a condition change.

With this in mind, we made our way to the mouth of Deer Bay. It was purely a gut feeling I had. "I'm going to win the tournament, right here in this bay," I pronounced with a slight delusion of grandeur. James simply nodded his head a few times. I sensed a little doubt. "Get your popcorn ready. I'm about to put on a show!" History would tell you that I was correct. I did have a knack of being entertaining to my fishing buddy. Problem was, it was usually hi-jinks and not trophy success.

The key on this bay was to utilize the uniqueness of its ability to grow very large lily that were widely distributed throughout the bay. This bay, compared to others we had fished, was very clear, with a beautiful carpet of red cabbage dancing on it's floor. I instructed James to motor us into the very middle of the bay, which averaged depths of eight feet. It was here that I felt we might find a larger specimen, whom, unlike its shallow four-foot or less occupying counterparts, hadn't been pressured by mindless double 10 chuckers. Don't get me wrong, double 10s have hooked me and many others a thousands muskies. But it seemed like our group had a ton of lookers and few hookers this year. Were these fish conditioned to the thumping of the double 10s? I heard from a few fellow experienced on Minnesotan waters that believe this is possible. Our group's collective experience on this trip, has swayed my opinion on the double 10.

An usually large lily pad, about twenty or so yards away, grabbed my eye. I used a Goldilocks Slop master for my next cast. This particular Slop Master was one that I had replaced the trailing Colorado blade on earlier in the week because a musky had somehow opened my split-ring, forcing me to replace it with an orange one I found in my hook box. That cast landed ten feet past the pad. It was a perfect view. The sun was to my back and lit up the red cabbage, setting the stage for my big moment that I knew was going to transpire. The musky hid in the cabbage bed beneath the large lily pad. As I reeled my spinner bait past the pad, I noticed a slight movement straight off the bottom. Everything went into a Matrix-like slow motion. The large musky flared his gills, revealing a red, fleshy cave with rows and rows of stalactites. My mind raced into a wet dream sequence where I battled the beast for an hour while it performed countless aerial jumps and surface barrel rolls. In the end, she was no match for my supreme rod and reel skills.

"SNAP OUT OF IT STUPID!" I think to myself. "Your ultimate goal awaits you at the end of the line! Set the F###ing hook and get her in the net!" Only then did my instincts take over. I set the hook so hard I thought my rod was gonna break in two. That moment bestowed fear over me. Fear of her getting away. "JAMES! GET THE NET!!!" I screamed like a crazed madman. I then proceeded to vent into the prototypical rant about how she was barely hooked and going to get off at any second. Even with all that blabber, for some reason this time, I really believed, it was going to finally happen. I peered over and James was dinking around reeling in his bait. This kicked in a full blown rage within me. This obsession of being the best and winning, making it two years in a row, was extremely important to me. I desperately craved everybody's respect for being a good musky hunter. I didn't feel I had done enough to earn any respect, but back-to-back titles would erase that fear from within me.

I fought her hard, all the way to the boat. My best guess had it between forty-eight and fifty-two inches, which would easily destroy Jerry's puny forty-six inch minnow. Another glance over found James struggling to get the extendable handle of the net pulled out, but it appeared tangled in the netting. "HURRY JAMES!" I bellowed. That's when my fear became reality. I secured a glimpse of her mouth, and she was barely hooked on the left side of her jaw. By now, the musky was at the boat and I was lost to know where to go with her. James hadn't gotten the net deployed yet, so I battled for what seemed like hours. Then, the shit hit the fan. Just as James put the net into the water, the musky head-thrashed underwater a mere three feet from the boat and spit my spinner bait. The musky must have been as shocked as I was that her prospective meal was striving to get away. In that very moment, everything reverted into slow-motion once more.

Surprisingly, I didn't panic. I knew my only chance was to act on the musky's instinctive nature. I sprung into a figure eight the second the bait jarred loose, and wasn't the least bit shocked when that worked. The musky froze dead-still the second my bait popped out, but now she was on a mission to make sure it didn't happen again. Its mouth was agape as she shrunk the distance from three feet down to 3 inches with a simple flip of its tail. My second chance battle was only a fraction of a second away. At that precise moment, my partner finally showed up with the net at the ready, but somehow only grazed the musky with the hoop of the net. The musky spooked violently under the boat, and off into parts unknown and out of my life, forever. It quite possibly was the worst trick Mother Nature ever played on me. I thought all was lost, only to be given the rarest of second chances, and then have my partner blow it for me.

"WHAT THE HELL WERE YOU DOING?!?!? YOU BLEW IT FOR ME! I'VE WAITED ALL YEAR FOR THIS VERY MOMENT, ONLY TO SEE IT STOLEN FROM ME, TWICE, IN LESS THAN THIRTY SECONDS?!?!" James placed the net back into the boat and rubbed his brow. "I'm sorry, Brad. I thought I could get her in the net," he apologized. I was fit to be tied. I knew it was one of those rare moments in life that could never be forgotten. I quickly went right back to fishing, but knew damn well it was over. Deep down my PMA had been stomped and was on life support.

We ended up fishing that whole bay for the next three and one-half hours in silence. We did raise two more muskies in the low forty-inch range. As the sun retreated on our last day of Canadian fishing, it's time of death was finally called. We had to start working our way back to the lodge to get supper going. On the ride back, I struggled to cool off. I probably hadn't said more than two words the previous few hours, and started feeling guilty about how I acted. "James. I'm sorry for how I reacted when the big musky was lost. I know things happen, and it's just fishing. Our group seems to have a lot of bad luck following it around," I admitted. James cracked a smile. "That's OK. I know how much you wanted to beat Jerry and win the Biggest Musky contest." When James mentioned that Jerry was to be the winner, a little red light flicked on inside my evil head. "How would you like to play a prank on your over confident brother? If he wins the Biggest Musky contest, I'll have to hear him gloat about it for an entire year. I've done that before, and trust me, it's not fun," I offered up. James' eyebrow cocked with interest and an evil grin of his own. "What do you have in mind?"

"Simple. We're probably gonna be the first ones back to the docks. Jerry will be the last. I'm gonna tell everyone the big musky story just as it happened. Then inform everyone not to tell Jerry that we lost the musky, but that I had actually hooked the winning fish and it measured forty-nine inches. We don't tell him until late tonight, after he's down in the dumps and I've had my chance to gloat and rub it in about being the champion two years in a row. The fact everyone will be in on it is just icing on the cake, he will be crushed!" In fairness to me, this sounded much better in person than in the moment. Looking back on it, it was probably a bit petty and a feeble attempt to fill an empty bravado. I was so infatuated with gloating in Jerry's face, I briefly lost what it meant to hunt with a group like this. It's rare to have a group of schmucks as great as these guys were to me. Yet, smashing their faces in whenever I could felt important. It took me a bit to realize that my availability to artificially gloat in Jerry's face was also taking away his opportunity to enjoy his actual success.

As the second boat motored into the bay, I saw that it was Steve and Allen. I knew they would be all-in, so I tell them my heart-breaking story and devious plan. Of course, they were all-in. "What are you going to do when Jerry asks to see the picture on your digital camera?" questioned Steve. "I already thought of that. I just happen to have the same SD card with last year's forty-eight inch musky picture on it. I'll just change the date on the photo. No way Jerry recognizes it's the same fish!" I said. "I don't know about this prank anymore. Seems a bit harsh," admitted James. "To me, harsh is just another way to show a buddy how much you care. Plus, we'll all get a good laugh out of it," I explained to James. As the rest of the guys trudged back into camp, the story was told and everyone understood that nothing was to be said until that evening at the main lodge.

Just as I had thought, Jerry was the last one in. I was like a kid waiting to unwrap the first gift on Christmas morning. "So, young man, how did you do?" asked Jerry. I could hardly contain myself, but had to stay calm and convincing, and keep a perfectly straight face in order for the prank to work. "You'll never believe it, Jerry. I hauled in a forty-nine inch musky today!" I announced, allowing a shit-eating grin to etch on my face. The color in Jerry's face deepened a few shades red. "Well, congratulations. Let's see a picture and hear the story!" I was taken aback a little. It wasn't exactly the heart crushing reaction I was wishing for. I convinced myself he was just keeping it together until he could return to his cabin and cry himself to sleep. After retelling my fairy tale for the tenth time, Jerry simply shook my hand and told me how happy he was for me. He even remembered that my now-fabled musky was my new personal best. Not until that moment did I feel a little jerkish about the whole prank. I quickly casted those thoughts aside and decided my inner voice didn't like to have fun. The prank was on like Donkey Kong, or something like that.

While cooking supper, Jerry kept asking me about the details of my record catch. I had to do my best to keep a Pinocchio nose from giving me away. After supper, the clan went up to the lodge, but I stayed back at the cabin to squeeze in a quick shower so I wouldn't have to do it that night. Upon my arrival at the lodge, I walked through the door and Tim, the resort owner, greats me with a hero's welcome, congratulations, and a hearty hand shake. Apparently, Jerry had told Tim that I had won the biggest musky contest with my forty-nine inch record-setter. At this point, the prank started to feel like I was pulling it on myself. I didn't know what to do. Tim was supposed to be in on the prank, not the one getting pranked. It was over. I was busted. All that was left to do was tell Tim what had really happened with my big musky that day, and how she became yet another one of my "how-she-got-away" stories. Every musky hunter on the planet has these sad tales. But for me, sometimes it feels like that's all I have.

I look over in Jerry's direction after the explanation to Tim. Jerry was completely dumbfounded at the sudden turn of events. "That's right, Jerry. You won, again. I had you beat and blew it," I admitted with my head sulking. Tim just laughed and shook his head. "You Americans sure like to fuck with your buddies, don't you. I'd have punched you in the nose for pulling a prank liked that." Tim meandered over to the stupefied Jerry. "Well, here's your custom-made Musky rod for the largest fish of your outing." Jerry shook Tim's hand, his mind still in a fog. "I can't accept this rod. My brother, James, had the biggest musky of the trip and lost it due to unforeseen circumstances. He's far more deserving than I am." Jerry cruised over and handed the rod to James. Jerry smiled and mentioned he was sorry for his loss, as if an immediate member of his family had just passed away. Only in the musky world could that type of pain be felt by all. As I retold James' musky story to Tim, he scratched his head in utter bewilderment. He had to be wondering who had caught a musky, who had lost a musky, who had the biggest musky, and who was just full of shit. Come to think of it, all those answers should have been pretty clear. "I can't take your rod, Jerry. I lost my musky and you hooked yours. It wouldn't be right," said James. "It's you who grasped a giant, not me. You deserve this rod. It would make me happy if you owned this rod," expressed a slightly emotional Jerry. With that, James understood Jerry's motives. He silently nodded his head and reluctantly accepted the trophy rod.

Now I feel like a huge douche bag. Tucking my tail between my legs, I ventured over and congratulated Jerry on his win, and gave him the prize money I'd been holding on to for our little tournament. Steve came over and shook Jerry's hand in appreciation for what he did for their brother. One by one, the entire group of men made their way to both Jerry and James and offer up their sincere congratulation and respect. I have to say, even I was quite impressed by what the ultra-competitive Jerry had just done. Really brought a new perspective to an old friend.

All the hi-jinks, all the miserable failures and heart-pounding victories, if I had learned nothing on all these adventures, I believe I did discover what it truly meant to be in a real group of men. Not just musky hunters, but a close knit brotherhood. Looking back, whenever a hand or some friendly advice was needed, every guy was eager to pitch in, or rally around each other in bad times. It wasn't just about busting each others chops every chance we had. (Though, that was part of it). It was about being there for one another and sharing in each other's victories, and sharing in our defeats. I will be forever grateful for being included in something that is ever-increasingly rare in today's society.

And in case any of you were wondering how journal recovery turned out, lets just say, not good. In fact I probably lost 25 percent of my entries which made for some of the days I wrote about in this book a little less detailed. What's far more important though, are the life long friendships forged in the search of the next Musky.

MUSKY TALE OF THE TAPE - AUGUST 2013

JERRY - 46" 44" 40.5" 36.5" 36" 30"

BRAD - 40" 40" 34.5" 27"

JAMES - 40.5" 40.5" 38" 36.5" 32" 30"

STEVE - 44.75" 40"

ALLEN - 43" 41.5" 27" 24"

JAN - 42"

JOE - 36" 31.5"

TRACY - 38" 37"

GARRET - 34"

WOLFY - 44.5" 34.5"

ROD - 41" 38" 37" 37" 37"

BUCKY - 39"

BY **BRAD MATHEWSON**

MUSKY HUNT-AUGUST 2015

CHAPTER XLIV

BLURIED MEMORIES

Unfortunately as fate would have it, tragedy stuck again and my musky diary was once again damaged almost beyond repair. My 2015 season is as the title suggests, just a blur. I seem to have more problems keeping my diary safe then a teenage girl does from the prying eyes of her mother. And with my musky memories stacking up like dried fire wood, it's getting harder to decipher which hazed misadventure goes with which trip and who drew the short straw and had the misfortune of fishing with me. Though you would be hard pressed to find a member of our group that would turn me down as a veteran net man, hook removing surgeon, and all around bullshitter.

It was an interesting trip, just not as memorable as the past. A month before our departure date I was driving home from a near by musky hole when my 1994 ShoreLand'r trailer made a horrific sound, I peered into my rear view mirror and to my utter amazement, it appeared as if I was towing a sparkler. Lucky for me I was able to limp my firework into a nearby auto repair shop and to my dismay they wouldn't or maybe couldn't help me. So I called a friend who brought me some tools and we Jimmy Rigged it up so I could drive 15 mph and limp it home.

Of course this had to be the year that it was my turn to be the caption of the ship. See Stew and I always took turns bringing our boats, mainly because we had the 2 oldest rigs out of the group so and it wasn't even close. Mine is a 1994 Aluma-Craft and Stews was a 1990 I believe leaky bath tub that should be in the scrap yard, but we're both cheap and they still run after 15 minutes of praying, cussing, and finally divine intervention. Put it this way, Stew's boat leaked more than the Titanic, I bet we pumped 30 gallons of water out of that hull each day it was on the water and the rougher it was the more the rivets would leak. If his bilge pump ever quit working, an iceberg would be a welcomed savior.

Late August had finally arrived and it was time for our annual trip to L.O.T.W. We were in Stew's truck hauling his boat as my axle, which took me 2 weeks to find, hadn't been delivered as promptly as promised. Oh, and there was more good news, an hour into the drive Stew informed me that he would need to cut our usual eight day trip short because he had promised his wife he would drive their daughter back to college. So instead of Friday – Saturday we would be leaving Friday morning, missing one full day of fishing. Not the kind of surprise I wanted to here once we were on the road. Though my boat mate did make the suggestion that I talk to our fellow musky hunters and inquiry about fishing three men in a boat. I almost fell out of my truck seat when he uttered those words. "Are you insane," I said. "Why not, what's the big deal, and maybe someone could give you a ride if you wanted to stay another day it's up to you," said Stew. I was flabbergasted by his suggestion.

Now this might not sound like that big of a deal to you twenty two foot Ranger boat guys, but we're fishing out of 16.5 foot Aluma-Craft and Lund boats with 60-90 H.P. Motors, with beam widths under 90 inches. I will reiterate my point in a story that was recently told to me by a member of my local musky club. Now I will preface this story by saying it was a kid that was the culprit in this story, but it's the number of fisherman in the boat not the age of the fisherman. So for the sake of the story we'll call our subject Bob.

Bob, his retired father, and Bob's son had planned a nice Father's Day musky outing on a local lake and they were fishing out of a 16.5 walleye style boat. They weren't on the water for more than a hour when Bob's nine year old son who was in the middle of the boat while Bob was on the front deck, made a back cast to the a spot the trio just finished working. When the kid came back into his side, casted his 6 inch Reef Hawg, struck Bob in the face and knocked him to the ground. Luckily for Bob his father saw the whole thing and yelled at his grandson to stop his casting. Fortunately he wasn't hooked in the eye or had his eye ball ripped out by rusty treble hook. One point of the treble hook did pierce is lower eye lid, in fact he showed me a picture of the Reef Hawg hanging from his eye lid while his child stood next to him with tears in his eyes. He was able to cut the hook and push it back out without seeking medical care. And besides a black eye and small cut, he was no worse for wear, but things could have go much worse.

This year for whatever reason seemed to be the year of the jerk bait with Bobbie baits and Suick's leading the way. One day Stew and I were casting on an isolated reed filled cove on the back side of Wolf Island and the brothers Derrick and Garret were fishing not 75 yards away. From our front row seats the big show played out on center stage. The dynamic duo were working a textbook location, it was a garage sized cove off of the main basin that was full of gorgeous coontail in 6 feet of water. And dead center of this musky utopia was a large fallen tree, an ideal ambush point for a toothy predator. Derrick the star of this show, was casting a plastic neon green Suick alongside the tree when she smashed his bait and with the bright lights on that fish, went air born and tail walked it's way toward the boat and to unexpected musky fisherman. Meanwhile Garret was in a battle of his own, trying to untangle his bait out of the net while his brother screamed instructions for him to net the fish. Suddenly Garret broke free of his bait carpet battle and made a well timed dip and scope, which only temporarily held the fifty to fifty four inch beast. And that's when all hell broke lose, see a fish that large and powerful isn't going to like being stuffed into a tiny 1980's nylon walleye net, I'd say that the relic held her for maybe 2 seconds. Once she started thrashing, the aluminum handle broke and the rotten net tore. Garret and Derrick tried to get a hold of her, but the hooks of the

BY **BRAD MATHEWSON**

Suick tangled in the net, she twisted, and the hooks popped out. Then probably in a state of shock, she pined on the surface for a good 5 seconds while the boys deployed the destroyed net in her direction, but the moment it touched her, she submarined out of their lives. Instantly angry and frustrated over the blown once-in-a lifetime musky boiled over and they both started bickering back and forth. Unbeknownst to them we had seen the whole shebang and were both doubled over in side splitting laughter over what had just transpired. It was like watching an old Three Stooges episode minus Moe. I looked over at Stew and say, "We should go over there before those two start throwing punches at on another." As we pull up Stew yells out, "That was quite a performance you two put on."

Both boys spun around, their eyes the size of diner plates, you could tell they were both embarrassed by their childish behavior towards one another, they were both good kids and this was a rare site. Their demeanor's quickly returned back to their jovial selves and they began to spin a tale of the one that got away while Stew and I listened and gave out some veteran advise, not that these two needed it. They were both in their early twenties and gung ho as all get-out. They really busted their butts running and gunning trying to cover as much water each day as possible. What's funny to me is their diet of pre-made peanut butter and jelly sandwiches, which they eat by the dozen and they would bring half gallon bags of milk with them in the boat and drink a gallon to a gallon and a half each every day. And somehow, they both sported six packs. It was a great motivator having the young brothers in camp, we all feed off their never-give-up high energy, which I'm sure contributed to there 15 combined musky total for the week.

Their father Tracy teamed up with Jan for a combined musky total of 19 fish, and Tracy caught twelve of them himself. Tracy fished one bait the entire week it was a brown sucker Bobbie bait that was at-least forty years old. When I asked him what the key was with the Bobbie, he said to work it as tight to cover as possible and the more tree branches and rocks he bumped into the more musky action he saw. By the looks of his bait after the trip I suspect he hit every damn rock in the lake, there wasn't a speck of paint left on it and its resemblance was that of a beaver gnawed stick. So this for me after all, ended the hot color dispute, the action he departed into that bait was definitely magic there's no doubt about that. As far as trophy fish are concerned Jan and Tracy raised more 50 inch fish than the rest of the group put together, only they kept all there spots top secret which isn't the way we normally operate, they were the first ones out and last ones back each day.

On the last day of the trip for Stewart and I, we did the traditional partner swap. I went with Jan and Stew went with Tracy. Now I was going to finally have a chance at a few of the 50 inch fish Jan and Tracy have been hoarding all week. The one fish in particular that they would talk about Jan had named Andre after famed WWF legend Andre The Giant, a massive musky that was so obese Jan guessed him to be in the fifty pound class. When I stepped into my buddy Jan's boat he bust open like a teenage girl talking about her first crush. I'm not surprised he and Tracy encountered so many trophy fish, they had more than Fifty years combined experience on the lake. Now one would probably assume after a long week of raising the same gigantic muskies over and over again that these neutral fish would have to eat, but they must have received a tip I was coming and headed for the main basin.

We fish every hot spot on Jan's milk run that day and never laid our eyes on their hit list fish. I did manage to catch a forty incher that had moved in on a big fish spot after the previous tenant skipped town. Yes I didn't catch my lifetime trophy fish with Jan that day, but I did learn a lot about where muskies like to hang out in the particular cold weather pattern we were having during this trip. See normally we have upper eighties to ninety degrees and humid conditions with a bout or two of pop up thunderstorms. On this trip it was much cooler with temps in the upper sixes to seventy degrees, with only one day reaching eighty and this weather pattern pushed in the week we arrived, kicking out the seasonably warmer air. So that took the muskies off their normal rock bite and pushed them deep into the weeds, in fact all Jan's hot spots were what we refer to as slop holes. Tiny isolated patches of thick coontail and cabbage adjacent to the main basin. Most guys would drive right past these spots. They were so small, they could only conceal a single fish. Stew and I were just as guilty, we really struggled to put fish in the boat, but guys get compulsive and we rely way to much on what worked last year.

Anyone can catch a few muskies when the bite is hot, but when mother nature throws you a knuckle ball, that's when the season vets that can adapt quickly with a wide variety of techniques will still succeed. Old mother nature served Stew and I a big slice of humble pie this year, but we'll be back with our PMA, and a few more tricks up our sleeves.

Now father time might have fogged up some of Stew and I's fishing details of the trip, but the memories I have of our cabin mates are permanently burned into my subconscious mind whether I wanted them or not. As I have stated before in this book, the aforementioned Hoelzel brothers are all building contractors with the exception being Stewart, and I am their cabinet maker. Jerry upon mentioning Canada with a past customer of ours had invited him and his buddy up to Lake Of The Woods for our annual week long musky hunt. The said customer, we'll just call him Bill and his buddy, we'll call Ted happily accepted the invitation, but informed Jerry that they weren't much into muskies, but would come fish walleyes and pike.

It takes a hardy soul to keep up with our crew of musky nuts, running and gunning for 13 hour straight and then not eating supper until 10 p.m. It tends to weed out guys rather quickly. So they ended up in our cabin which was fine by us, they were both retirees so we knew they wouldn't be up at all hours of the night partying and would surely be to bed early, ensuring all roommates would get a good night sleep, unlike some of the other cabins and mates. When it came to cooking, cleaning, sharing food and drink you couldn't ask for two nicer guys, but as the week wore on their comfort level with us, let's say, got a little too comfortable. I thought it was just a case of bad timing when I walked into the cabin after a long day of fishing and as I shuffled past the bathroom, there was Bill shirtless on the toilet in the middle of a major transaction. I excused myself and quickly averted my eyes and went about my business of starting supper. Not 2 hours later as I went to fetch a bottle of Whiskey from my room which was apparently not so conveniently located adjacent to the rest room, it was like deja vu all over again, only Ted had taken the place of Bill on the throne.

After he had finished I went into the bathroom just to make sure that the door hadn't been removed, but it was still there and it was in good working order maybe be these two weren't sure of how a door works. The next day in the boat I told Stew what I had seen and he chuckled that he had witnessed the same thing only in a number one transaction. We both chalked it up as old men not having their wives around and not caring because it's just a bunch of bros up north fishing for a week. All that changed when I walked into the cabin and spotted Bill naked stepping out of the shower the next day. Now things have gone too far so I politely said, "you need to close the door dude, no one wants to see that." I was equally shocked when he responded, "What's the big deal we're all guys here." Then if that wasn't the icing on the cake he proceeded to walk from the bathroom to his bedroom in his birthday suit, a site I will never forget, but wish I could. For the whole rest of the trip Stew and I would either see one of these guys using the toilet or see them bare ass naked. I guess as some people age their sense of shame goes away and is replaced by total unapologetic wrinkled nudity.

MUSKY TAIL OF THE TAPE-AUGUST 2015

Brad - 38" 36" 37, 40

Stew - 34.5" 31" 38" 36.5"

Jerry - 38" 43" 40" 41" 44" 44.5" 44.5"

Garret - 37" 34" 38.5" 28" 32" 36" 42" 46.5" 40" 20"

Derrick - 38.5" 22" 37" 40" 44" 28"

Bill - 32"

Chris - 38" 37" 38" 25" 38" 37.5"

Tracy - 40.5" 33" 26" 38" 40" 33" 37" 38" 38" 26" 49" 37"

Jan - 20" 35" 34" 43" 32" 48" 32"

Rod - 35" 41.5" 34"

Bucky - 31.5"

Ted - 0"

BY **BRAD MATHEWSON**

MUSKY HUNT- AUGUST 2016

MY LAST MUSKY ADVENTURE EVER??

After my disappointing 2015 season where L.O.T.W basically kicked my ass, it was time to implement a new plan, my fishing partner had informed me he won't be joining me on our 2016 season. And after seeing the numbers Tracy had put up with 12 fish in the boat, my goal was to have him as a partner in 2016. In fact I put the bug in his ear about teaming up with him the night of my last day in Ontario. Tracy had been coming up to L.O.T.W. long before the Hoelzel clan and his vast knowledge of the lake and its toothy inhabitants are second to none. I feel isn't very important to always be learning and to try and hang out with people who have more experience in a subject than my self. So I might gleam some information from them and hence become a better musky hunter. The plan of attack was to wait until January when musky fishing is on everyone's back burner. On the day I contacted him I was thrown back to my teenage years when I called a girl for the first time to ask her out on a date, only I didn't have to go converse with a overly protective father. It was a nerve racking call at first, but Tracy's a very easy going laid back guy who doesn't seem to stress over much and soon a half an hour flew by and it was like talking with a old friend. Up until this call, I hadn't had much more than a pleasant exchange at the docks on how many muskies each boat caught, but he seemed like a genuine nice guy. In fact I had more in-depth conversations with his two boys, who were both raised right and would gladly give their shirts off their backs to help someone out. After our chewing of the fat session was over he said he wasn't sure if he would be going in 2016, but if he did go he'd like to join up with me in this rig, and that I should call him in the spring. So I waited until May 1st to touch base with him once again and he accepted my invitation and now I was off to the big Canada dance, BUT WHAT WILL I WEAR.

Finally back in Canada with my new partner, I was ready to set the lake on fire. I was in the boat of a L.O.T.W. Pro who tore up the lake the prior season and I was going to learn so much and crush the numbers board, and who knows maybe my first fifty incher? Then fours days in a reality came crashing in on me as our weather wasn't the norm. We were battling 50's - 60 's for temperatures when there usually in the 80's - 90's, but we had the same issues in 2015. So the muskies should be buried in the thick weeds once again, right? Nope the water level in the lake had dropped by 2 feet from 2016 and the once four foot area's with nice weeds had turned into two foot dead zones with brown dead weeds and no fish. The crazy action filled milk run Jan and Tracy had put together in 2015 was now just sour milk along with my hopes of a fifty inch musky. And for Tracy's secret weapon, the brown Bobbie bait, it seems it's magic had dried up over the long cold winter. In my own attempt at recreating Tracy's 2015 campaign, when I returned from Canada I quickly snatched up all 4 Bobbie baits from the 60' – 70's on eBay. I was even fortunate to find the same brown colored Bobbie as Tracy and at $35 a piece, that was a price I was willing to pay for success.

CHAPTER XLV

WHITEFISH BAY ADVENTURE

That night while beating our collective heads together and drinking our sorrows away, we spread out the Sabaskong Bay map on the kitchen table, hoping something would jump out at us. "Tracy I have the solution to all our problems," I said. "What's that," said a very skeptical Tracy. So I went on to explain how a couple years ago Jan and his son-in-law Joe had headed north up through Turtle Lake and had taken the Marine Railway portage over land and into Whitefish Bay. They told of seeing no other boats and caught a ton of northern and seeing a few larger musky, it was the kind of place with low numbers, but with the real possibility of a truly giant fish due to the abundance of Lake Trout. "Sounds like an adventure, I've been to the portage before but it was out of service," said Tracy.

So the next morning had us up and on the lake before most of the crew could roll out of the fart sacks. We couldn't have asked for better conditions as a warm front had pushed in overnight and the day was going to be cloudy with highs around 80 and low humidity. Before we entered Turtle Lake we spotted a couple familiar faces, it was James and his son Danny, they were staying at King Island. They were fishing the rice beds around the Hay Island area. As we pull up, they both had shit-eating grins, so we knew they had just boated a big fish. It turns out Danny had just caught and released his new personal best 48 inch musky. So after a short B.S. session of looking at digital cam pics and back slapping, Tracy and I thought we too would give the area an hour of fishing before we were to continue on our journey.

Just as we began fishing, an ear splitting sound seemed to be headed our way, it sounded a lot like a small air plane. It turns out to be an Air-boat, followed closely behind by a 24 foot Rough Neck John boat. We could see it was a couple members of the First Nations tribe and by the looks of it they were going to be harvesting rice today. If you've never seen rice being harvested before, its very interesting. Gone are the days of the traditional rice collecting, during the olden days they would use a small canoe that was propelled through the rice beds with a long push pole by a person on the stern. The "knocker" or person sitting down, gently bends the rice stalks over the boat and then uses 2 cedar sticks to gently tap the rice kernels off the stalk catching the grain in a blanket.

My, oh how things have changed, instead they use an air boat that's propeller driven with a large metal scoop attached to the bow that knocks the ripe rice off the plant and into a the scoop bucket. When the front of the air boat is full a guy pulls up, typically in a large John boat, and the rice is manually shoveled in large grain sacks and stacked into the John boat. Then the whole process starts again, the guy running the air boat will make a couple overlapping passes over the area that he previously harvested from to insure he didn't miss any rice. Now they claim the new way of harvesting doesn't damage the plants, it just bends them over and then they pop right back up after each pass. But Stew and I went back in the areas after the air boat passed over them and all we saw were busted up plants, so that's clearly a big lie.

We went back to fishing and eventually made it back to the spot were Danny had released his big fish, when I spotted a large musky fining on it's side against a rice bed. She had some significant damage on her fins and her back when I seized her tail in order to keep her in a upright position. I slowly worked her back and forth trying to carefully pump lifesaving oxygen through her gills but whenever I thought she was strong enough to swim on her own she would go belly up. Tracy and I both knew her prognosis looked bad, if only our boat was equipped with a large 60 inch live well. I've know of guides that fish Lake St. Clair that revive musky in large tanks by pumping in lots of fresh water and a strong aerator. Now I'm not saying for sure the fish had been dropped, but to us it sure looked like it, as its back was missing a large portion of protective slime. Finally thirty minutes after working on this fish James and Danny showed back up as they were done fishing the area, they seemed surprised that Danny's fish was in my hands. I told them we gave it 30 minutes so its the least they could do is give it the same, all parties know these things happen, but its our duty to exhaust all options in reviving a musky. There's a saying I've heard in situations like this before and its, "turtles have to eat to," well this is true, but what a waste of a trophy class fish.

So off we jet into Turtle Lake, as adventure awaits us, the new lake seems to be fairly clear and looks rather fishy, but we're onto bigger things, though the temptation to wet a line in new water is strong. When we arrive at the portage it's 10 a.m. The relic of a contraption looks old and worn by the 4 seasons it must endear. We had heard rumblings of it's poor design and constant breakdowns from locals. We were both very nervous about the rust, broke parts, and general lack of maintenance that was even obvious to the untrained eye. The railway includes a single cart and a track that runs overland between Sabaskong Bay and Whitefish Bay. Boats drive onto the carriage cart and people use a hand crank, which is a giant wheel that runs a gear box that's connected to a series of pulleys and a long cable. "Lets give it the old college try," said Tracy. So with that he drove the boat up onto the cradle which seemed to be a tad narrow for Tracy's musky ship. In order to get it on the cradle fully though, he had to power load it like you see all the guys in glass boats do.

The cradle had four vertical poles, one located on each corner with a 2x4 bolted onto each one, which looked like an attempt at narrowing up the cart in order to keep larger crafts from portaging over. Tracy had been to the portage years earlier, but it was in disrepair and claimed the cradle didn't have the aforementioned 2x4's. As the boat lurched forward the now 2x4's acted as a wedge, so there we were slightly stuck. I told Tracy to put the motor in reverse and give it full throttle, but nothing happened. In a last feeble attempt, I sprung onto the cart and tried rocking the boat up and down while trying to push from the bow, but nothing happened, well except a deep belly laugh from Tracy. "Is this the adventure you so desperately wanted," said Tracy. I just held my tongue and pondered a solution to our predicament. As I rested my butt on the rusty track an answer to our problems popped into my empty head.

Here's the plan we're not going to try and turn around, now its time to dig in and push forward. We need to get this boat into Whitefish Bay so we can get fishing, we're burning daylight. I tell Tracy, I want him standing on the bow of the boat in order to more balance the weight on the cart. And I was going to man the spinning wheel of death until I'm wore out in which we'd flip flop places. Only five minutes in, the immense weight of the craft and Tracy has worn my arm muscles to the point of trembles, thankfully my effort had taken us to the ¼ way point. Once the old switch-a-roo was complete, we were back in business once at the half way point we did one more Chinese fire drill and I was back at the wheel. The screeching emanating from the dilapidated pulleys was so soul piercing, I

think I developed permanent hearing damage as I had ringing in my ears that lasted for hours. Now at the peak of the rise, gravity should become our ally and the force of momentum should knock our jammed boat off the carriage cart. What we didn't consider was the safety factor, see Tracy was still standing on the front casting deck as our now rocket ship hit warp speed only seconds after cresting the hill. I had to let go of the now crazed Las Vegas roulette wheel and suddenly everything went into a slow motion blur. As the boat was about to career into Adam's ale, Tracy and I locked eyes and telepathically he said to me, "Why the fuck didn't I stay on shore." And just like that the shit hit the fan and the front of The USS Crestliner submarined into Whitefish Bay and Tracy flew ass-over-tea-kettle and crumpled into the back deck floor. "Tracy are you all right?" I yelled.

A muffled groaning emanated from inside the boat confirmed my worst fear, that he had been injured in one of my hair ball schemes. As Tracy got up like a 90 year old man who just fell down a flight of stairs like a rag doll, I felt a sense of extreme guilt wash over me for it was my coaxing that brought us here. "I'll live, there's no reason to cry over spilled milk, we came up here for adventure and now we have one," said Tracy now learning over the steering console. I could tell he was in a lot of pain as he winced and grabbed at his knee when he walked, but he was determined to press on.

Now we fish and begin the arduous task of finding muskies in a very low density body of water, but we were informed if we did run into muskies they would be very large. The water color

BY **BRAD MATHEWSON**

was as described to us as gin clear, in fact so clear, you cold see bottom in 25 feet of water very easily. With water so clear one would assume weed growth would be excellent, but that surely wasn't the case at all in fact the weed was quite sporadic. Though it seemed every time we found lake salad we found fish, only they were of the Northern pike variety and in very high concentrations. Tracy and I both casted the large sized spinner baits, but you couldn't make a cast without one of us hooking into a pike.

The other unique attribute we noticed, there didn't seem to be a gradual taper of the lake bed, it just seemed to drop 20 feet only a couple feet from shore in most of the area we explored. While on the hunt for Mr. Toothy, Tracy and I had the good fortune to stumble upon three accent rock paintings, done in some kind of red paint which I'm told is red orche. My research indicates the red dye was produced by heating Limonite, an iron ore of yellowish brown color that once fired, would turn red. From there it could be crushed and with a little water or rendered animal fat would make a paintable paste. The Anishinaabe natives of the area would create these paintings to tell a story; it could be a birth, a successful hunt, or a good day fishing; it was their way of capturing a moment in time just as we use our cameras. These beautiful pictographs date back hundreds of years, the ones we were lucky enough to find were protected under ledges where the sun's rays and snow and rain couldn't easily destroy them. I remember seeing fisherman and his catch of fish, a hunter and a deer, and some sort of snake.

Now I'm not going to get into First Nations treaty rights but since a "loophole" appeared when a local (Kenora) fish plant was granted a multi-species quota in order to make and sell fish patties. The plant has taken advantage of the rights of First Nation, paying them to supply the plant with walleye and whitefish. And from what I've been told, the placement and daily checking along with quotas of fish harvested have been largely unregulated by the local government. Our group of ten to twelve guys have all seen ghost nets, a net that has been long abandoned, killing thousands entangled fish as they float around the lake. Tracy and I watched local natives check their net shortly after lunch and what we saw was very shocking. For one we almost ran our boat into it as the only thing marking its placement where a few soda bottles.

We decided to stay and watch them with binoculars check their nets from a quarter-mile away as we ate our lunch in a shaded cove. They would throw some fish into the boat and others they would (gill) a process of cut the gills in order to bleed out a fish only the gilled fish were thrown back into the lake. Soon after the checking of the net began dozens of eagles and pelicans appeared out of thin air to feast on the buffet of senselessly killed fish. When they were done and motoring away, we drove over to find out what species of fish they thought was garbage. Now most of the evidence had been consumed by the birds or sunk to the bottom to be eaten by turtles or lake sturgeon, but we did find over a dozen northern pike with their gills cut finning on the surface. Tracy and I were both fighting mad at such a seemingly blatant waste of a resource and total disregard of life.

by **BRAD MATHEWSON**

After losing our appetites over such a disgusting middle finger to mother nature, it was time to continue or hunt for Es-ox Masquinongy. With not much more than a mosquito fart for breeze and the cloudless sky, with the oven set to broil, the fishing was tough. Having spent a few hours working the traditional shallow water bite, we need a new venue. So after carefully reviewing our map we quickly identified four humps I wanted to check out. Once on top of the first hump which topped out at five feet surrounded by fifty feet of water, it finally happened.

Tracy raised a mid forty inch musky. I myself never saw her as she followed for a short ways until she spotted the boat and then quickly vanished. Tracy and I gave the area a good lashing hoping to entice her into biting, but it was not to be. "On to the next spot," I shouted. I was fired up now that we had confirmation there were truly muskies in Whitefish Bay. This spot was a bit more complex than the first, it consisted of a point on mainland and extended into a rocky finger thirty yards out into a lake, a small drop off, and then a large rock hump. We spent a good hour working the area with absolutely nothing to show for it. So on to spot number three, it was a reef marked with a milk jug that would easily take your lower unit off and totally ruin your day. The pickup sized rock topped out at two feet and dropped off to forty five feet on one side and fifty five on the other. On my first cast something slammed my white spinner bait, I set the hook and the quarry came unbuttoned.

On my subsequent cast my bait was crushed once more and this time my swing to the heavens rang true. The battle was short as the fish succumbed to my nine foot musky tamer, only to our chagrin it wasn't a musky, but a thirty eight inch fat and sassy northern pike. Though all wasn't lost, we end up catching three more pike off that spot. Our final spot was a hump in a neck down that came up to three feet before dropping off all sides into fifty feet of water, but it was more of the same. We caught four pike and raised no muskies.

BY **BRAD MATHEWSON**

CHAPTER XLVI

STRANDED & CART BROKEN

As the burning torch in the western sky hovered above the horizon, Tracy indicated our time here was done. With a turn of the key we set the water on fire, blazing back toward the portage only a few miles away and a follow up meeting with the wrenched death sled. Back to the portage I noticed something was different, someone else had used the crossing as the carriage was now on the Turtle Lake side. I hopped out of the boat and tried to spin the operation wheel and it just spun freely with the cart not moving so much as a inch. Thankfully I thought as I spotted an in-case-of-help sign with a 1-888 number printed under it. Only problem was my phone had no bars to call out and Tracy had the same issue. Upon further inspection of the dilapidated contraption we found out what the problem was, the cable had snapped. So there we sat, it was 7:30 p.m. and we had a hour and a half before it was dark. The only people we had seen on the water all day were two Native Canadians checking nets and that was seven hours ago.

The idea of sleeping in the boat, while thousands of blood thirsty mosquitoes feasted on our exposed legs and arms was out of the question, and if we did have to stay I would have to turn to cannibalism as our food and snacks were gone. Sorry Tracy, but I'm not going to sleep on an empty belly, it messes up my sleep schedule. It seemed if we wanted out of this predicament we would have to find help, before the darkness of night hindered our search. But this area of White Fish Bay only had a few cabins that we had seen. The first two cabins had seen better days as they were both abandoned with roofs that had caved in after many winters of heavy snow fall. Now the third cabin we motored up to held a glimmer of hope as my eyes caught a sliver of light through a window that clearly had a objection to Windex.

There was no boat at the dock, but Tracy pulled up, and I jumped out and heard a loud crack as the rotten boards stressed under my 185 pounds. One fall and I'd need to update my Tetanus shot, as rusty nails protruded from every direction have been worked back out after years of wave action that flexed and twisted the old dock a fraction of an inch each day. Once off the dry rotted dock I could just make out a faint foot path in the two foot high weeds and scenes from the 1972 movie

BY **BRAD MATHEWSON**

Deliverance took over my imagination. With a shaky hand I wrapped on the torn screen door and waited with bated breath for an axe wielding psychopath wearing a suit made of skin from the last sorry fisherman who dared knock on his door. A full minute later with no one seemingly home, my hope of getting off Whitefish Bay before nightfall was doubful and my spirits were crushed.

So with a quick about-face, I marched back toward our vessel. Suddenly my ears perked up to the sound of a man with a thick French accent and broken English said, "can I help you?" To say I was startled by the sudden broken silence of the evening, would be a giant understatement. Now when I spun around I was fully expecting him to be wielding a machete at the very least. But the man who stood before me wore tattered jeans that he actually wore out, not the $100 pair that come pre-ripped and worn out that the kids wear now a days.

His hair was gray and slicked back like Fonzie from Happy Days. He was of slim build and weathered face, I would guess a man of eighty years. And to appease this American in our relentless stereotyping of people from every culture, the old Canuck was holding a Moosehead beer in one hand and a cancer stick in the other. I stuttered out that we were marooned on Whitefish Bay due to the boat portage contraption now being in a state of disrepair. With that he broke into snicker that swiftly turned into an all out roll on the floor, side-splitting belly laugh, that was so violent in nature he spilt his beer and made me question the man's sanity. After a solid minute of utter enjoyment at our expense the old-timer stated, "that thing hasn't worked in a year I'm surprised you got that big walleye boat across it. Looks like you two boys are in a bit of a pickle" he said, still giggling. "Fortunately I have a solution. Go back the way you came three quarters of a kilometer and on your left hand side you'll see a small weedy cove, if you go slow, you will see a channel cut through the rice bed. Now follow the little channel until it opens up into a bay and you'll see a resort, they will be able to help you out." I thanked the old Maple Leaf and he just shook his head and said, "Americans."

BY **BRAD MATHEWSON**

CHAPTER XLVII

LOST AND NOW FOUND

Back at the boat I told Tracy to floor it before the crazy old man has a change of heart and decides to make us into a couple of lamp shades. "So where are we going?" said Tracy. "We're going back the way we came," I said. When we reached the ¾ mile marker in my head I told Tracy to slow down to a crawl as we slowly motored passed the rice bed cove and with nightfall fast approaching neither one of us could spot the pathway back to civilization. Soon the cove was a distant memory, "Tracy we need to turn around and get right in the rice bed on the next pass, maybe we missed something," I said. "Yeah or this is the wrong cove and that maple syrup drinking Canadian has sent us on a wild goose chase. He's probably watching us now with his binoculars, giggling like a school girl, "said Tracy. Now with a totally different sight angle, I could now see a faint path and as we motored deeper into the cove I could see where plants had been bent over and broken off. The further we traveled the more defined the channel became until suddenly the right path way opened up into a bay. It was an utter shock to the system, like the feeling as Dorothy in The Wizard of Oz opens the door to her once black and white filmed flying house and a vibrant world of gorgeous color explodes through the doorway. There on the far end was a resort and a few cabins lining the shore.

I looked over at Tracy and a sense of relief washed over us. Starting with the desolate utopia we had prayed we'd have the fortune to discover before twilight enveloped us. It was the last remaining day of August, and the last of the tourist season was coming to a close as tomorrow would bring September and the coming of fall shall commence begin. The green cabins were part of a resort named Vic & Dot's Camp which we would soon discover is located off of the Trans Canadian HWY 71, the same highway as the resort we're staying at. In fact only a hop, skip, and a jump down the road. Tracy and I dock the vessel and we're both elated to see lights on in the main office. We go in and meet a man named Robert the grandson of the former owner Vic & Dot.

After telling him our animated Indiana Jones adventure story, he smiles and explains our lodge is just down the road, and if we would have just trailer-ed the boat over, we could have saved an hour and a half boat and portage time. He then pulls his flip phone from his right breast pocket and begins to dial, as he informs us he's buddies with our lodge owner.

BY **BRAD MATHEWSON**

Soon he is engaged in a good old-fashioned belly laugh at our expense, with our host and reiterates with said party, just how much time we wasted driving to the portage when we could have simply trailer-ed to Whitefish Bay.

I believe it was a whopping thirty minute wait when the cavalry show up to rescue us. Once our resort owner hung up his phone he looked out the window and just so happened to see Tracy's two boys, Derick and Garrett, pulling up to the dock. He enlightened them on our situation and gave them the elementary directions to Vic & Dot's just down the road. The boys pulled up right at dark driving Tracy's truck and towing the trailer, the two knew the drill and quickly backed the trail down to the landing and power-loaded the boat.

We thanked Robert for his help and we were back at the resort in no time flat minus $15 for a boat landing fee, which was really only a one way launch. When we returned to our resort ,the boys played out the roles in reverse and had the boat landed and secured to our assigned dock number. As Tracy and I supervised his boys, I felt a hand on my shoulder and I look over and there's a hand on Tracy's also. It was like being back in high school when you were caught doing something stupid and you knew a long-winded lecture was coming. "Why the hell would you drive almost an hour to that shitty boat portage that hasn't worked in a year, then dick around for a half hour to portage the boat? All you had to do was tell me your plans of wanting to fish Whitefish Bay and I would have simply told you to trailer the boat 15 minutes down the road and put in at Vic and Dot's, saving yourselves a lot of time,"said Tim. That's when I piped in and said, "If we had discussed with you our intentions for today, we wouldn't have had an adventure." Tim just shook his head in total bewilderment, laughed, and said, "Fucking Americans."

BY **BRAD MATHEWSON**

CHAPTER XLVIII

TACTIC CHANGE

A new day begins and a new tactic is on the docket. This is our last day of fishing and we desperately needed to make up for the lack of success, especially when compared to Tracy's previous year, a record breaking catch. When we climbed into the boat that morning I explained my game plan that I've always wanted to try, that I've used with positive results while fishing river current for small mouth bass. "I'll keep an open mind to anything," acknowledged Tracy.

So I instructed him to drive us to the Split Rock Narrows and stop when we arrived to the location where the lake narrowed down to a hundred yards wide. The dramatic neck down created an impressive current when the wind was just right and today's conditions were absolutely perfect. Steep rocky banks on the south shore that quickly descended into forty four feet of water and loaded with ideal ambush points such as shelves, cracks, and broken rock. The menu for this area included walleyes, crappie, and perch. Now I've fished the area before with some luck, but we always just spot casted to cracks while control drifting twenty yards out from shore.

But my idea was to take jointed perch Shallow Raiders and hug the shore with the boat floating 1 to 2 feet out. Tracy and I would both share the front deck making perpendicular casts along and still maintain proper control of our craft. Fishing in this manner keeps your bait in the strike zone longer. Plus the erratic action and water displacement of a jointed bait when bumping structure, with a slight pause when you do encounter a barrier, can really play into a musky's aggressive nature.

This technique has been killer for me chasing river smallies, why couldn't it work on muskies also? Upon arrival, my partner and I dig through our suitcase sized musky boxes looking for jointed crank baits. I find two, a yellow & brown, and the other in the traditional perch pattern. Tracy comes up with none as he forgot his crank bait box at the dock, so being the generous soul that I am, I loan him the traditional colored perch Raider.

I drop the trolling motor down to set up for the first controlled drift and we're really hugging the shore which is only two feet away. And Tracy fires a rocket, a foot off the bank and is bumping rock from the initial crank of his Abu Garcia, then it happens. On a short pause after hitting a large ledge rock, his line goes from slightly slack to taunt. Our bad luck has changed as Tracy brings the fish to my now awaiting net and in slides a healthy forty two in musky. "Now we were on to something," I said. With-in thirty seconds of resuming our drift, Pow! My yellow and brown Raider is pounded and I'm on the board with a forty inch fish "GAME ON," I shouted as I released my musky. I felt like I was L.O.T.W legendary guide Bill Sandy.

On our second drift Tracy hooks a nice musky and gets her all the way back to the boat and she comes unbuttoned, a solid forty five incher for sure. We drift the rest of the way down to the curve then motor back, and on our third pass tragedy struck. I had a upper forty inch fish strike and had a solid hook set. I fought that fish almost into Tracy's open net until my bait broke in two with the musky swimming away with my back treble hook and bait body. My heart fell into my chest with anger and sadness as I hope the broke bait and hook wouldn't cause the musky any harm.

Frantically I search the bowels of my bait box, but I couldn't summon another jointed bait. Tracy looked in compartments of his boat and discovered the same color bait, only problem was it wasn't jointed it was a straight flat-sided Shallow Raider so I shut my mouth and snapped it on and got back to work.

Now on the fourth pass, Tracy raises two muskies, both in the low forty inch range. On the fifth cast a musky explodes out of the water and hit the boat as he begins his figure eight, moments.

Later he's got a thirty eight inch fish in the net, on MY BAIT. And Tracy's luck continues, on the sixth pass he sticks another musky, this one a thirty six incher. If that wasn't crazy enough Tracy raised four more muskies during the seventh and eighth pass, with my lonely bait not getting so much as a sniff.

BY **BRAD MATHEWSON**

CHAPTER XLIX

JEALOUS JERK

To say I was fit to be tied, would be a very accurate characterization of myself at that moment in time and I deeply wanted to take my bait back. Loathing in anger at the makers of the Jointed Raider for making such a weak product and pissed at myself for not having a back up bait in the same color pattern. My new friend Tracy read my deflated PMA, slumped over demeanor, and crushed ego. A pout session, I'm ashamed ever took place. "You know Brad I have a crank bait box back at the lodge and I think I have the same hot bait just sitting there, plus it's only a twenty minute boat ride there," said Tracy. Jealousy had overtaken my normal rational mind, so I eagerly jumped at the opportunity laid before me. All the way back to the dock the little devil on my shoulder was dancing the jig, now that I had my bait back in hand. The bait that had been so amazing for Tracy. But hey, he was going to retrieve his box that should've never left the boat in the first place I told myself. And besides, the muskies aren't going anywhere. Once at the dock Tracy had to run into the main lodge basement to retrieve his tackle box.

Fast-forward 45 minutes after we left musky central, we're back and I have my bait and Tracy has a whole box full of crank baits, but not a matching jointed lure like the one he forfeited back into my greedy hands. I could tell by the frantic digging through baits he wasn't pleased by the whole situation but he stayed his normal calm self in the face of my shitty selfishness.

When Tracy's frantic search was over I offered my dud bait that I had been using that started this whole fiasco, he politely declined. Now it was my turn to slay a boat load of muskies and over inflated my ego. On our first drift, there was a sense of electric magic in the air, but also a bit of guilt. It was like having Joe Bucher's secret bait that he keeps under glass with a sign that reads, BREAK GLASS ONLY IN THE EVENT YOU'VE BEEN SKUNKED TODAY!!!! But to my befuddlement the first pass produced zero musky sightings and so we pulled the trolling motor up, cranked up the big motor ,and we're off to give it another run. "The muskies must have been daydreaming on that drift," I say to Tracy. So we give her another go and another and another. We fish up and down that ledge rock for the next two hours with nothing in return.

"IT'S OVER," I shout. What seemed almost too good to be true is done. The feeding window had slammed shut and with it broken our self confidence into tiny shards. Embarrassed and deflated I slinked back into my boat seat, I was trying to wrap my head around why I would let us leave a hot bite, and sadly the answer was obvious. Things weren't going my way and I was plain old jealous of all the action Tracy was receiving while fishing with my bait. Simple as that. Deep down I knew I had ruined a good thing, I was certain that we were going to have hours of fish catching opportunity, but it probably only lasted forty five minutes.

CHAPTER L

REMORSE

In my heart I knew I had broken one of the cardinal rules of teamwork in a musky boat and it saddened me. I had become what I hate most in people, GREEDY. Each musky that is caught and landed is a team effort ensuring both the safety of the fish in proper netting, handling and unhooking, and that of the fisherman as he or she isn't injured by a thrashing hooked musky. It's a shared success with hero pics and a healthy safe release that lends to someone else in enjoying the same moment in the future.

One of the hardest things to do, as for most men, is to admit you were wrong and say those very simplistic words, 'I'm sorry.' But I manned up and told Tracy I was sorry for my crabby mood and I should have never let us leave a hot bite. And sorry because I couldn't handle the simple fact that someone was having more success than I was, regardless if they were using my bait or not. My actions had sabotaged a musky feeding frenzy, the likes I might never witness again. Deep down I knew I had done wrong by Tracy and I hoped he could somehow forgive my poor display of sportmanship and to a bigger extent, friendship. "I understand where you were coming from and accept your apology. If I were in your same shoes, I would've wanted my bait back. Also our fishing window was much short than I had anticipated," said Tracy.

What Tracy and I accomplished in only 45 minutes was nothing short of amazing, but what 'could have been' keeps creeping into my head. In the flicker of time we managed to boat four muskies and raise seven more, I can only imagine if we each had jointed perch Shallow Raiders. I believe we could've put up double digits.

Regrettably, the rest of the day's fishing activities was a total bust, though Tracy did manage to entice a thirty incher back to the boat. And so another beautiful sun has set on what might have been my last time fishing musky on Lake Of The Woods... more on that later.

The numbers for the whole group were way down this year compared to last. And the big girls were all on hiatus this trip, in fact only one fifty incher was raised out of our group of ten. Steve and his son Allen tied for largest musky as they both caught forty eight inchers only minutes apart in the same weedy cove. It was the same cove where two years earlier James and I were fishing when he lost a mid fifty inch hog when it barrel rolled next to the boat, severing the line with its gill rakers.

MUSKY TALE OF THE TAPE-AUGUST 2016
Brad - 40" 38" 39"
Tracy - 42" 40" 36" 38"

BY **BRAD MATHEWSON**

CONCLUSION

I've spent many a day gazing at the elegance and the amazing world beneath the surface of the Lake of the Woods over the years. I've made references to the lake being very similar to a woman, in that they can be beautiful on the outside, but the special ones are even more so inside her soul. Canada's Lake of the Woods, specifically Sabaskong Bay, forces you to appreciate the simple things in life. The sky, so incredible and vast, allows you to view her seemingly endless natural beauty for miles in every direction. The curvature of the Earth is accentuated on such a large body of water. It's hard to get an understanding and appreciation of Mother Nature and her offerings until you've spent time in her bosom. Staring blankly into those puffy cotton balls in the sky can be mesmerizing. Witnessing these creature-like apparitions, emerging from Mother Nature's breathe, transcend high above and bring to life by one's own imagination like a child. My own dreams consisted of a musky eating on a full moon, a Greek warrior riding his horse into battle, and even fleeting images of loved ones lost long ago in nature's ever-changing Etch A Sketch. The only place you can truly be yourself is in your own mind. Lake of the Woods, though far and away, brings you closer to home.

It's now 2020 as I finish writing this book and a lot has changed in my life. I haven't fished musky since my last trip to L.O.T.W. August of 2016. In the early summer of 2017 I suffered a severed Labrum tendon in my right shoulder and six weeks later while awaiting my much needed surgery, I suffered the same injury to my left shoulder. Rehabbing surgeries 11 weeks apart shut down my 2017 season. Then tragedy struck again and I fell only a few short months after my left shoulder repair and caused a second degree separation of my collar bone. That was only the half of it as I had re-torn my left Labrum only the doctors missed it and didn't discover it until 2018. So back in I went for my left shoulder repair number 2. It all went well until 39 days out I heard a pop while working with my physical therapist. I had my third left shoulder surgery in July of 2019 and this was more involved where they had to detach and reattach my left bicep tendon and I'm still not 100% back from that fillet job. So for you folks keeping track, that's 4 shoulder surgeries between October of 2017 through July of 2019, three on the left and one on the right.

Not to mention the daily grind of work, whisking the kid off to daycare, and struggling just to stay afloat in this chaotic world, doesn't typically allow you the luxury of appreciating all that life has to offer. But the wilds of Canada's unspoiled

BY **BRAD MATHEWSON**

Lake Of The Woods permits me a return to memories of my younger days. Like lying in the fresh cut grass watching the clouds drift by wondering if that cloud looks like a sea turtle or a flying dinosaur. Everyone needs their own special place where they are allowed to dream the day away. I know where my heart belongs. Do you?

I don't know if I'll ever hunt muskies again, but writing this book helps me remember the good times and gives me closure on my Lake Of The Woods adventures.

A musky hunter's day is an easy one. Cast, retrieve, figure eight, and repeat. If only life were only so simple...

Thank you to my wife Laura for being ok with my musky obsession and for never complaining when I wanted to stay one more hour on the water because of a coming moon phase. Your understanding of my need to lock myself in my office, and your freshly baked Oatmeal raisin cookies are what helped me get this book done. I couldn't have found a better net women than you.

And to my adopted brothers, The Hoelzel Boys Jan, Jerry, James, Stewart, and Steve; some of the best multi-species fisherman in the state of Wisconsin. You guys took this musky slim wet behind the ears novice, and turned me into a hardcore 12 hour fishing machine. Without your guidance and never-give-up Positive Musky Attitude, I would never would have made it past day one of your daily musky marathon boot camps that you put on in your boats each day. I especially appreciate your patience when I'm snagged on a rock for the 100th time each day and then moving us closer so I can get unstuck and in the process ruining yet another honey hole. Honestly they should rename the place Lake Of The Rocks, those damn rocks always seem to jump up and bite my hook on every cast...

And I'd like to thank my brother-in-law Jeff Wagner for your first edit of this book. Your ideas and chapter names helped inspire a renewed love of writing, which made rewriting this book as enjoyable as the first time.

Lastly, I'd like to thank Shawn Brook Williams for his never-ending editing of my - their, there, there's, they're. And for his magnificent vibrant cover, illustrations, and professional layout. My old cross country teammate helped me make it to the finish line in spectacular fashion.

THE END FOR NOW.

ABOUT THE AUTHOR

Author **Brad Mathewson** grew up in Northeast Wisconsin in the small town of New London, WI, a stones throw from the famed walleye factory, the Wolf River. It was on this river and it's many acres of wet public hunting grounds he spent many a skipped school time chasing deer, coyotes, beaver, and wetting a line for anything dumb enough to take a worm. As the need for adventure and challenge grew, the appeal of Musky fishing and its nickname "The Fish of Ten Thousand Casts" drew him in like a moth to a flame. And soon he was using all his over-time money buying baits and traveling to the famous Lake Of The Woods in Ontario, Canada.

When he's done casting for muskies in the summer, he likes to travel to Wyoming and Montana hunting mule deer, elk, and antelope.

Brad is a 2012 Northeast Wisconsin Natural Resources Award winner, 2013 Hoelzel L.O.T.W Biggest Musky Award (bad luck ruined a repeat in 2014), Husband of the Year Award 2009, 2010, 2013, 2015, 2017, 2020. Father of the Year Award 2016, 2017, 2018, 2019, 2020. Super Dad Award nominee 2016-2020.

He is married to a very forgiving and patient woman named Laura and they both have their hands full with their 4 year old son Tristan. As an amateur naturalist, most of his free time now-a-days is spent teaching his son about everything mother nature has blessed us with and what better place to do it than in her waters, woods, and sky.

— *Brad Mathewson*

CONTACT BRAD

bradmathewsonoutdoors@gmail.com
facebook.com/muskyslayersbiblebook